SPARTA

SPARTA

The Rise and Fall of an Ancient Superpower

Andrew Bayliss

Profile Books

First published in Great Britain in 2025 by
Profile Books Ltd
29 Cloth Fair
London ECIA 7JQ

www.profilebooks.com

Typeset by James Alexander/Jade Design

1 3 5 7 9 10 8 6 4 2

Printed and bound in Great Britain by
CPI Group (UK) Ltd, Croydon, CRO 4YY

A CIP catalogue record for this book is available from the British Library.

Our product safety representative in the EU is Authorised Rep Compliance Ltd., Ground Floor, 71 Lower Baggot Street, Dublin, DO2 P593, Ireland.
www.arccompliance.com

HB ISBN 978 1 80081 601 5
TPB ISBN 978 1 80522 749 6
Ebook eISBN 978 1 80081 603 9

Contents

ETRURIA

Adriatic Sea

Naples

Taras

Segesta

SICILY

Selinus

Syracuse

Mediterranean

0   500

Kilometres

The Ancient Eastern Mediterranean

Black Sea

Amphipolis

Byzantium

X Aegospotami

PHRYGIA

X Arginusae

LYDIA

Aegean Sea

Thermopylae X Plataea
Delphi   Thebes
          Eretria   Sardis

Megara   IONIA

Corinth Athens   Ephesos

lympia   Aegina   Delos Samos

Argos   Naxos

Sparta

CYCLADES

CRETE

Sea

Cyrene

⊙ City state / Major city
• Settlement
X Battle site

The Ancient Peloponnese and Surrounds

Thermopylae ✗

Delphi ●

Sicyon ⊙

Elis ⊙

Mycenae ⊙

Tiryns ⊙

Olympia ●

Mantinea ⊙   **Argos**

Tegea ⊙   *Thyrea*

Aulon (?) ●   ▲ Mt Parno...

Mt   **Pellana** ●

Ithome ▲   ● Sellasia

MESSENIA   Thouria ●   **Sparta** ⊙

I o n i a n   S e a

Pylos ●   Mt ▲   Geront...
Taygetus   ●

Methone ●   **LACONIA**

Helos (?) ●

M e d i t e r r a n e a n   Gytheum ●

S e a

Cape
Taenarum

✗ Battle site
⊙ City state
● Settlement / village
▲ Mountain

Author's Note

Sources

We have no contemporary Spartan sources to tell the true story of Classical Sparta. The only sources written by actual 'Spartans' are a few hundred lines of verse by the poets Tyrtaeus and Alcman, which were written too early, and a few snippets by the third-century BCE scholar Sosibius, which are too late, and are mostly preserved in much later sources. The rest of our sources, ranging from the Classical period to the Byzantine era, were written by non-Spartans – admirers, critics, actual enemies in the case of the famed Athenian historian Thucydides – who typically present Sparta as a radically unique and unchanging society.

Modern scholars often talk of the 'Spartan mirage' – coined as *le mirage Spartiate* by the French scholar François Ollier – to describe the idealised, stereotyped and distorted picture of Spartan society that was created by largely non-Spartan sources. While we cannot simply splice together snippets from sources separated by the best part of a millennium, it would be dangerous to reject all the later ones that focus on the 'otherness' of the Spartans. The very existence of the Spartan mirage tells us that there really was something different about the Spartans.

This book will follow the general principle that most experts today take, by starting with contemporary sources such as Herodotus, Thucydides and Xenophon who experienced Sparta at first hand, before resorting to later and potentially less reliable sources like Plutarch. Only when we lack more contemporary sources will later writers be used alone. Readers will find that even the most reliable of sources for Sparta have their weaknesses. When it comes to Sparta, we have to take great care when using *all* the sources.

Endnotes have been used to point readers to the key sources of information for the facts and details about Spartan society. They appear less frequently in the narrative elements of the story to avoid overwhelming non-academic readers with notes and references. These references follow a version of the specialised citation method for ancient Greek and Latin sources used by Classicists. Rather than citing page numbers for ancient texts, Classicists provide the name of the ancient author, the title of the work (but not if only one work by the author survives), and then references to books, chapters, sections or line numbers. These divisions differ, depending on whether the author is writing prose or verse, or the length of the work in question. This system works because no matter how long the translation of the Greek text turns out to be, any modern translation of, say, Herodotus' *Histories* will always have nine 'books', and Book 1 of Herodotus will always have precisely 216 'chapters'. Similarly, Xenophon's *Constitution of the Lacedaemonians* (*Lac. Pol.* for short) will always have fourteen 'chapters', and Isocrates' sixth speech, *Archidamus*, will always have 111 'sections'. So, when a note refers to 'Herodotus 1.82', Xenophon, *Lac. Pol.* 14, or Isocrates, *Archidamus* 81, any reader will be able to find the exact references, regardless of whether they are reading the original Greek text in a specialist Classics publication, or a translation into English (or any other modern language).

There are two exceptions to this rule: the 'Stephanus' and 'Bekker' systems, which are used for Plato and Aristotle respectively. Plato's works are ordered by title, using a numbering system based on the 1578 edition of Plato's complete works translated by Joannes Serranus and published by Henricus Stephanus. Aristotle's works are likewise ordered by title, with a numbering system based on the edition of his complete works published by the Classical philologist August Immanuel Bekker between 1831 and 1837. Readers wishing to track down references to Plato and Aristotle for themselves will be able to find them using any translation that follows these numbering systems.

Ancient Monetary Values

The ancient Greeks used a monetary system based on the 'drachma', literally 'as much as one hand can hold'. In the Classical period the most universally accepted currency was the Athenian drachma, which weighed 4.3 grams. The drachma was equal in value and weight to six silver 'obols'. The term *obolos* reportedly derived from *obelos*, the Greek word for 'roasting spit', the reasoning being that six roasting spits was the most someone could hold in their hand. The Greeks also used the 'stater', which equalled two drachmas, and the talent (*talanton*), which was equal to 6,000 drachmas.

While it is impossible to calculate exact modern equivalents for this ancient Greek currency, we can produce a rule of thumb based on the fact that a skilled worker's wage in Classical Greece was probably around 1 drachma per day. At the time of writing, an average skilled worker's wage in the UK is £14.53 per hour ($18.72 per hour in the US), which would make a day rate of approximately £109 (or $150). Therefore, approximate modern values for ancient Greek money will be calculated on the assumption that 1 drachma is worth approximately £100 or $150.

Prologue:
Honour and Duty

'Corinthian'-style bronze helmet (*c.* 500–450 BCE) of the sort that Othryadas would have worn at the Battle of the Champions. The nail-holes in the top and cheek-pieces indicate its display as a trophy or victory offering.

As the light faded, his energy ebbing with it, the Spartan soldier Othryadas felt his opponent's shield drop under the pressure of his own. His gaze, scarcely visible beneath the heavy bronze helmet that covered all but his eyes and mouth, met his adversary's. Disciplined for warfare by his city's rigorous upbringing – the world's first compulsory state-run education system – Othryadas knew exactly what to do.

Grunting with exertion, he plunged his short stabbing sword into the exposed flesh between the base of his opponent's helmet and the top of his bronze breastplate. As the fighter from the neighbouring city of Argos slumped to the ground, his soul bound for the underworld, Othryadas realised, to his horror, that he was the only Spartan still standing. After hours of fighting, 299 of Othryadas' fellow citizens had fallen, leaving him to face alone the two surviving Argive champions, Alcenor and Chromius. Spartans may have called themselves the *homoioi* ('peers'), but Othryadas was on his own.[1]

Steeling himself for one last effort, Othryadas planted his feet firmly on the ground, readying himself either to win a glorious victory against the odds, or to join his opponents in what the Spartans called a 'beautiful death' in combat. War poems written many decades before by the seventh-century BCE Spartan elegist Tyrtaeus had taught generation after generation of Spartans that 'it is a beautiful thing for a good man to die, falling in the front ranks fighting for his fatherland'.[2] But the Argives differed. Rather than face Othryadas head-on, Alcenor and Chromius simply declared themselves the winners and ran home to Argos to celebrate their 'victory'.

Othryadas remained on the battlefield, carefully stripping the armour from the bodies of the Argive dead. He then carried these spoils back to his own army's nearby camp, where he remained at his station, as was required of a Spartan soldier. According to the later Spartan king Demaratus, Spartan law called for citizens to remain at their place in the line of battle, and to either conquer or die.[3]

The next day, both sides disputed the result of what would later be dubbed the 'Battle of the Champions'. Around 545 BCE, Sparta and Argos were squabbling over a hinterland between their two city-states known as the Thyrea, which the Spartans had recently occupied. To resolve the conflict, the Spartans and Argives had agreed that both armies would withdraw while two sets of 300 elite champions battled, fearing that if the full armies were nearby, the temptation to intervene would prove too great.[4]

The Spartans would have had no difficulties selecting their 300 champions. The best graduates of the Spartan upbringing were selected to join an elite Spartan infantry unit known as the 'knights' (hippeis), which served as an official bodyguard for Spartan kings. The rivalry between this 'special forces' unit and the Spartans who missed out was legendary, with violence regularly spilling out into the streets of the city-state. Any young adults who refused to desist when older Spartans intervened were hauled before the authorities, and stiff fines were dished out to ensure that respect for Spartan law was maintained.[5]

The object of the Battle of the Champions was to avoid a great loss of life on both sides; nonetheless 597 men died – perhaps as much as 5 per cent of the male citizen population of both Sparta and Argos. The Argives, understandably enough, claimed that they had won the duel because more of their men had survived. But the Spartans argued that *they* were the victors, because Alcenor and Chromius had run away. They stressed that Othryadas had remained on the field of battle and despoiled the dead – a clear indicator of triumph in ancient Greek combat.

With neither side willing to relent, the full-scale pitched battle the Spartans and Argives were hoping to stave off became inevitable. This was likely one of the first significant battles in ancient Greece between heavily armed infantrymen called 'hoplites', a name derived from the 30 kilograms or so of bronze armour (*ta hopla*) each foot-soldier wore for protection. The hoplites fought in a ranked formation known as a 'phalanx' – as the poet Tyrtaeus described it, 'pressing shield against shield, / crest on crest and helmet to helmet / and chest to chest'.[6]

The thousands of hoplites in both armies would have worn a bronze helmet with full face protection known as the 'Corinthian', which was usually topped with a horsehair crest. Allowing in little sensory information, such helmets would have created a state of heightened psychological alertness. Both phalanxes of hoplites would have worn breastplates, made from either bronze or a composite made from layers of linen or hide; bronze greaves would have protected their lower legs. But their primary defence was a large, bowl-like wooden, bronze-faced shield called an *aspis*. Later sources suggest that the Spartans emblazoned the Greek letter *lambda*, for 'Lacedaemon', their own name for Sparta, on the face of their shields. The uniformity would have likely produced a chilling effect on the enemy. Indeed, the fifth-century BCE comic playwright Eupolis describes an Athenian being 'terrified' by the sight of the 'flashing lambdas'.[7] But at the time of the Battle of the Champions, the Spartans probably had personal emblems on their shields.[8] Vase paintings from the time show other Greeks carrying shields adorned with lions, bears, snakes and scorpions.

A hoplite's main offensive weapon was a long, iron-headed ash spear. In case their spear broke, they also carried stabbing swords. Spartan swords were notoriously short. When a foreigner once asked why this was so, he received the blunt reply, 'So that we might reach our enemies with our hands.'[9] Spartan soldiers all wore red cloaks and tunics – partly because red was considered the manliest colour, and partly because it would conceal bloodstains.[10] The Spartans' use of uniforms for their soldiers was hitherto unparalleled, and focused the enemy's attention on their intimidating conformity.

In the era of the Battle of the Champions, the Spartans fought in five regiments known as *lochoi*. The regimental names that have been preserved vividly convey the Spartan wartime mindset: 'Devourer', 'Ravager', 'Rager', 'Thundercloud' and 'Leader of the Centre'.[11] Later sources tell us that each *lochos* was commanded by an officer known as a *lochagos* (literally 'leader of a *lochos*'), and was divided into smaller units known as 'sworn bands' (*enōmotiai*), led by an officer called an *enōmotarchos* ('ruler of the sworn band'). Orders were passed down from the Spartan king to senior officers called 'polemarchs' (*polemarchoi*), then to the *lochagoi* and finally to the *enōmotarchoi*, who told the rank and file what to do. The formality of this command structure was unmatched at the time, and helped the Spartans to carry out manoeuvres that contemporary professional drill instructors considered difficult.[12] Due to the parallels with modern military practice, many modern translations render the Spartan officers as colonels, majors and captains.

The Spartans' comparative professionalism may have been decisive in the pitched battle that decided the fate of the Thyrea. The fighting was brutal, with heavy casualties on both sides, but this time the Spartans emerged unambiguously victorious.

The Argives were so humiliated by their defeat that they shaved their heads in mourning; they also instituted a new law requiring male Argives to keep their hair short, and denying women the right to wear gold jewellery, until Argos recovered the Thyrea. It would take two long centuries of keeping their hair cropped and doing without gold adornments before the Argives got the Thyrea back.[13] Meanwhile, to celebrate their victory, the Spartans began wearing their hair long as a kind of uniform.[14] Later sources explained their characteristic long hair as designed to make them look 'freer' and 'scarier',[15] or to make handsome men more handsome and ugly men more frightening.[16] Many ancient artworks represent Spartans with elaborately plaited locks. The best example is a bronze statuette of a Spartan warrior from around 510–500 BCE, now held at the Wandsworth Museum in Connecticut. But not all artworks depict Spartans with neat hair: one Spartan shown on a wine-mixing jug from around 420 BCE has long locks hanging wild and curly over his shoulders and torso.

*   *   *

After their victory, the Spartans would have buried their dead in a communal tomb near the battlefield where they had fallen, rather than bring them home to Sparta. One of their Argive enemies would later jeer about the fact that there were many Spartan dead – like the men who fell in the Battle of the Champions – buried near Argos. But the Spartans were untroubled, replying, 'But not one of *you* is buried in Sparta.'[17] The message was clear: while the Spartans had fought many battles near Argos, the Argives hadn't once invaded Spartan territory.

Spartans who died in war were permitted to have memorial stones at home; indeed, only Spartans who died in combat were remembered in this way.[18] These memorials were required to be small and largely identical.[19] Archaeologists have found twenty-four small and largely unadorned Spartan funerary inscriptions bearing only the name of the deceased and the words *en polemōi*, 'in war'.

Although the Spartans won the day, Othryadas did not join his fellow citizens in celebrating. Ashamed that he alone of the 300 champions had survived, he committed suicide. Othryadas may have been trying to avoid joining the ranks of men in Sparta dismissed contemptuously as *tresantes* – literally 'those who flee', but often translated as 'tremblers'. These men were compelled to shave off half their beard and to wear patchwork cloaks, presumably to make them look ridiculous and to mark them out; they also tended to be the last picked for ball games, banished to 'insulting' positions in religious choruses, and forced to yield to younger men – a striking inversion of Spartan norms, whereby younger men always gave way to their elders.[20] The treatment Spartans meted out to cowards may well have been intended to shame them into committing suicide, as Othryadas did.

*   *   *

Over the centuries that followed, many Spartans – especially senior officers – would ensure that they achieved a beautiful death in combat rather than suffer the sting of shame Othryadas felt at surviving his fallen comrades. Most famous is another group of 300 Spartans: the legendary men commanded by King Leonidas, who faced up to hundreds of thousands of Persian invaders before sacrificing themselves for Greek freedom at the Battle of Thermopylae in 480 BCE.

A cursory look at the story of the Spartans' doomed attempt to hold off the Persians – whom the Greeks at the time explicitly called 'barbarians' – at the narrow pass of Thermopylae shows why the Spartans are often seen as heroes to be emulated.[21] Leonidas and his 300 were tasked with leading just 7,000 of their fellow Greeks to hold back a massive Persian army until reinforcements could arrive. The invading army was composed of men from across the Persian king Xerxes' vast realm, which stretched from the Balkans to the Indian subcontinent. There were combatants from forty-six nations, including the Persians, Medes, Babylonians, Assyrians, Bactrians, Indians, Libyans, Egyptians, Ethiopians and Scythians. Popular legend had it that Xerxes' army was three million strong, and that the accompanying pack animals alone drained a large lake.[22]

The Spartan defenders were nonetheless undaunted by the odds against them. When they were warned that Xerxes' army boasted so many archers that their arrows would darken the sky, one of them – Dienekes – responded tersely, 'Good, we'll fight in the shade.'[23] Later, less reliable sources attribute other glorious quips to the Spartans. When someone asked Leonidas why there were so few Spartans at Thermopylae, he responded that there were 'many enough to die.'[24] One Spartan hoplite Leonidas tried to send home with a message retorted, 'I came with you to fight, not carry letters.' Most famously, when Xerxes demanded the Spartans surrender and hand over their weapons, Leonidas reportedly shot back just two words: *molōn labe*, 'come and take them.'[25]

The resilience and good humour shown by Leonidas and his men under such immense pressure was not mere bravado. For two whole days, ensconced in the pass, they repelled wave after wave of Xerxes' best troops, killing tens of thousands of Persians in the process. The narrowness of the pass enabled them to make up for their small numbers by fighting in relays. They even refused to rest, with the older and younger men vying to outdo each other in displays of courage and prowess.[26] The Spartans – whom the Athenian playwright Aristophanes vividly described as fighting like angry wild boars, with 'froth' dripping from their jaws and running down their legs[27] – fought so bravely that Xerxes jumped from his seat three times in fear for his army.[28]

At the end of the second day, however, the Spartans were betrayed by a local named Ephialtes, who told Xerxes about an alternative route over the spine of the mountain that would allow the Persians to circumvent Leonidas' position. When Leonidas learned of the danger, he dismissed his allies and ordered the Spartans to remain with him and fight to the death in order to buy enough time for their allies to withdraw safely. On that final day at Thermopylae, the Spartans fought bravely to the very end, with only their allies from Thespis in support.

By the end of the day, most of the Spartans had broken their spears and were fighting only with swords or knives. Finally, some fought with just their bare hands and teeth as they faced the Persians, who bore down on them on all sides. Even then, the Spartans proved such formidable opponents that many Persians preferred to shoot them down with the arrows rather than fight hand-to-hand.[29] At the close, the Persians probably did darken the sky with their arrows.

* * *

It is often argued that without the Spartans' iron will defying the Persians at Thermopylae, the glories of Classical Greece that followed – Athenian democracy; the Parthenon; the tragedies of Aeschylus, Sophocles and Euripides; the comedies of Aristophanes; the philosophy of Socrates and Plato; the practice of writing history itself – may never have come to pass. In his essay 'The Hot Gates', the novelist William Golding so closely connected the later flourishing of democracy at 'shining Athens' with the self-sacrifice of the Spartans at Thermopylae that he was moved to write, 'A little of Leonidas lies in the fact that I can go where I like and write what I like. He contributed to set us free.' In a similar vein, in his graphic novel 300, Frank Miller writes of Leonidas and his men rescuing the world from 'the dark, stupid ways' and helping to 'usher in a future that is surely brighter than we can imagine.'[30]

This image of the Spartans as courageous freedom fighters, the ancient world's fiercest soldiers, has made them popular icons to be revered, even emulated, by many throughout the ages down to today. Lord Byron was so inspired by Leonidas and his men that he sought to summon three proper Spartans to help liberate Greece from the Ottoman Turks in his *Don Juan*:

> Earth! render back from out thy breast
> A remnant of our Spartan dead!
> Of the three hundred grant but three,
> To make a new Thermopylae![31]

Leonidas' famed retort, *'molōn labe'*, has become an unofficial slogan for North American firearm enthusiasts campaigning against gun control, and one can buy T-shirts, caps, stickers and guns emblazoned with the phrase. In the United Kingdom, a group of 'Eurosceptic' Members of Parliament styled themselves the 'Spartans,' to symbolise their resistance first to the UK's membership in the European Union, and later to Covid-19 restrictions. Mark Francois MP even self-published a book entitled *Spartan Victory: The Inside Story of the Battle for Brexit* to commemorate what he saw as a heroic emulation of Leonidas and his 300.

In popular culture, Spartan hoplites have starred in feature films such as Rudolph Maté's 'swords and sandals' epic, *The 300 Spartans* (1962), and Zack Snyder's *300* (2006), which stars Gerard Butler as Leonidas. Based on Frank Miller's graphic novel, the latter film grossed $450 million at the box office. The Spartans have also been the focus of best-selling novels; Steven Pressfield's *Gates of Fire* (1998) has sold more than one million copies worldwide and is even a set text at the US Marine Corps Basic School at Quantico, the United States Naval Academy at Annapolis, and West Point. Popular computer games allow players to virtually embody Spartans – *Assassins Creed Odyssey* (2018) centres on Sparta during the Archidamian War (431–422 BCE), with gameplayers controlling either Kassandra or Alexios, two exiled Spartan mercenaries descended from Leonidas; the *God of War* franchise sees players control Kratos the Spartan, a demigod son of Zeus who battles Greek and Norse gods; and in the first-person shooter video game franchise *Halo*, players control super-soldiers codenamed 'Spartans'.

The Spartans' vaunted physicality has led to countless sports teams across the globe taking their name. The most notable is the Czech soccer team AC Sparta Prague, who have won their national league thirty-three times, and the varsity teams of Michigan State University (MSU) have been known as the Spartans since 1926. The 'Spartans' brand has been so successful that MSU have utilised it for the entire institution, even using a stylised Corinthian helmet as the university logo. There is also the global phenomenon known as the 'Spartan Race' – with 250 events held annually in more than forty countries across the Americas, Europe, Africa, Asia and Oceania – which requires competitors to 'run, crawl, jump, and swim' and overcome a series of obstacles. Explaining the decision to call the event the Spartan Race, founder Joe de Sena wrote, 'The Spartans seemed to personify everything we stood for. They were strong, resourceful citizens with no tolerance for bullshit. They were known far and wide for their ability to defeat much larger military forces through force of will. They focused on mind and body in equal measure.'[32]

Yet all these admirers of Sparta would probably be discomfited to learn that Spartan-style courage in the face of overwhelming odds inspired the leaders of Nazi Germany, too. During the last days of the Battle of Stalingrad in 1943, the Luftwaffe chief Hermann Göring invoked an epigram that was written in memory of Leonidas and his men – 'Stranger, go tell the Spartans that here, obedient to their orders, we lie'[33] – telling German troops from the Sixth Army: 'If you go to Germany, tell them you have seen us fighting in Stalingrad, obedient to the law.'[34] In April 1945, in the closing days of the Second World War, Adolf Hitler himself told his close lieutenant Martin Bormann, 'A desperate fight will always be a worthy example ... just think of Leonidas and his three hundred Spartans.'[35]

More recently, the far-right ultra-nationalist Greek political party Golden Dawn (1985–2020) painted itself as the inheritor of the Spartan tradition. The hymn of the party, which was the third most popular in the Greek parliament in the 2015 election, ran: 'Trackers of ancient glories, sons of brilliant struggles, we are the New Spartans.' At the party's annual torch-lit celebration of the Battle of Thermopylae in July 2008, Ilias Kasidiaris, then a Golden Dawn MP, stated: 'We are Sparta's shield, patiently guarding the body of Greece.' Since the party's recent demise (it was banned after being declared a criminal organisation), a new far-right group calling itself 'The Spartans' has emerged, criticising the colonisation of Greece by 'invaders' and the alteration of its ethnic mix by hordes of 'barbarians'. The choice of the latter term illustrates how powerful the story of the Spartans' resistance to the Persians remains in the popular consciousness.

All this raises the question: what did the ancient Spartans 'really' stand for? Does the image of the Spartans as single-minded freedom fighters stand up to closer scrutiny? Was there more to Sparta than these one-dimensional stereotypes suggest – another side to Sparta that modern admirers might like to know about, or another side that they might prefer not to see?

*　　*　　*

Indeed, there was far more to Sparta than the relentless focus on its martial prowess and the 300's doomed stand at Thermopylae typically leaves room for in the public imagination. On the positive side, Sparta had what is recognised as the first state-run education system, which was compulsory for all the sons of Spartan citizens. In addition, Sparta is almost unparalleled in the pre-modern world as a city-state where women were permitted to own land in their own right and had a clear voice; Simone de Beauvoir once singled out Sparta as 'the only Greek city in which woman was treated almost on an equality with man'.[36]

The focus on Spartan heroism at Thermopylae has also tended to obscure some horrific aspects of the ancient city-state. Modern 'Spartophiles' may be unaware of the stories of Spartan elders inspecting newborn babies and dumping the weak or disabled unceremoniously off the edge of a cliff, or the fact that Spartan husbands could share out their wives as breeding stock.[37] That the Spartans' freedom was based on the ruthless exploitation of tens of thousands of slaves known as 'helots' should give even the most ardent admirer pause. So too should the *krypteia*, a brutal rite of passage where young men were sent into the countryside armed with a knife and ordered to eliminate the strongest of the helots. With this knowledge, it becomes rather disturbing that the instructors on the Spartan Run's training programme, the 'Agoge' – invoking the Roman-period name for the Spartan upbringing – are called 'Krypteia'.

The Spartans' image as the defenders of freedom at Thermopylae also overlooks the fact that after the Persians' ambitions of conquest in Europe were ended, the Spartans made their own ill-fated attempt at regional domination. In the century that followed the Persian Wars, the Spartans vied with the other great Greek power – Athens – for leadership of the

Greek world. During the so-called Peloponnesian War against Athens (431–404 BCE), a war the Spartans themselves cast as a fight for freedom and autonomy against Athenian tyranny, they shamelessly bargained away the freedom of the Greeks of Asia Minor in exchange for Persian assistance against Athens. Worse still, in 387 BCE, ten years after launching a campaign to re-liberate those Asian Greeks from Persian rule, the Spartans abandoned them for a second time to secure Persian backing for a treaty that guaranteed Spartan dominance over mainland Greece. During this time, the Spartans made it clear to everyone that the only freedom they were really interested in was their own.

If we attempt to peel back the layers of legend, what do we find? This book examines how the city of Sparta grew from a collection of five villages in a remote corner of southern Greece into a world superpower, its rise to power as dramatic as its sudden collapse. It is a story filled with heroic acts like those at Thermopylae, great military victories against the Persians, Athenians and other Greeks, breathtaking arrogance towards Greeks and foreigners alike – as well as the Spartans' delusions of grandeur, their crushing defeats at the hands of their fellow Greeks, and their horrific atrocities, particularly against the helots.

The tale shows why, despite its brief florescence – from only 700 BCE to 371 BCE – Sparta has captured the imagination of so many over the millennia, from poets and politicians to freedom fighters and footballers. It also shows why we should be careful when we choose our heroes.

1

The Origins of the Spartan State

c. 1000–600 BCE

Marble pyramid stele (*c.* 600–570 BCE), with relief depicting Helen and Menelaus. The couple hold a wreath, symbolising their reunion.

To chart the rise and fall of the Spartans, we need to start at the beginning of their story: who were they, and where did they come from? Put simply, the Spartans were the inhabitants of Sparta, a small city in the Peloponnese, a large island peninsula joined to the south of mainland Greece by the Isthmus of Corinth.

Somewhat confusingly for the modern reader, however, the inhabitants of Sparta did not call themselves 'Spartans'. Rather, they called themselves the *Spartiatai* or the *homoioi*. The former name is often rendered Spartiates, and the latter as 'equals' or 'peers', or even 'similars'.

The place name Sparta is also seldom used in our sources. Sparta was usually referred to in writing as 'Lacedaemon'; readers of translations of the great ancient Greek histories by Herodotus, Thucydides and Xenophon will thus often find references to the 'Lacedaemonians'. This is because Sparta was not merely the villages that made up the city, but a 'city-state' comprising both the urban centre and the surrounding countryside. The ancient Greek term for such a city-state is *polis*; there were more than 1,000 *poleis* (the Greek plural), not just in what we know as Greece but throughout the ancient Mediterranean. Each Greek city-state controlled a territory circumscribed by mountains or sea, or by proximity to another city-state. Each was fiercely independent, and border wars were common. All the Greek city-states seem to have possessed similar institutions: a central marketplace (*agora*), annually elected magistrates, a council of elder citizens, an assembly of citizen-soldiers, and public buildings such as gymnasia, wrestling schools, theatres and temples to the gods.

Adding another layer of complexity to the identity of the Spartans, the region where the city of Sparta lies was also known as 'Laconia', which it still is to this day; Spartans therefore often appear in our sources not as Spartiates or Lacedaemonians, but 'Laconians'. And if that was not baffling enough, the Spartan *polis* was not only the city of Sparta and the region of Laconia; from around 700 BCE to 369 BCE it also included the neighbouring region of Messenia, to the west of the Taygetus mountain range. This gave the Spartans yet another name for the territory they controlled: the '*Lakōnikē gē*', or 'Laconian land'.

At the height of its power, Sparta would be a truly gargantuan *polis*, comprising roughly two-fifths of the whole Peloponnese. By way of comparison, its great political and military rival Athens – itself vastly larger than most other *poleis* – was less than three times its size. No wonder the Athenian playwright Euripides described Spartan territory as 'large for many, but for twice as many, more than large.'[1] Other famous and powerful *poleis* that were far smaller than both Sparta and Athens included Thebes, Byzantium (the European half of modern-day Istanbul) and Argos, Sparta's great Peloponnesian rival. In fact, research suggests that Spartan territory was nearly a hundred times larger than the vast majority of Greek city-states. In terms of its size, then, Sparta really was an ancient Greek superpower.

In spite of this, the urban centre of Sparta was decidedly unimpressive. Thucydides, an Athenian former general who was living in exile from his homeland, travelled to the city while conducting research prior to writing a history of the Peloponnesian War (431–404 BCE). Expecting to find a grand city that resembled his hometown, he was stunned to find little more than a cluster of four villages – Pitana, Limnae, Mesoa and Cynosoura – built up around a low mound of marls and clay. Thucydides later claimed that these villages (which Spartans called *obai*) made a 'deficient show'.[2] In fact, he was so unimpressed with what he saw that he predicted, somewhat presciently, 'if the city of the Spartans were to become deserted and only the temples and foundations of building remained', future generations would find it hard to believe that Sparta was as powerful as it was.

Anyone who has visited the remains of both ancient Sparta and Athens would find it hard to disagree. Built on several metres of 'mudstone', the Spartan citadel barely merits the title *acropolis* – literally 'high city' – when compared with the grandeur of the 150-metre-tall Athenian acropolis. Not only did Sparta entirely lack what Thucydides called 'costly temples or edifices' to rival the Athenian Parthenon, it also lacked a circuit wall to demarcate and protect it. The absence of walls was so unusual at the time that a foreign visitor in the fourth century BCE asked the Spartan king Agesilaus how the Spartans managed without them. Agesilaus pointed to the Spartan citizen army and retorted, 'These men are Sparta's walls.'[3]

But what ancient Sparta lacked in architectural grandeur it more than made up for with its breathtaking natural setting. Sparta lies in the heart of the Eurotas valley, an alluvial fan wedged between the Taygetus and Parnon mountain ranges, bounded by the high mountains of Arcadia to the north and the Laconian gulf to the south. The Taygetus mountain range is a spectacular sight, rising steeply to loom over the city. Although its peak is half the height of Mont Blanc at a relatively paltry 2,407m, Taygetus feels more imposing than it should; it is effectively two mountain ranges that run in parallel – a lower range of schist and marble cliffs rises to terrace-like uplands, with even steeper limestone slopes above them. Taygetus extends a hundred kilometres south from the Arcadian plateau to Cape Taenarum. The southernmost point in mainland Europe,

Taenarum was believed to be the site of a gateway to Hades, where the souls of the dead languished for eternity.

The Parnon mountain range to the east of Sparta, a tangle of rocky foothills and valleys topped by limestone peaks, is far less imposing. The range runs ninety kilometres south to the Malea peninsula, and the surrounding seas were notoriously treacherous. The great hero Odysseus was blown off course while rounding Malea on his return from Troy; thus began his decade-long 'odyssey' – which likely explains a saying recorded by Strabo, the ancient geographer and philosopher: 'But when you round Malea, forget your home.'[4]

Situated between these ranges, the Eurotas valley is prime agricultural land, and the river, which reaches the sea in a marshy delta, is one of few in mainland Greece that flows in the summer. In antiquity, Sparta would have been laced with orchards and gardens, and the surrounding countryside would have been sown with barley, wheat and pulses, as well as grapes and olives. Today the main agricultural output of the region is citrus fruit, mulberries and olives, but wheat, barley and maize are cultivated too. The warm climate and fertile soil near modern-day Sparti yield two harvests each year. No wonder, then, that modern scholars think that the name 'Sparta' might derive from the Greek verb *speirō* ('I sow'), making Sparta 'the sown land'.

The Eurotas valley is a rift valley, formed by massive tectonic subsidence. Like much of the eastern Mediterranean, the land around Sparta is also strikingly seismic; Strabo singled the region out as 'good for earthquakes.'[5] Because of this, the Spartans appear to have paid particular reverence to the god Poseidon, who was known throughout Greece as 'the Earthshaker'. A catastrophic earthquake that struck Laconia in the 460s BCE, reportedly demolishing the whole city of Sparta except for five houses, was thought to be caused by Poseidon's fury at the sacrilegious killing of suppliants at his temple at Cape Taenarum.[6] A tremor at the wrong time would halt a Spartan army in its tracks, in the belief that the god was expressing his displeasure at the mission.[7] Nonetheless, Sparta's position – described as 'hollow, surrounded by mountains, rough and difficult for enemies to invade'[8] – created a secure home base, providing the real explanation as to why the Spartans chose not to invest the time and resources required to build a wall around their city.

*   *   *

How did the Spartans come to settle in this fertile-but-earthquake-prone spot in the Peloponnese in the first place? According to varying traditions, the Greek race was born when the god Zeus was so angry that the king of Arcadia had sacrificed a human child to him that he tried to destroy humanity with a great flood. As in the stories of Noah in Genesis and Utnapishtim in the *Epic of Gilgamesh*, the gods ensured that one family survived: the immortal Titan Prometheus warned his mortal son Deucalion to build a large chest and fill it with sufficient food supplies to ride out the flood. After nine days, the waters subsided, and Deucalion and his wife, Pyrrha, touched down at Mount Parnassus in central Greece. There they regenerated the human race by casting stones over their shoulders, from which people sprang. But Deucalion and Pyrrha also had a biological son, Hellen, who became the progenitor of the race we call 'Greeks', but who called themselves 'Hellenes'.

As with all myths, there are conflicting traditions, but in the most standard version, Hellen and the nymph Orseis bore several children: Aeolus, Xuthus and Dorus. Xuthus in turn went on to father Achaeus and Ion. These two generations include the mythical progenitors of the different Greek ethnic groups we find in the Classical period: the Aeolians, Dorians, Achaeans and Ionians. The Spartans, like Othryadas and the three hundred at Thermopylae, identified as 'Dorians'. But the earliest Spartans mentioned in Greek myth – the men from 'the swarming hollow of Lacedaemon'⁹ who accompanied the Spartan king Menelaus to Troy to recover his wife Helen after her abduction by the Trojan prince Paris – were most definitely 'Achaeans'. Homer's epic poem the *Iliad* tells the story of the ten-year Trojan War between the 'long-haired Achaeans', led by Menelaus' elder brother Agamemnon, and the Trojans, led by King Priam's son Hector.

The story of how the Spartans came to identify as Dorians is wrapped up in a myth about how the 'Achaean' descendants of Heracles – known as the Heraclids – returned to their rightful home in the Peloponnese after being persecuted by Eurystheus, the king of Argos. The legend goes that, after Eurystheus drove them out of the Peloponnese, the Heraclids were initially granted asylum by the Athenian king Theseus. When Eurystheus subsequently attacked Athens, he and his five sons were slain in the fighting; Heracles' eldest son, Hyllus, then led the Heraclids back to the Peloponnese to reclaim the Argive throne. But when a terrible plague struck, Hyllus travelled to Delphi to consult the Pythia – a priestess of the god Apollo who acted as a medium between humans and the god himself. Throughout the Archaic and Classical periods (800–322 BCE), all the Greek *poleis* would consult the oracle at Delphi before making any major decision. The Spartans were especially prone to follow the oracle's advice, even if it meant acting against their better judgement.

Apollo warned Hyllus that the Heraclids would need to wait until 'the third fruit was ripe' before they could return to the Peloponnese. After hearing this, Hyllus led them to Doris, a small river valley wedged between Mount Oeta and Mount

Parnassus in central Greece, where Dorus had reportedly settled his people,[10] and Dorus' son Aegimius, the king of the region, gave them refuge. Hyllus assumed that the 'third fruit' meant three annual harvests, so after three years had passed, he confidently led the Heraclids home to reclaim their kingdom. But it was still not to be: Hyllus was killed in battle. Realising that the 'third fruit' was not three harvests of crops, but rather three generations of men, the Heraclids left the Peloponnese again, returning to Doris to wait it out.

Once three generations had passed, Heracles' great-great-grandsons – the brothers Temenus, Aristodemus and Cresphontes – gathered an army to invade the Peloponnese. This time the Heraclids had grand ambitions. Rather than merely seeking to reclaim Heracles' kingdom of Argos, the three brothers planned to carve up the whole Peloponnese. By this time the king of Argos was Orestes' son Tisamenus, who was also the legitimate king of Sparta as the grandson of Helen and Menelaus. The Heraclids defeated Tisamenus and set about dividing up the Peloponnese. As the eldest, Temenus received Argos, while Cresphontes and the twin sons of their other brother Aristodemus – Procles and Eurysthenes – gained Messenia and Sparta respectively. The myth thus conveniently explained why there were two royal houses – the Agiads and the Eurypontids – who reigned over Sparta simultaneously.

But while this story might explain how the Achaean Heraclids became the rulers of the Peloponnese, it doesn't explain how the Spartans came to be Dorians. The answer to this question lies in a footnote to the myths: the Dorians who had given the Heraclids asylum invaded the Peloponnese with them. The earliest extant source for this story is, in fact, Spartan. The seventh-century BCE poet Tyrtaeus wrote that 'Zeus granted this city [Sparta] to the Heraclids, with whom, leaving windy Erineus [i.e. Doris], / we arrived at the broad island of Pelops.'[11]

This origin story positioned the Spartans and the other Dorian Greeks as outsiders, later arrivals who displaced the Achaeans. Significantly, it made them far later arrivals than their Athenian rivals, who believed themselves to be born from the earth itself, and therefore – as Plato puts it – 'pure-blooded Greeks, unadulterated by barbarian stock'.[12] When a sixth-century BCE Spartan king, Cleomenes, once tried to enter the temple of Athena on the Athenian acropolis, a priestess tried to deny him entry on the grounds that it was illegal for Dorians to enter an Athenian temple. But – invoking the legend that the Spartan kings were Achaeans descended from Heracles, not Dorians – Cleomenes barged straight in, blithely telling the priestess, 'Madam, I am not a Dorian, but an Achaean.'[13]

*   *   *

Of course, the stories of Menelaus and Helen and of the return of the Heraclids to Sparta are only myths. To fully understand Sparta's origins, we must turn to the archaeological record.

The evidence we need comes from the Bronze Age and the so-called 'palatial' period of Mycenaean culture in Greece (1400–1200 BCE), which roughly coincides with the time when the ancient Greeks believed the Trojan War took place. During this period, at least ten states were likely ruled by a 'lord' or *wanax* from large complexes that archaeologists designate as 'palaces'. The title *wanax* has been found written on clay tablets inscribed with a pre-alphabetic script, known as 'Linear B', composed of syllabograms, logograms and punctuation; they record shipments of goods into and out of the palatial centres. First deciphered in the 1950s, they are now recognised as the earliest attested form of the Greek language.

The Mycenaean palace sites were characterised by monumental fortifications built from massive limestone boulders.

This style became known as 'Cyclopean', after the belief of later Greeks that the walls had been built by the mythical one-eyed giants.[14] The palaces themselves, usually built from large rectangular dressed stones, were dominated by a central rectangular hall, with a ceiling supported by four columns, a monumental central hearth and walls decorated with frescoes. The Mycenaean sites also featured monumental-style 'tholos' tombs – underground, corbel-vaulted structures that were thought to house the remains of Mycenaean 'royals'. Such tombs have been found near Sparta at Amyclae and Pellana. Material evidence discovered in Mycenaean palaces reveals remarkably similar pottery, terracotta figurines, ivories, jewellery and seals across sites.

Linear B tablets bearing the words 'ra-ke-da-mi-ni-jo' and 'ra-ke-da-mi-ni-jo-u-jo' (the Linear B forms for the later Greek terms 'the Lacedaemonian' and 'the son of the Lacedaemonian') have been found at Thebes, in central Greece, showing that the name 'Lacedaemon' dates back at least as far as the Mycenaeans. But while archaeologists have long tried to find evidence of a Mycenaean palace with a link to Menelaus and Helen, there are no references to the name 'Sparta' in the published Linear B tablets – and little Bronze Age archaeological evidence has been found at the site of the city of Sparta itself. The closest we have to a connection is the fact that Mycenaean grave offerings including pots, beads and semi-precious stones have been found just south-east of modern Sparti, close to the banks of the Eurotas, at a site called 'Psychiko'. The most exciting find there is the remains of a warrior's 'boar's tusk helmet' of the type worn by Odysseus in Homer's *Iliad*, 'cleverly adorned all around with rows of white tusks from a shiny-toothed boar, the tusks running in alternate directions in each row'.[15] Such helmets have also been found in Mycenaean-period graves at Mycenae and Dendra in the Argolid region of the Peloponnese, and at Knossos on Crete.

For a long time, archaeologists hoped to find evidence of a proper Mycenaean palatial complex at the site of a substantial settlement at Therapne, only a couple of kilometres south-east of Sparta, known since antiquity as the 'Menelaion'.[16] Strong evidence of cult activity from the late Bronze Age to the Classical period has been discovered at the site, where Helen, Menelaus, and Helen's brothers Castor and Pollux (together known as the 'Twin Gods') were all worshipped.[17] In fact, the oldest surviving Spartan inscription is a dedication to 'Helen, the wife of Menelaus' inscribed on an oil flask dating to 675–650 BCE found at the Menelaion. But the search for a Mycenaean palace there has always been in vain.

Recent findings suggest that a more likely candidate for the urban home of the Mycenaean 'Lacedaemonian' is much farther away from Sparta, at the site of Agios Vasileios some twelve kilometres south of modern Sparti. Although archaeologists have not yet found definitive proof of a palace complex, the recent unearthing of a substantial settlement with monumental structures, a large courtyard, a Linear B archive including a hundred tablet fragments, fresco fragments and large quantities of finely decorated pottery suggests that this is most likely the site of the 'palatial' centre of Mycenaean Lacedaemon. Therefore, if there really was a Bronze Age Menelaus, we can safely say that he wouldn't have lived in the city that came to be known as Sparta.

* * *

Could the Spartans have displaced a Mycenaean-era 'Menelaus' as part of a Dorian invasion, as the myths suggest? There *is* evidence of serious upheaval across the eastern Mediterranean at roughly the time when the ancient Greeks believed these mythical events took place. In mainland Greece, there are clear signs of destruction at major Mycenaean centres like Mycenae and Pylos, but also near Sparta – at Therapne and Agios Stephanos in southern Laconia, in what appear to be approximately simultaneous violent conflagrations. At around the same time, Linear B writing, fine pottery making and other advanced skills were lost throughout the Mycenaean world. In fact, there was no more writing of any kind in mainland Greece until the Greek alphabet was adopted in the eighth century BCE. In addition, population levels in Mycenaean Greece appear to have fallen by as much as 75 per cent between 1250 and 1100 BCE, with a considerable number of sites being abandoned altogether.

The collapse of Mycenaean society also seems to have coincided with clear cultural change. Whereas Mycenaean housing – like that at the Menelaion – had been multi-roomed and rectangular, later housing tended to be one-roomed and circular. Burial practices changed from multiple tomb complexes to individual inhumations, and even cremation. Archaeologists also note the sudden appearance of quite different pottery that was not made on a wheel, known either as 'handmade burnished ware' or, more dramatically, as 'barbarian ware'. Other material changes include the appearance of slashing swords of a style developed in northern Europe and new metal clothing fasteners known as *fibulae*, which might imply new arrivals in southern Greece from colder climates.

When the evidence for these disruptions came to light in the late nineteenth century, some archaeologists were quick to see it as proof that the Mycenaean kingdoms had been overthrown by migrating Dorians from the north. The Dorians were thought to have swept into the Peloponnese, sacked the Mycenaean citadels and introduced their language and customs. But more recent archaeological excavations have unearthed 'barbarian ware' in pre-destruction deposits at Mycenaean palatial sites; it also turns out that the 'new' round houses were common in the Mycenaean world prior to 1600 BCE – they simply hadn't been spotted by archaeologists. Thus, what seemed to be the strongest evidence of new practices from abroad is actually evidence of cultural continuation.

In addition, linguistic studies have shown that the change from the Greek recorded in Linear B tablets to Dorian Greek dialect does not fit the story either. If the 'Achaeans' in Homer's epics were the real Mycenaean Greeks and the Dorians were later invaders, the Greek in Linear B tablets should have been 'Achaean', and Dorian Greek should be a different dialect. But this is not the case. Arcadian, rather than Achaean, is the later dialect closest to Linear B Greek, and the Achaean and Dorian dialects are loosely related, rather than different languages. Even the fact that Mycenaean sites were destroyed doesn't fit the myth; after all, the returning Heraclids were not said to have destroyed the cities of Argos, Messene and Sparta, but rather took them over as their birthright. Finally, the chronology of the supposed Dorian invasion doesn't work; the Dorian king Aegimius was said to have adopted Heracles' son Hyllus, yet his natural sons Pamphylus and Dymas fought alongside Heracles' great-great-grandsons when they returned to the Peloponnese. For the story to work, the Dorian princes would have needed to be hundreds of years old.

Today, most archaeologists and historians doubt that the Dorians arrived as a distinct ethnic grouping and replaced the Mycenaeans. It is more likely that the collapse of Mycenaean culture occurred due to a combination of factors, such as earthquakes, climate change, disease and social unrest, as well as an invasion. In the chaos that followed, what really happened was forgotten. Sometime later, the people who lived throughout the region came to identify themselves as 'Greek', while also developing distinctive dialects, religious practices and cultural norms within that broad cultural grouping. The Ionians, said to be descended from the Athenians, colonised the Aegean islands and southern Asia Minor. The Aeolians, who lived in central and northern Greece, colonised the northern Aegean, while the Achaeans lived in the northern Peloponnese and colonised southern Italy. The Dorians – including the Spartans – inhabited most of the Peloponnese and colonised the Aegean islands of Aegina, Melos, Thera, Rhodes and Cos, as well Cnidus and Halicarnassus in Asia Minor, Crete and much of Sicily.

Rather than reflecting what really happened, the story of a Dorian invasion was what myth experts call a 'cognitive artefact' – a way in which humans try to imagine their past when they don't know the truth of what happened.

*　　*　　*

So, what *do* we know about the Spartan state before 700 BCE? The answer is frustratingly little. Archaeology tells us that by the tenth century BCE, its key features were in place: the four villages of Sparta and Amyclae were settled, as were other locations in Laconia that would become important regional communities: Geronthrai, Pellana and possibly the Spartan port of Gytheion. At some point during the ninth or eighth centuries BCE, the four villages of Sparta unified to form what would become the urban centre of the city-state. The evidence for how it was arranged is thin, but archaeologists suggest that it likely consisted of open villages of simple houses with rough stone foundations and clay walls, with wooden posts supporting thatched roofs.

By the eighth century BCE, the village of Amyclae, located about five kilometres south of Sparta, was incorporated into the Spartan 'city' as a fifth *obē*. Although the Amyclaeans became proper Spartans, they maintained a somewhat separate identity. For example, they would always return home to celebrate the annual Hyacinthia festival in honour of Apollo and his beloved youth Hyacinthus, even when away on military campaigns.[18] Later tradition held that Amyclae was an 'Achaean' city that had needed to be 'conquered' by the Dorian Spartans.[19] In line with this idea, it has even been suggested that the myth in which Apollo accidentally kills Hyacinthus[20] is a metaphor for the cultural change brought about by the Dorian conquest. But the fact that Hyacinthus was worshipped in many Dorian cities and not just Sparta makes it far more likely that Amyclae's 'Achaean' status is little more than a myth attempting to explain why the two parts of the city of Sparta were separated by five kilometres.

We do not know precisely what happened next as the Spartans' power grew, but at some point they seem to have taken control of much of Laconia. The residents of the towns near Sparta came to be known as the *perioikoi*, literally meaning 'those dwelling around'. The *perioikoi* were free men and they shared the designation 'Lacedaemonians' with the Spartans, but they were not equal in status; they had no control over foreign policy and were required to follow the Spartans in war.

At some point, the Spartans also enslaved some of the population of Laconia and began to call them 'helots'. Exactly how the distinction between *perioikoi* and helots came about is not clear. We can safely ignore later folk etymologies that claim the helots were *perioikoi* from the southern Laconian town of Helos who were enslaved after they rebelled against the Spartans.[21] The Greek word for 'helots' is actually *heilōtai* and not *helotai*; the name of the town would have needed to be 'Heilos' for this story to work. Nonetheless, linguistic experts believe the term probably derives from the Greek verb *haliskomai* ('I take'). Each year the Spartan authorities declared war on the helots[22] – a strong suggestion that the helots were indeed local

Greek inhabitants who were conquered and enslaved.

The fact that the Spartans owned and exploited so many human labourers did not mark them out as unusual at the time. Slavery was a widespread and accepted practice in ancient Greece and other contemporary societies; indeed, in the fifth century BCE there were probably as many as 80,000 slaves toiling for the Spartans' great rivals the Athenians. Unlike the helots, however, the majority of the Athenians' slaves would have been non-Greeks purchased in slave markets, whether as victims of warfare, piracy, debt, punishment for crimes, child abandonment or sale, or even voluntary self-enslavement. The wealthiest citizens in Athens may have owned as many as fifty slaves, but many Athenians would have been far too poor to afford to own even one. What singled the Spartans out was the ruthlessness with which they conquered and enslaved their fellow Greeks, in order to ensure that each of their own citizens possessed a captive, self-reproducing human workforce.

Nonetheless, the Spartans were not the only later arrivals to Greece who conquered the aboriginal inhabitants of the regions where they settled. Plato, for example, likens the helots to the 'Penestae' in Thessaly, in central Greece, who were said to be the original Achaean inhabitants enslaved by Thesprotian invaders from north-west Greece,[23] while Aristotle compared them to the *klarōtai* in Crete,[24] locals who were forced to work on the land by Dorian invaders, in exchange for the payment of fees.[25] However, the Spartans did something that the Thessalians and Cretans could not: they used helot labour in Laconia as a springboard to further expansion. After subduing the rest of Laconia, the Spartans turned their attention to their Dorian cousins in Messenia, with hopes of enslaving them too.

*   *   *

According to the mythic tradition, the grudge between the Spartans and the Messenians went back to when Heracles' descendants returned to the Peloponnese and divided the region between them. As the eldest, Temenos received Heracles' ancient kingdom of Argos. The rest of the prime lands in the Peloponnese – Messenia and Sparta – were to be shared between Cresphontes, and Aristodemus' twin sons, Eurysthenes and Procles. To determine who received which lands, tokens made from baked clay were dropped into a pitcher of water; Messenia would go to whoever's token was drawn first, leaving Sparta to the loser. But Cresphontes, who was not prepared to leave the decision to chance, switched the twins' kiln-baked token with one that was sun-dried. The counterfeit token dissolved in the water, ensuring that Cresphontes' token was drawn.[26]

The reason why Cresphontes wanted Messenia was obvious. As the Athenian playwright Euripides later put it, Messenia was 'a land of fair fruitage ... watered by innumerable streams, abounding in the pasturage for sheep and cattle.'[27] The prime agricultural land in Messenia is the central Pamisos Valley, dominated by Mount Ithome. The Pamisos river rises from two large springs at the foot of the Taygetos mountain range, emptying into the Messenian gulf in a wide, fertile delta. The valley is split by the Skala ridge east of Ithome, forming a lower portion known in antiquity as Makaria ('blessedness'), and an upper portion – the Stenyclarus plain, where Cresphontes is said to have held his royal palace.

The Spartans would later claim that the Messenians murdered Cresphontes and that his sons begged them for help. According to this self-serving story, the Spartans then accepted Messenia as a 'gift' in return for their intervention.[28] Yet whatever later attempts they would make to justify their actions, the Spartans' conquest of Messenia was, first and foremost, a land grab. It is surely no coincidence that it took place during a period when population increases were putting pressure on resources in the Greek mainland, leading many poorer citizens to seek new homes abroad. This period of colonisation between 800 and 550 BCE saw hundreds of Greek cities pop up around the coastal regions of the Mediterranean. Some of them were close to home; Chalcedon and Byzantium together grew into modern Istanbul, and then there were Reggio Calabria, Naples and Taranto in southern Italy, and Zancle in Sicily. Other colonies were as far away as Marseilles in France, Cyrene in Libya, Varna in Bulgaria, Tomis in Romania and Odessa in Ukraine. So rather than finding new resources abroad, the Spartans chose to take those of the Messenians – a process modern historians sometimes refer to as 'internal colonisation'.

It is essentially impossible to provide a historical account of the Spartan conquest of Messenia. Our main source is Pausanias, a Roman-period geographer and travel writer, who was writing nearly nine hundred years after the events he was describing. On the plus side, he describes Messenian sites and monuments in detail, and he had read a wide range of local histories, folklore and inscriptions, and the verses of the seventh-century BCE Spartan poet Tyrtaeus, who wrote exhortatory elegiac poems and anapaestic war songs to inspire the Spartans during their attempts to conquer the Messenians. But much of Pausanias' narrative is based on sources that were not written until after the Messenians were eventually liberated. So rather than reflecting actual history, Pausanias recorded a myth-history that had been 'worked up' by the Messenians themselves. Unsurprisingly, these stories usually paint the Spartans as the bad guys.

All we can say for certain is that the later generations believed that the initial war of conquest lasted just shy of twenty years. This idea is preserved in the surviving fragments of Tyrtaeus' poetry, which claim that 'we took spacious Messene, a good thing to plough, good to plant. For nineteen years they fought over it, unceasingly, always stout-hearted and spirited, the spearmen fathers of our fathers; and in the twentieth they, abandoning their rich fields, fled from the great mountains of Ithome.'[29] We know little about what actually happened; although Pausanias describes rousing victories on land by the Messenians and a long siege of the Messenians on Mount Ithome,[30] his narrative is tainted by echoes of later factual events involving the Spartans that occurred elsewhere in Greece.

We should probably accept Pausanias' claim that when Ithome fell to the Spartans, the defeated Messenian nobles fled, taking advantage of their ties to well-to-do families in Arcadia, Argos, Sicyon, and Eleusis near Athens. The ordinary Messenians who were scattered throughout their old farming communities had no such luck. The victorious Spartans forced them to work on the land they had once owned, requiring them to send half of their produce to Sparta. Evoking the true horror of these ordinary Messenians' fate, Tyrtaeus describes them as 'Like asses worn down by great burdens / bringing to their masters out of dire necessity / half of all the crop their tilled land bears.'[31] Anyone who has seen a tired old donkey will understand the simile only too well.

These harsh conditions eventually led the Messenians to rebel. The timing is probably linked to a serious defeat the Spartans suffered at the hands of Argos at the Battle of Hysiae in 669 BCE.[32] The details of this defeat are murky to say the least, but it seems that at the same time the Spartans were conquering the Messenians, the Argives were embarking on their own quest for regional domination. After defeating the Spartans at Hysiae, the Argive king Pheidon drove out the Elean organisers of the Olympic Games and presided over proceedings himself. Pheidon also established a standardised system of weights and measures across much of the Peloponnese.[33] Later sources claimed that Pheidon took the leadership of the Greeks away from the Spartans,[34] but in reality the Spartans had not yet gained the leadership. The Spartans would eventually take the leadership from the Argives, but that was a long way off. With the Spartans reeling from their defeat at Hysiae, the Messenians seized the opportunity to rise up against them. It would take the Spartans ten long years to put down.[35]

To inspire the Spartans during the long struggle, Tyrtaeus reminded them that Messenia was 'spacious' and 'good to plough'.[36] He also recalled their past defeats and victories, stressing that they had 'learned well the rage of painful war', and 'been with those fleeing' as well as 'those pursuing'.[37] As we have already seen, Tyrtaeus' most memorable verses told young Spartan soldiers that it was 'beautiful' to die fighting for Sparta.[38] Tyrtaeus even urged the young soldiers to 'hold the black goddesses of death dear like the rays of the sun'.[39] No wonder then that Leonidas, the hero of Thermopylae, reportedly said that Tyrtaeus was 'a good one to slaughter the lives of young men'.[40] This laconic saying essentially meant that Tyrtaeus encouraged young Spartans to go and get themselves killed.

Although the surviving fragments of Tyrtaeus' poetry date to the period of the Messenian war, we have very little reliable evidence about the war itself. One Tyrtaeus fragment mentions a battle near a 'trench',[41] which seems to fit with a claim of Pausanias' that in the third year of the war, the Messenian general Aristomenes led the Messenians against the Spartans at the so-called 'Battle at the Great Trench'. Another snippet of historical reality might be buried in a story Pausanias tells about the Messenian women garlanding their leader Aristomenes with ribbons and flowers while singing, 'To the middle of Stenyclarus plain and to the hilltop Aristomenes followed after the Lacedaemonians', after he had won a great victory over the

Spartans at the 'Battle at the Boar's Tomb'.[42] This may well be a folk song that endured the long centuries of Messenian servitude, one that was only sung when their Spartan masters were out of earshot. The notion that the Messenian rebels dug in on Mount Eira in the north of the Stenyclarus plain also makes sense in the context of a long rebellion.

However, the rest of Pausanias' narrative, which centres almost entirely on the seemingly miraculous achievements of the rebel leader Aristomenes – who was later worshipped as a demigod by the Messenians[43] – is just as unreliable as his narrative of the initial conquest. Nonetheless, no discussion of the Spartan conquest of Messenia could be complete without at least mentioning the absurd tale of Aristomenes' miraculous escape after being struck in the head in battle. The story goes that Aristomenes was captured with scores of his men, and the Spartans threw them all into the Kaeadas gorge – a seemingly inescapable chasm on Mount Taygetus into which Spartans cast criminals and prisoners of war.[44] While all of Aristomenes' men plunged to their deaths, the great hero himself escaped unscathed. Pausanias claimed that Aristomenes was rescued by an eagle, which flew beneath him as he fell;[45] the later writer Polyaenus claimed that Aristomenes floated down to the bottom of the ravine on his shield.[46] But that's not the most entertaining part of the story. Aristomenes initially gave up, assuming there was no escape from the chasm. But when he spotted a fox gnawing on his fallen comrades, he realised that there must be a way out. So he grabbed hold of the fox by its tail, holding on tight when it ran off, protecting himself from its teeth with the folds of his cloak. And so, according to the Messenians, Aristomenes escaped to fight another day.

Yet the Spartans had their own version of this story. They said that when they captured Aristomenes they cut open his chest to make sure he was dead. When they did, they found that his heart was 'hairy'. According to the Roman naturalist Pliny the Elder, the hairiness of his heart explained why Aristomenes was so extraordinarily brave.[47]

Despite Aristomenes' heroics – real and imaginary – the Spartans were ultimately able to put down the Messenian rebellion, securing the prime lands in the Pamisos valley and the Stenyclarus plain for themselves. In the process, the Spartans made themselves all very wealthy men, explaining why they kept a tight grip on Messenia for three long centuries. The Spartans would later argue that their long occupation of Messenia justified its acquisition in the first place. Even after the Messenians were liberated in 369 BCE, the Spartan king Archidamus would complain, 'But we took Messenia before many other Greek cities were even founded.'[48]

As terrible as it sounds to us today, enslaving the helots was the first crucial step on Sparta's path to superpower status. Slave labour allowed Spartan citizens to access the considerable agricultural resources of Laconia and Messenia without needing to work themselves. In fact, the Spartans were even able to fix the property qualification for citizenship sufficiently high that no Spartan citizen should ever need to work for a living again. Over the centuries that followed, the Spartans became increasingly rich, allowing them to devote their time to leisure activities such as athletics and games, as well as an increasingly communal lifestyle, which helped them become – as the Spartan king Demaratus put it to Xerxes – 'as good as anyone in the world'.[49]

2

Utopia on the Eurotas

Sixth-century BCE Laconian-style bronze figurine of a warrior, found at the sanctuary of Zeus at Dodona, Greece.

The foundations for Sparta's long-term success lay within a tough collective lifestyle that bonded citizens together. Life in Sparta was so harsh and austere that today we use the term 'spartan' to describe things that are plain, unadorned or lacking in comfort. But the toughness of their lifestyle was only one element of the Spartans' success. The rigidly hierarchical nature of Sparta's social structure, which masked tensions within and between citizens, the *perioikoi* and the helots, was also crucial to Sparta's long-term power. So too was the stability of its government, which kept the city-state free of the civil strife that plagued other Greek *poleis*. Together, the Spartan lifestyle and system of government created a tough, well-organised society, which contemporary and later writers could paint as a real-life – albeit austere – utopia.

'We all know that Sparta has the best constitution,' the fifth-century BCE Athenian Spartophile Critias enthused.[1] Plato – Critias' contemporary and fellow student of Socrates – felt that a 'god' must have been watching over Sparta when the Spartan constitution was set up.[2] The third-century BCE historian Polybius praised Sparta for combining 'all the excellences and distinctive features of the best constitutions', so that each part was checked by the others.[3] Even Aristotle, who was by no means an admirer, grudgingly admitted that many of his contemporaries considered Sparta to be an ideal blend of kingship, oligarchy and democracy.[4]

More modern admirers of the Spartan way of life have included Niccolò Machiavelli, who was 'firmly convinced' that the way to set up a long-lasting and stable republic was to constitute it like Sparta.[5] Jean-Jacques Rousseau deemed Sparta to be a 'Republic of demigods rather than men' – particularly admiring the fact that Spartans deemed 'rough labour' to be recreation.[6] During the French Revolution, Robespierre was likewise inspired, claiming that 'Sparta shines like a lightning-flash amid vast darknesses'.[7] Across the Atlantic, the US Founding Father Samuel Adams hoped that the United States could become 'the *Christian* Sparta'[8] – yet his cousin, the second US president John Adams, disagreed, deeming aspects of Sparta's communality 'stark mad'.[9] A close examination of the Spartan way of life shows why the two cousins reached such radically different conclusions.

* * *

The lifestyle of the Spartan citizens, who were known as Spartiates, was designed to foster a communal identity. The Spartiates called themselves the *homoioi* ('equals'), and to reflect that shared status they adopted a uniform appearance, keeping their hair long and wearing red cloaks and tunics when abroad and plain undyed clothing at home.[10] Every Spartiate was required to serve in the army until the age of sixty, and throughout their lives they were expected to share in communal activities, with citizens exercising and hunting together during the day, and dining together in mess clubs in the evenings. Citizens aged between twenty and thirty even slept together in barracks each night.[11]

Only sons of Spartan citizens who had been trained in the Spartan upbringing were eligible to become one of the *homoioi*. This communal upbringing saw Spartan boys separated into 'herds', with training undertaken in two separate phases – first as *paides* (literally 'boys') when they were between seven and fourteen, and then as so-called *paidiskoi* when they were aged fourteen to twenty. This training prepared them for their future role as hoplites; as the fourth-century BCE historian Xenophon described, 'from the beginning of boyhood they are taught the discipline for land warfare'.[12] The collective upbringing helped the Spartans develop what social psychologists call an 'in-group' identity. It was also an equalising measure: by taking the education and training of Spartan boys away from their fathers and handing it to a state official – the *paidonomos* ('boy-herder'), who had the authority to punish the boys as he saw fit, even to the extent of being given a staff of young adults called 'whip-bearers' – the Spartans ensured that the sons of richer and poorer citizens had the same tough start in life.[13]

Spartan boys in training had their hair shorn off and were only occasionally allowed to bathe in the Eurotas.[14] They weren't allowed to wear shoes, so that they would learn to run and jump faster than those who did, and were forced to make do with a single item of clothing all year round, to train them to endure both extreme heat and cold.[15] To remind them of their inferior status, the Spartans required teenagers to walk in the streets in silence, their gaze fixed to the ground and their hands inside their cloaks.[16] Only once they had completed their gruelling rite of passage would they be able to look and act like Spartiate gentlemen.

Their food intake was also strictly limited. According to Xenophon, the Eirens – twenty-year-olds on the cusp of adulthood who oversaw the boys when the boy-herder and other adults were unavailable – furnished them with only enough food for them not to be 'fat or sluggish'. They were supposed to know what it was like not to have enough, so they would be able to work hard without eating and make their rations last longer.[17] In fact, Spartan boys were so poorly fed that they needed to steal extra food to survive. Some readers might be familiar with the apocryphal tale of the Spartan boy who 'stole' a fox cub and hid it in his cloak. When the fox turned 'savage', the boy remained steadfastly silent while his insides were clawed and bitten out, rather than cry out and be caught stealing.[18]

Although modern scholars tend to doubt the veracity of this particular story, we have no reason to doubt that Spartan boys did indeed steal food.[19] Xenophon even describes a conversation he once had with the Spartiate Cheirisophus about the merits of Spartan theft. When the two were discussing how best to 'steal' higher ground from the enemy during combat in Asia, Xenophon suggested that Cheirisophus was best qualified to lead the operation because Spartans practise stealing from an early age; Cheirisophus retorted that as the democratic Athenians were experts at 'stealing' public funds, surely Xenophon was better qualified.[20] The practice might seem bizarre, but Xenophon provides an explanation: the light rations made the boys better able to keep going on an empty stomach; stealing made them 'more resourceful and better fighters' by preparing them for future ambushes. Furthermore, a boy would be beaten if he were ever caught in the act, to punish him for 'not carrying out properly what he is taught to do'.[21] The boys even learned to work as part of a team in their stealing, with the older ones doing the stealing while younger boys acted as lookouts.[22]

A considerable part of a Spartan boy's education involved bodily exercises. Spartan youths spent much of their time competing in athletics, wrestling, boxing and the *pankration* (a mix of boxing and wrestling not unlike modern mixed martial arts). But Plato also attests to 'group fights with bare knuckles,'[23] which some modern scholars have linked to a Roman-era ritual bare-knuckle battle between teams of boys. After sacrificing a puppy to the war god Enyalios and releasing trained fighting boars, two teams of Spartan boys would enter a sacred grove of plane trees, which was surrounded by a moat, and try to drive their opponents into the water by kicking, punching, biting and gouging.[24] Spartan boys may even have duelled with knives; we know they carried curved blades – the *xuēlē* – which they used as a makeshift woodcutter and strigil. Xenophon recalls meeting a certain Dracontius who was exiled from Sparta as a boy for accidentally killing another boy with his blade.[25]

Spartan boys honed their sporting skills at various competitions held throughout Laconia, in particular during an annual contest held in honour of the goddess Artemis Orthia from at least the fourth century BCE. One such 'competition' involved boys 'stealing' cheeses placed on the altar of the goddess, which was guarded by defenders armed with whips. It was a matter of honour for the boys to steal as many cheeses as they could, with the whipping intended to make the point that a short period of pain was worth enduring in the pursuit of honour.[26] A fourth-century BCE inscription atop a dedication of five sickles commemorating one youth's successes in the games in honour of Orthia reads: 'Victorious Arexippus dedicated these to Orthia, manifest for all to see in the gatherings of boys.' Archaeologists have also found vast numbers of bronze, lead and ivory figurines that youths on the cusp of adulthood seem to have dedicated to the goddess Artemis Orthia, perhaps as part of this festival. Hundreds of fragmentary clay masks have also been unearthed, which might have been worn by youths dancing in honour of the goddess.

When Spartans reached adulthood, they would adopt the uniform appearance described earlier – long hair and red clothing – further cementing their in-group identity. The early king Charilaus was said to have explained that Spartans chose to wear their hair long because it was the least expensive of all possible adornments,[27] while Xenophon claims there was no point in a Spartan trying to make money to spend on expensive cloaks, since they adorned themselves through the good conditions of their bodies.[28] Spartan cloaks were often described as *phaulos* (literally 'slight' or 'insufficient'), suggesting that they were thin and shabby. But their long hair and red cloaks showed the outside world that Spartans were gentlemen of leisure. The ancient Greeks didn't believe it was possible for any man with long hair to perform manual labour,[29] while producing the red dye for their cloaks, like the Tyrian purple later worn by Roman emperors, was incredibly laborious. It required extracting and heating the hypobranchial glands from murex shellfish, and more than 10,000 of these molluscs were needed to produce just one gram of dye. With their elaborate hairstyles and expensively dyed but shabby cloaks, the Spartans presented a collective image of modestly dishevelled rich men – not unlike a cash-poor modern country squire wearing a battered, but once expensive, tweed jacket.

To maintain their citizenship, all Spartiates were obliged to dine together in the evenings, in mess groups called *pheiditia* – a term derived from the word for 'thrifty'. A bronze figurine from around 530–500 BCE (now in the collection of the British Museum) that shows a long-haired, bearded man reclining on a dining couch while leaning on one elbow and holding a shallow dish in his left hand may be a representation of a Spartan dining in a mess hall. To join one of these groups, Spartans had to pass a unanimous secret ballot by existing members,[30] and supply monthly contributions of foodstuffs from their estates in Laconia and Messenia. Modern scholars have calculated that each Spartiate would have needed to own at least 15 hectares of land to meet their mess contributions, making them *all* wealthy by ancient Greek standards. We can safely say that no other Greek *polis* boasted such a large population of citizens with that level of wealth.

Astoundingly, given the paucity of Spartan source material we have, we know exactly how much of which foodstuffs each citizen had to provide each month: 45 kilograms of barley, 3 kilograms of cheese, 1.5 kilograms of figs, a small amount of pork (roughly equivalent in value to £160 or $250 today) and 37 litres of wine.[31] The Spartan main meal comprised unbaked barley burgers and 'black broth'. This black broth wasn't made from coffee, as Sir Henry Blount, the seventeenth-century 'father of the English coffeehouse', suggested it might have been,[32] but rather by boiling pork in salt and blood – hence its other name, 'blood soup'.[33] The broth was so unpleasant that a visitor from Sybaris, a Greek city in southern Italy that was notorious for its luxury (hence the modern word 'sybaritic'), remarked that he no longer considered the Spartans to be brave after trying their food, because 'anyone in their right mind would prefer to die ten thousand times than share such a poor living'.[34]

However, there was absolutely nothing frugal about the portion sizes. Scholars have calculated that the monthly contributions would have produced more than double the number of calories required by an adult male to maintain a healthy body. Given that Spartan citizens were expected to be comparatively slim, they must have been training very hard to require that level of calorie intake.

There was also an 'afters' course, which was not covered by the required monthly food contributions. This consisted of game from hunting (wildfowl, deer and boar), lamb or goat from the Spartans' flocks, or perhaps even wheaten bread.[35] The last was a luxury product at Sparta; only the very wealthy would have had sufficient land to grow wheat in addition to the barley required for the main meal. Hunting would have been useful in conditioning Spartan men and boys to kill with bladed weapons, and the communal element of the activity would have helped foster trust – a vital quality in a hoplite phalanx where the shield of the man standing beside you could mean the difference between life and death. The Spartans reputedly shunned cakes and sweetmeats, with the fourth-century BCE king Agesilaus once dismissively passing the latter to his helots because such extravagances were alien to free men.[36]

Although the Spartans had a reputation for being abstemious with alcohol,[37] the reality is that they were far from temperate. In fact, the monthly wine contributions for the messes were equivalent to nearly 1.5 bottles of modern wine for each diner – every single night. When it was watered down, as was normal ancient Greek practice, the volume drunk would have been astonishing. The wine flowed so freely in Sparta that visitors from the island of Chios – men who were themselves notorious for heavy drinking – drank so much that they ended up vomiting in one of Sparta's public buildings. Spartan citizens were expected to control themselves, so the authorities instituted a rigorous investigation to make sure none of the *homoioi* had made the mess. When they confirmed that the Chians were responsible, they ensured no further embarrassment for either party, issuing a face-saving proclamation giving the Chians permission to be 'filthy'.[38] To ensure that they understood the consequences of drunkenness, Spartan boys were sometimes invited to the adult messes to watch the helots drink unmixed wine.[39] Rather than not being allowed to be drunk, it was probably the case that Spartans were not allowed to be *seen* to be drunk.

No Spartan citizens – not even the kings – were exempt from communal dining. Ancient observers regarded this measure as 'democratic'.[40] Nonetheless, the rules were a little more flexible for the kings than for ordinary citizens. They were permitted to eat in their own mess, with dining companions of their choice – so-called 'Pythians', because they also acted as the kings' official envoys to Delphi, the home to Pythian Apollo. The kings also received a double portion of food with which they could entertain guests.[41] After leading the Spartans to victory at the Battle of Mantinea in 418 BCE, the Eurypontid king Agis asked for his meal to be delivered to his home, so that he could dine with his wife. When the authorities refused him this special treatment, Agis was so furious that he refused to make a state sacrifice the next day; in return, the authorities issued him a fine.[42]

Although Sparta is sometimes compared to a military camp in the ancient sources,[43] in reality it looked more like a community of gentlemen landowners. As mentioned before, when the Spartans set the rules of citizenship (some time prior to the late sixth century BCE) they fixed the property qualification so high that citizens would never need to work for a living. Consequently, the Spartan citizen body comprised only men who were wealthy enough to buy the bronze armour required, but also to have the leisure time required to keep their bodies strong by engaging in such gentlemanly pursuits as gymnastic exercises, sprinting (including while wearing armour), long-distance running, the *hoplomachia* (mock fighting in armour), dancing in armour, and playing team ballgames such as 'battle-ball' (*sphairomachia*),[44] in which two teams vied to catch a ball and throw it over the heads of the opposition until one team pushed the other over a line. Hunting and horse-breeding for chariot racing were also popular activities for Spartans. All this sport, which kept citizens fit and strong, is probably what Xenophon meant when he said that the only 'work' permitted for Spartan citizens was that which promoted 'freedom for the *polis*'.[45]

The Spartans so excelled at sports that between the first Olympic Games in 776 BCE and around 500 BCE, they dominated some of the key events at the ancient games, which were held every four years at a sanctuary dedicated to Zeus. As is still the case today, winning brought great honour to both the athletes and their home states. Unlike in the modern Olympics, only men could participate, and they competed naked. The Spartans were apparently the first Greeks to strip naked for exercising.[46] At the fifteenth Olympic Games, in 720 BCE, Acanthus the Lacedaemonian scandalised his fellow Greeks by casting off his loincloth and racing to victory in both the two-stade sprint (a race equivalent to 384 metres) and the *dolichos* (approximately 4,800 metres). Before Acanthus stripped off, the Greeks had been 'ashamed' to compete naked.[47]

At Sparta, there was a strong focus on the good physical appearance of both men and women, which was by no means unconnected to all their naked sporting activities. The Spartan poet Tyrtaeus encouraged young Spartans to risk their lives in combat, promising that if they died young, they would remain forever beautiful: 'for the young everything is seemly, so long as he has the splendid flower of lovely youth, for men a wonder to see, and lovely to women when alive, and handsome too when they have fallen in the front ranks.'[48]

The Spartan officials known as ephors ('overseers') reportedly inspected the young men in the nude every ten days to ensure they had not grown fat. A Spartan named Naucleides, who had become 'extremely corpulent', was even made to stand in the middle of the assembly to shame him into changing his ways.[49] When the reforming kings Agis IV and Cleomenes III tried to revive Spartan greatness in the third century BCE, they did so by boosting the number of citizens with the 'finest looking' of the *perioikoi*.[50]

Spartan women were also expected to be physically attractive. The reputation of Sparta's women for beauty goes back to Helen, whose physical perfection caused the ten-year Trojan War. Indeed, Homer referred to Sparta as a 'land of beautiful women'.[51] The beauty of Spartan maidens is emphasised in the surviving fragments of the poet Alcman's *Maiden Song*. The chorus of unmarried young Spartan women single out Agido and Hagesichora as first and second in 'beauty', making it clear that they are the most eligible of the bachelorettes. The need for

Spartan brides to be beautiful is apparent in the stories of the sixth-century BCE king Ariston stealing his best friend's wife because of her immense beauty,[52] and the fifth-century BCE general Lysander seeking to swap his fiancée for a prettier one.[53]

Spartan girls participated in sports, including running, wrestling and jumping, to ensure that they would bear 'sturdy' babies.[54] Later sources add that girls were required to sing and dance naked, with the male citizens watching on.[55] They were also notorious for what was known as the 'rump jump' or *bibasis*, whereby they would jump up and kick their own buttocks, first with one foot, then the other, followed by both at the same time. There were even competitions, with an epigram recording one Spartan girl's proud boast: 'I managed one thousand jumps in the *bibasis*, more than any other girl.'[56]

Rather than competing naked like the men and boys, Spartan girls protected their modesty by wearing short tunics. Nonetheless, these tunics exposed their thighs, earning them the sobriquet 'thigh-flashers'.[57] A bronze figurine from c. 530–500 BCE, found at Dodona and currently on display at the National Archaeological Museum in Athens, depicts a Spartan girl running or dancing, her short-sleeved tunic hitched above her left thigh. Other bronze figurines, thought to represent wrestlers, depict Spartan girls bare-breasted, wearing only triangular loincloths. Plutarch even claims that the occasional nudity of Spartan maidens incentivised Spartan men to marry, out of 'amorous necessity'.[58]

Given the importance of sport in Sparta, it is no wonder that Spartans had such success at the Olympics, allowing them to erect numerous monuments across Olympia to celebrate their victories. Few have survived intact, but the Roman-period travel writer Pausanias recorded the texts documenting some of the more remarkable Spartan achievements. The sprinter Chionis – a veritable Usain Bolt of his day – won seven

Olympic running titles in the seventh century BCE: four in the stade sprint (192 metres) and three in the two-stade race. The Spartans were sensitive enough about their reputation for athletic prowess to later add a note explaining that Chionis did not also win at the footrace in armour, because that event had not yet been invented.

Sparta also produced some remarkably successful Olympic wrestlers, most notably Hetoemocles and his father Hipposthenes, who between them won eleven Olympic wrestling titles in the eighth and seventh centuries BCE.[59] The Spartans are also known to have tasted success in the pentathlon, boxing and the *pankration*, but later tradition had it that the Spartans started shunning the latter two sports, in which it was permissible to admit defeat, because they did not want to encourage the idea that it was ever acceptable to concede victory.[60]

Song and dance were also crucial communal aspects of Spartan life. Choral singing was so important that the great Greek lyric poet Pindar described how 'councils of old men are pre-eminent there, and the spears of young men, and choirs and the Muse and Festivity',[61] while the fifth-century BCE tragedian Pratinas of Phlius compared the Spartans to cicadas.[62] One of the highlights of Spartan religious festivals was the so-called *trichoria* (literally 'the three choruses'). 'We were once valiant young men,' a choir of old men would sing, after which a chorus of men in their prime would respond with 'But we are the valiant ones now; put us to the test, if you wish'; then a third choir of boys replied, 'But we shall be far mightier.'[63] Choruses in Athens were usually comparatively small, with between twelve and fifty members; if all the male Spartans sang in three large groups – literally thousands at the height of Sparta's citizen numbers – the effect would have been truly remarkable.

The Spartans would also learn the *pyrrhichē*, a form of dance performed while wearing hoplite armour,[64] which involved simulating dodging blows and missiles by swerving and ducking, leaping and crouching, as well as assuming attacking postures.[65] Spartan boys also learned the *anapale* ('wrestling dance'), in which they would perform wrestling movements in time to music.[66] At the end of a hard day of physical training, a flute player would strike up a tune while tapping a beat with his foot; the young men would follow one another in a line, performing 'figures' in rhythmic steps, sometimes specifically martial and at other times those of choral dancing.[67] All these dances would have helped prepare Spartan boys and young men for the rigours of hand-to-hand combat.

Where Sparta most resembled a military camp was in the lack of freedom of movement it afforded those of its citizens who were not participating in military service or sporting competitions abroad. The implication is that the authorities wanted to ensure that as many as possible were on hand to defend the city if required, although Plato claims that the reason Spartans under the age of thirty were not normally allowed to travel abroad was a fear that they would 'unlearn' Spartan ways.[68] Isocrates even suggests that this restriction on movement extended to all adult Spartans fit for military service,[69] meaning everyone aged between twenty and sixty. Spartan citizens in their twenties also seem to have lived in barracks, rather than at home.[70]

*   *   *

The distinctive Spartan upbringing and way of life forged a strong group identity. It being human nature to divide the world into 'us' and 'them', the Spartans were naturally unable to view everyone from Lakonike as part of their 'in-group'. We have already seen that they distanced themselves from certain other residents of Lakonike: the *perioikoi* and the helots. But the *perioikoi* – the inhabitants of all the towns in Laconia and

Messenia except for Sparta and Amyclae – were an unusual case. For the Spartans, they were both 'us' and 'them', sharing the designation 'Lacedaemonians' with the *homoioi*, while also being viewed differently.

The relationship between the Spartiates and the *perioikoi* was unusual for the time. Regions far smaller than Lakonike, such as Arcadia just north of Sparta or Boeotia in central Greece, typically consisted of dozens of *poleis*, which were either fiercely independent or formally bound together in a federal league. But the *perioikoi* were neither citizens of fully independent *poleis* nor equals in a league with the Spartans. They were free to trade with the outside world, but had no control over foreign policy and were required to follow the Spartiates into war. The Spartan authorities could even put them to death without trial.[71] For this reason, academics sometimes treat them as 'second-class' Spartan citizens.

The majority of perioikic communities were located in Laconia. Sellasia and Pellana in the north provided a buffer between Sparta and their Arcadian neighbours. To the southeast, in the central Eurotas valley, were Geronthrae and Croceae; the former has magnificent Mycenaean 'Cyclopean' masonry, while the latter was a source of 'lapis Lacedaemonius' (also known as 'Spartan basalt'), a greenish stone that was popular for decorative sculpture in Roman times. To the south were the port towns of Gytheum, Las and Taenarum, most notable for quarries where *rosso antico* and black marble were mined. In the west were Thalamae and Oetylos, while Thyrea (taken from Argos at the Battle of the Champions), Tyros, Prasiae, Kyphanta, Zarax, Epidaurus Limera, Prasiae and Boeae lay in the east. Zarax and Epidaurus Limera had splendid fortification walls that are still visible today, while Boeae was an important site for processing the *murex brandaris* shellfish, producer of the dye that the Roman naturalist Pliny the Elder described as 'the best in Europe.'[72] Offshore to the south was the island of Cythera, said to be the birthplace of Aphrodite, the goddess of love.[73] There were also a smaller number of communities of *perioikoi* in Messenia: Aulon, Cyparissia, Pylos and Methone on the west coast; Asine, Korone, Kardamyle and Pharae scattered around the gulf of Messenia; Thouria and Aethaea in the heart of the Pamisos Valley. The Skiritai, who lived in villages to the north of Sparta and served separately in Spartan armies, fighting as an advance guard, were also considered *perioikoi*.

Modern scholars suggest that the *perioikoi* owned around 30 per cent of the arable land in Lakonike; their small landholdings compared to the Spartiates reflected their inferior wealth. Whereas all Spartiates were landed gentry, only some of the *perioikoi* would have been wealthy enough to afford the bronze armour necessary to serve as hoplites. Most of them would have been engaged in economic activities that were denied to the Spartiates: manufacturing, overseas trade and the exploitation of mineral resources. The *perioikoi* likely made the Spartans' pottery, including a special military drinking cup called a *kōthōn*, which Critias praised as the most serviceable drinking cup for military campaigns because it was the easiest to carry in one's knapsack and had a special lip that trapped impurities.[74] The *perioikoi* would also have imported the copper and tin required for the Spartans' bronze arms and armour. They were probably even responsible for much of the surviving 'Spartan' art found in museums throughout the world today – most notably the high-quality, black-glazed ceramic vessels that were widely exported in the sixth century BCE, particularly to Samos, off the coast of Asia Minor, and Etruria in central Italy.

It has been suggested that without the *perioikoi*, Sparta would have never been more than an average military power, because the wealthiest of them boosted Sparta's armies by serving as hoplites in the phalanx. Indeed, over time, the Spartans became increasingly reliant on their military contribution. At the Battle of Plataea in 479 BCE, the Spartans and *perioikoi* were evenly matched. By 418 BCE, at the Battle of Mantinea, the *perioikoi* outnumbered the Spartiates around three to two. By the time of Sparta's disastrous defeat at Leuctra in 371 BCE, there were more than twice as many *perioikoi* as Spartiates. Many modern experts think that as the Spartans became more reliant on their neighbours, they allowed them to fight alongside them. It seems likely then that the *perioikoi* also wore red in battle, or the enemy would have been able to tell them apart.

It would also make sense for the *perioikoi* who served as hoplites to have received proper training; otherwise they would have been a liability in combat. For this reason, some modern scholars think the wealthiest may have paid for their sons to take part in the harsh Spartan upbringing, as *trophimoi* (literally 'foster-children') – a term that refers to foreigners who were sent to Sparta to be trained alongside Spartan boys. Given that the legal status of the *perioikoi* was no different from that of foreigners, the label could have easily included them.

*   *   *

Isocrates claimed that the Spartans enslaved the souls of the *perioikoi* as thoroughly as they did the bodies of the helots,[75] and the ultimate key to Sparta's success was the exploitation of the group the Spartans considered the real 'them': the underclass of helots.

The primary role of these slaves was – as Aristotle bluntly put it – to 'farm the land for the benefit of the Spartiates.'[76] To illustrate the difference in the groups' roles, the sixth-century BCE Spartan king Cleomenes claimed that Homer was 'the poet of the Spartiates', while another poet of roughly the same period, Hesiod, was 'the poet of helots'. Cleomenes explained that this was because Homer, who told the stories of the great Achaean heroes Achilles, Ajax, Agamemnon, Menelaus and Odysseus, taught 'what was needed to fight', while Hesiod, whose most famous work was a didactic poem about agriculture, passed on only 'what was necessary to farm'.[77]

By toiling on their masters' estates in the Sparta basin and the Helos plain in Laconia, and later the Pamisos Valley and the Stenyclarus plain in Messenia, the helots provided the Spartans with the large quantities of foodstuffs they needed to maintain their status as citizens. The helots have even been called the 'alimentary canal' of Spartan society, with the flow of produce providing what was needed for them to thrive,[78] but this analogy underplays the unequal and hateful nature of the relationship. For that reason, the Spartans might be better viewed as parasites, feeding off the forced labour of their helots.

Not all helots were farmers or herdsmen. Some of them also performed domestic duties – the type of activities that would have been performed by chattel slaves elsewhere in Greece. We hear of male helots serving as household servants,[79] watchmen[80] and grooms,[81] while helot women are known to have acted as nursemaids and made clothing for their owners.[82] The Spartans even made use of the helots in warfare, demanding that they carry the Spartiates' equipment while the army was on the march.[83] Helots even served as hoplites when the Spartans began to struggle for manpower in the fifth and fourth centuries, but employing them in war evidently carried a risk. When they were at home, the Spartans would remove the armstrap from the helots' shields to prevent the slaves from using the equipment against them. During campaigns this was unfeasible, however, so the Spartiates made sure to always carry their spears with them for protection.[84]

Although helots laboured for individual masters, with the richest Spartiates owning perhaps as many as 125 helots, the communal nature of Spartan society meant that poorer Spartiates were allowed to borrow helots from wealthier citizens as and when they required.[85] One source even suggests that helots could be beaten by any Spartiate, not just their owners.[86] This sharing of helots probably explains why later sources characterise them as 'public slaves in a manner' or as existing somewhere between free people and slaves,[87] which has led some modern experts to characterise them as 'serfs'.

Life for the helots was brutal. As we have already seen, each year the Spartan authorities would declare war on them, granting themselves permission to kill them as they pleased. As horrific as this sounds, the Spartans' brutality is confirmed by the Athenian philosopher and statesman Critias, who actually *praised* the Spartans for giving themselves 'the right of killing.'[88] The Spartans also forced the helots to wear dogskin caps and leather jerkins, and gave them a fixed number of beatings each year regardless of whether they had done anything wrong, to remind them of their inferiority. If any helot appeared to be too physically robust to be a slave, they had him put to death, before fining the master who had allowed it to happen.[89] We have already seen how helots were sometimes forced to get drunk to demonstrate to young Spartans the perils of overindulgence. The Spartans also forced helots to perform ignoble songs and dances, and helots were outright forbidden to sing the dignified songs the Spartans sang.[90]

By far the cruellest – not to mention the most terrifying – aspect of the helots' lives was the threat of arbitrary killing by the young Spartan adults participating in the *krypteia*. According to Aristotle, the young adult Spartiates thought to be the 'smartest' were periodically sent into the countryside with daggers and necessary rations, with orders to hunt down and kill the most dangerous helots. Sometimes they would hide during the day and spend their nights killing any helots they found on the roads. At other times they would cross the fields where the helots were labouring, and simply do away with the strongest of them.[91] It is little wonder, then, that some modern admirers of Sparta prefer Plato's version of the *krypteia*, which makes no mention of the Spartans terrorising the helots. He describes it as 'astoundingly harsh training for endurance: in winter unshod and without bedding, and without attendants, each attending himself, both by night and day, wandering across all the country'.[92]

Whatever the truth of this ritual, the helots were more than just victims – they represented an existential threat to the Spartans. With modern estimates suggesting that there were between 75,000 and 150,000 helots living alongside a maximum of between 6,000 and 9,000 Spartiates, it is easy to see why Thucydides claimed that, for the Spartans, 'considerations of security against the helots were always paramount'.[93] Aristotle likened the helots to 'enemies lying constantly in wait'.[94]

Consequently, in Laconia, modern archaeological field surveys have found evidence to suggest that the Spartans tried to limit the helots' capacity to conspire against them by keeping them dispersed in small family groups or hamlets, rather than allow them to mingle in larger slave townships. Overseeing and controlling these scattered helot labourers would have been relatively easy for Spartiates, as most of their estates in Laconia lay adjacent to the five villages that made up the 'city' centre. Even their estates on the prime lands of the Helos plain were close enough to Sparta to be visited in one day.

Rather surprisingly, however, surveys conducted in Messenia – far away from Sparta on the other side of the imposing Taygetus mountain range – have found evidence suggesting helots lived in large settlements there, perhaps for as many as 3,000 people. Quite why the Spartans would have allowed the Messenian helots to mass in such numbers, so far away from direct supervision, is difficult to explain. Some modern experts have seen this as evidence that relations between the helots and the Spartiates might have been less hostile than the sources suggest. Some even suggest that these helot townships were self-running, overseen by helot 'headmen' who would maintain order for both the helots and their masters. It may simply be, though, that the surveys in Messenia have been looking in the wrong place – beyond the Aigaleon ridge, which separates the Pamisos valley from the coastal strip near the Perioikic town of Pylos, rather than in the prime agricultural lands in the Pamisos valley and the Stenyclarus plain where the main Spartiate estates likely were.

In the Stenyclarus area, at Kopanaki and Basiliko, archaeologists have uncovered two large, two-storey Classical-period structures, which have been tentatively identified as the main buildings of large Spartiate 'estates' or 'plantations'. The eleven-room structure at Kopanaki measures 30 metres by 17 metres – so large by the standards of the time that it was initially mistakenly identified as a Roman-period villa. Pottery sherds found at the site suggest the building dates from the second quarter of the sixth century to the first quarter of the fifth century BCE, at which time it was violently destroyed. The remarkably similar structure of a building found at Basiliko (in terms of shape and size, chronology and pottery types), less than ten kilometres away, sits on a gentle slope overlooking the Pamisos Valley. It too was initially misidentified by archaeologists, this time as a small fortress. But its similarity to the Kopanaki mansion suggests that both buildings served a similar purpose. Given their location in prime agricultural land, it is tempting to see these buildings as evidence that Messenian helots worked in large numbers under direct supervision on huge plantations, rather than living in large self-regulated townships.

As their communal lifestyle required Spartan citizens to be

in or at least near the city of Sparta for most of the year – hence the need for Spartiates to get permission to be away from the city – there must have been some sort of system whereby managers were left on the plantations. One of our later sources mentions the terms *mnoia* and *mnoionomoi*, respectively defining them as 'group of slaves' and 'leaders of helots';[95] this suggests that helots were clustered in groups, with leaders to ensure that the estates ran smoothly. These leaders could well have been helots themselves, engaging in what has been called 'privileged collaboration' with their masters. It might also be that some masters spent harvest time on their estates to ensure they received a fair share of the produce. The large buildings at Kopanaki and Basiliko could, in fact, be country mansions, where the landowners stayed while overseeing their helot workers.

Despite the hostility between the helots and their masters, some helots managed to acquire their freedom – usually in return for military service. As Spartan imperial ambitions grew in the fifth and fourth centuries BCE, they increasingly offered helots freedom in return for serving as hoplites, adjacent to them in the phalanx. After completing their military service and gaining their freedom, these fortunate souls gained the title *neodamodeis* (literally 'new members of the *demos*'), but despite their promotion in status, they did not become members of the Spartan *demos*. Rather, they were free men who were subject to the Spartans, not unlike the *perioikoi*. We know that the Spartans settled one group of these *neodamodeis* on the border between Lakonike and Elis, presumably because the Eleans were hostile to the Spartans at the time.[96] This might suggest that the primary duty of these freedmen was to provide a buffer against Sparta's enemies. The *neodamodeis* may also have been required to capture runaway slaves, before returning them to the Spartiate estates.

We might even know the name of one such freed helot.

Fragmentary inscriptions from the Temple of Poseidon at Cape Taenarum from *c.* 450–430 BCE record the manumission of Laconian slaves – one of them for a slave called Kleogenes, who was freed by his owner Theares. Given that chattel slaves in ancient Greece were normally foreign captives, and Kleogenes has a Greek name, some experts argue that he must have been ethnically Greek. As we have already seen, the helots were said to be Greeks conquered by the Spartans, rather than captives from abroad. Kleogenes may well have been a helot, freed by his Spartiate master.

That any helots were ever willing to fight for the Spartans is a wonder – and not just because of how badly they were treated by their masters. Thucydides reports a truly horrific atrocity. The story goes that the Spartans once invited the helots to name those among them who had most distinguished themselves in war, with the promise of freedom as a reward. Some 2,000 helots volunteered, donning garlands and processing around the temples, but the entire episode was an elaborate hoax. The Spartans had calculated that those helots who were singled out would be the 'most spirited', and therefore the ones who were most likely to rebel. They executed every one of them – and in secret, so that no one ever knew what happened to them.[97]

Some modern scholars doubt that this massacre ever happened, partly because Thucydides is uncharacteristically vague about the details. Some focus on the fact that he describes the massacre taking place around the time that 700 other helots known as the 'Brasideioi' took up arms and fought alongside the Spartans under the command of Brasidas, in return for freedom. Why would they have done that so soon after such a horrific massacre? Others suggest that Thucydides' source was probably a former Messenian helot who gained his freedom following a revolt – and who may have told Thucydides this nightmare tale to darken Sparta's reputation. As an Athenian,

Thucydides would have been only too happy to believe the worst of the Spartans, so he may have been an easy target.

We can't discount the possibility that the Spartans really did intend to free the helots, only to panic when so many vigorous ones took up the offer. Or it may be that the Spartans themselves promulgated the story. As we've already seen, they terrorised the helots with the threat of the *krypteia*, so the story of such a massacre would have made the helots even more afraid of their masters.

Although there were active helot rebellions, for the most part the Spartans kept them under control. A particularly revealing story comes from a time when some helots did rebel, shortly after the Spartans' defeat by the Thebans at the Battle of Leuctra in 371 BCE. The following summer, the Thebans invaded Laconia, prompting a full-scale helot rebellion. But when the Spartans offered the prize of freedom to any helots who wanted to help fight the invaders, more than 6,000 of them answered the call.[98] Some of these helot hoplites were captured while fighting alongside their masters. When the Thebans told the helots that they were now free and could finally sing the songs they were prohibited from singing, the helots politely declined, telling the Thebans that their Spartan 'masters' would not approve.[99]

The refusal of these helots to accept their freedom can be interpreted in different ways. Some scholars have seen their behaviour as a sign of their fear of their masters, while others regard it as 'Stockholm syndrome'-style loyalty. It might be that many helots did not want to be free *from* the Spartans, but simply free *within* Spartan society. Whatever the case, the story shows the pressure placed on the helots in Sparta. The Spartiates needed them to be sufficiently in awe that they would not feel able to rebel, even when the numbers were stacked in the helots' favour.

* * *

The other key factor in Sparta's success was the stability of its government. Whereas most other ancient Greek states were governed by a democracy, an oligarchy – literally 'rule by the few' – or an autocrat, either a king or a 'tyrant', Sparta's government was seen to be a mix of all three, with each element cancelling out the excesses of the other two and preventing the type of civil strife between rich and poor that afflicted the vast majority of Greek *poleis*.[100]

Sparta resembled a monarchy in that there were kings, but the fact that there were two of them, from two separate royal families – the 'Agiads', named for Eurysthenes' son Agis, and the 'Eurypontids', named after Procles' son Euryphon – means that it was actually a dyarchy. Nor were Sparta's kings autocrats; they could be fined, exiled or deposed, and their influence was further limited by the fact that there were always two of them ruling at any one time. Their main role was as military commanders, priests of Zeus and keepers of oracles from Delphi.[101] The Agiad king Cleomenes took this latter role so seriously that he stole scrolls recording oracles from the Athenian acropolis.[102]

There was, however, an oligarchic element to Spartan governance: a small ruling council of Elders called the *Gerousia*. The council was formed of the two kings, in addition to twenty-eight Spartan citizens over the age of sixty. All served for life, having been chosen by acclamation based on their excellence. Xenophon hailed this office, arguing that it ensured that Spartan citizens continued to uphold high principles even in old age,[103] while Plato praised the Spartans for restricting the powers of the kings by giving the Elders equal weight.[104] There were some dissenters, however: Aristotle argued that life-tenure was dangerous, on the grounds that the mind could grow old as much as the body.[105]

Political commentators at the time saw an element of democracy in the important elected office of 'ephor'. Literally 'overseers', five ephors were elected each year from the citizen body. With repeat office apparently unlawful, it seems likely that the majority of Spartiate males would have served as an ephor at some point during their lifetime. At the beginning of each year, the ephors would order citizens to 'cut' their moustaches and obey the laws of Sparta.[106] Although many surviving sculptures show Spartans without moustaches, Athenian comedians frequently portrayed Spartans with exaggeratedly hairy upper lips,[107] so it seems likely that this law was often flouted.

The power of the ephors is evinced in the fact that they were the only Spartan citizens not obliged to rise when one of the kings approached. The ephors also exchanged monthly oaths with the kings, in which the latter would swear that they would 'reign according to the established laws of the state'. The ephors responded, 'While you abide by your oath, we will keep the kingship unshaken.'[108] Although this suggests that the kings and ephors acted in opposition to each other, one tradition had it that the Eurypontid king Theopompus had created the ephorate in order to preserve the kingship for posterity – giving the people some of his powers in order to keep them quiet.[109] When his wife complained that he ought to be ashamed to pass down a smaller kingship to his sons than the one he inherited, Theopompus responded, 'I do not, for I hand it on more lasting.'[110]

Another democratic element in Sparta was a citizen assembly where Spartiates could vote on bills put forward by the Elders. As with voting for the Elders, decisions were made not by a show of hands, but by shouting.[111] The citizens in the assembly were not allowed to discuss or amend bills; the role of the assembly was effectively to rubber-stamp decisions that had been made by the Elders. This arrangement came about because the Spartan citizens had previously played too active a role in the decision-making process, 'twisting' the resolutions put forward by the Elders. Consequently, a blunt amendment was inserted into Sparta's constitution: 'If the people choose crookedly, the kings and elders shall set it aside.'[112]

*   *   *

The entire Spartan way of life was said to have been devised by an ancient lawgiver named Lycurgus. Prior to him, the Spartans were reputedly the most badly governed of people;[113] indeed, Lycurgus' father, the Eurypontid king Eunomos, was killed after being struck by a cleaver while trying to stop a brawl. When Lycurgus' elder brother Polydectes died shortly afterwards, Lycurgus acted as regent for his nephew Charilaus, using his authority to establish a new constitution for the Spartans – and changing their way of life in the process.[114]

Lycurgus reportedly travelled to Crete, Egypt, Spain and even India as he sought inspiration to cure Sparta's ills. Once he had finally come up with a plan, he travelled to the oracle of Delphi and sought approval from the god Apollo. Today we call his constitutional brainchild the 'Great Rhetra' – *rhētra* being both a word that literally meant 'saying' and the Spartan word for 'decree'. Lycurgus' decree divided the Spartans into tribes and *obai*, established a council of Elders, and introduced regular citizen assemblies. The power, from that point on, belonged to the people.[115]

Lycurgus was also said to have redistributed the lands of Laconia into 9,000 equal 'plots' known as *klaroi* for the Spartans, with 30,000 smaller plots being allocated to the *perioikoi*.[116] He also reportedly banned gold and silver currency, instead imposing a system of iron 'spits'. This unwieldy currency was almost impossible to hoard in secret – a whole cart of spits was needed to make up 1,000 drachmas' worth, the same value as only 250 small silver coins used elsewhere in Greece.[117] The iron currency was worthless outside Sparta,[118] and it could not be used for anything else – when red-hot, the iron was quenched in vinegar to make it brittle.[119] Lycurgus' final equalising measure was to introduce a rule that required citizens to dine in common messes.[120] After Lycurgus died, a statue of him was erected, and from then on he was worshipped as a demigod.[121]

Many readers will never have heard of Lycurgus, but he has something of a global reputation as a lawgiver. The young Eugène Delacroix commemorated him in a mural, *Lycurgue consulte la Pythie*, which he painted on the ceiling of the central dome of the library at the Palais Bourbon in Paris; statues of him also stand in the Hall of the Four Columns in the same building, and outside the Palace of Justice in Brussels. Since 1950, a marble relief portrait of Lycurgus has sat above the gallery doors of the House Chamber in the US Capitol building in Washington, DC, alongside twenty-two other figures 'noted for their work in establishing the principles that underlie American law', including Moses, Pope Innocent III, Napoleon and Thomas Jefferson.

However, despite his enduring reputation, we can't be certain the Lycurgus even existed. Even in antiquity, the Spartans and other Greeks were unable to agree on the details of his life. Herodotus claims that Lycurgus was not regent for the Eurypontid Charilaus, but rather for the Agiad Leobotes.[122] Some traditions placed him as living in around 1000 BCE, but others claimed he was integral to the establishment of the Olympic Games in 776 BCE.[123] The seventh-century BCE Spartan poet Tyrtaeus does not seem to have mentioned Lycurgus at all – which is odd, because by the time Tyrtaeus started writing his now-lost poem 'Good Order' about the Spartan way of life, Lycurgus should already have reorganised Spartan society. Most tellingly, there's no way Lycurgus could have banned gold and silver coinage at any point between the eleventh and seventh centuries BCE: it hadn't yet been invented, the earliest use of precious metal coinage in Greece dating to the late seventh century BCE. Clearly, then, Lycurgus did not make all these changes, but the important thing is that later generations for some reason came to *remember* that he did. The myth of him bringing order was a sort of official fiction, designed to convince both themselves and outsiders that Sparta had always been well governed, and populated by happy, unified citizens.

* * *

The depiction of Sparta as an austere, wealth-free utopia was far from accurate. But the strong group Spartan identity allowed them to divide and conquer – both literally and metaphorically – the other residents of Laconia, while also masking the inequality that threatened the long-term stability of the citizenry.

Having between 6,000 and 9,000 hoplites who were not required to work also helped the Spartans develop ambitions for further conquest. Elsewhere in Greece, citizens were required to fight for their homeland when required, but only those who could afford the expensive bronze armour were able to fight as hoplites. At Athens, for example, poorer citizens would row on warships or fight as light-armed skirmishers. But in Sparta things were different, because every citizen was able to afford the armour. Even as a small elite within a large *polis*, the Spartiates represented one of the largest hoplite forces in all Greece. Combined with the *perioikoi*, the Spartans were able to put together a truly formidable fighting force. They would use it to dominate their fellow Peloponnesians in the centuries to come.

3

Sparta's Rise to Dominance

600–520 BCE

Interior, black-figure Laconian wine cup, by the 'Hunt Painter' (*c.* 550–540 BCE), depicting two young Spartan soldiers carrying a dead comrade from the battlefield.

The conquest of Messenia in the mid-seventh century BCE laid the foundations for Spartan dominance in the Peloponnese. However, due to a lack of contemporary sources, it is hard to say with any confidence anything about what happened in Sparta until around 570 BCE, by which time the city-state was already starting to be recognised as the dominant military and political force in the region. The Spartans' sustained successes in the key events at the Olympic Games between 720 and 600 BCE suggests that during this period individual Spartans were taking advantage of the wealth that conquering Messenia had provided, devoting their daily lives to sport rather than working for a living. But we can't say confidently that the Spartans had *already* transformed themselves into a society of wealthy gentlemen calling themselves *homoioi*. That probably came after they had attained regional dominance. And how they attained that dominance takes us from the realm of myth-history, like that recorded by Pausanias, and into actual narrative history.

Our key source for Sparta's rise to dominance in the Peloponnese is the first ever surviving history – that written by Herodotus of Halicarnassus in the fifth century BCE. Despite his reputation for exaggeration, Herodotus is one of the more reliable sources when it comes to Spartan society and customs. He visited Sparta around 450 BCE, and the Spartans welcomed him warmly. When he was there, Herodotus talked with the grandchildren and children of the Spartans he describes – sometimes even the key protagonists themselves.

*   *   *

The first event in Spartan history that Herodotus recounts is their attempt in around 570 BCE to conquer the whole region of Arcadia, to the north-west of Sparta.[1] At first glance, this might have seemed rather ambitious, particularly given that Arcadia comprised more than thirty different *poleis*. But as Herodotus puts it, there were 'many, not few' Spartans, they were no longer content 'to remain quiet', and they had come to look down on the Arcadians.[2] Clearly, two generations of exploiting the Messenian helots had given them a strong sense of self-importance, but their desire to conquer Arcadia might suggest that their booming population was putting pressure on resources in both Laconia and Messenia.

Having decided to conquer and enslave the Arcadians, the Spartans did what they always did before any major action: they consulted the oracle at Delphi. When they asked whether their efforts would meet with success, Apollo's reply wasn't exactly what the Spartans wanted to hear, but it seemed positive nevertheless:

> You ask Arcadia of me? I will not give it.
> There are many men in Arcadia, eaters of acorns,
> These will stop you. But still, I do not begrudge you;
> I will give you Tegea, to dance with beating feet,
> And fine plainland to measure out with rope.[3]

Apollo's apparent promise that they would take Tegea's high-quality agricultural land emboldened the Spartans. But even without that assurance, the Spartans would have considered Tegea a soft target; the largest recorded Tegean army was the 1,500 hoplites they sent to Plataea in 479 BCE, whereas the Spartans sent 5,000 Spartiates and 5,000 *perioikoi* to the same battle.[4] Tegea was also a good strategic target, located on the main road to the Isthmus of Corinth; control of the region would improve Sparta's access to central Greece.

Confident in Apollo's apparent promise of conquest, the Spartans marched against the Tegeans carrying iron fetters, with which they planned to chain up the vanquished foe. But as was often the case, Apollo's prophecy was more ambiguous than it first seemed. The Spartans did indeed end up beating the Tegeans' fields with their feet and measuring them with ropes, just as Apollo had foretold – but not as their new masters. For the Spartans lost what modern historians have dubbed 'The Battle of the Fetters', and those who were taken prisoner ended up wearing their own fetters while they were put to work on the Tegeans' fields. Herodotus saw the fetters that the triumphant Tegeans dedicated to the goddess Athena Alea when he visited Tegea more than two hundred years later.[5] Pausanias saw them too, when he visited the temple half a millennium later.[6]

The fact that the Spartans went to battle carrying iron fetters strongly suggests that they intended to turn the Tegeans into helots, as they had done to the defeated peoples of Laconia and Messenia. Presumably this means that the Spartiates meant to divide the Tegeans' lands among themselves, which would certainly have increased both Sparta's geographical extent and the wealth of its citizens. Nonetheless, redistributing the landed wealth of the Tegeans among themselves would not have increased the number of Spartan citizens; it would simply have made the same number of citizens even wealthier. To extend Sparta's power they would need either more soldiers, or a different plan.

Initially, the Spartans seem to have stuck to their plans of conquest, but despite their numerical inferiority, the Tegeans proved to be difficult opponents. Indeed, Herodotus claims that the Spartans were 'always doing badly' in their conflicts with them, and many years later, at the Battle of Plataea (479 BCE), the Tegeans tetchily reminded the Spartans that they had often defeated them in the recent past.[7] Later sources recall a bad defeat for the Spartans when they attacked Tegea in winter. It was snowing, and the Spartans were particularly discomforted because their bronze armour was too cold to touch in the freezing conditions. Safe inside their own city, the Tegeans built a large fire which they used to warm their armour before they marched out to face the Spartans, and so had the better of the fighting.[8] In their desperation, the Spartans turned once more to Apollo at Delphi. This time they asked which god they needed to placate to defeat the Tegeans. Apollo told them to bring the bones of the hero Orestes, the nephew and son-in-law of Menelaus, 'home' to Sparta.

Although they now had a potential solution to their plight, the Spartans had a big problem: no one knew where Orestes' remains were buried. They consulted Apollo, but again the reply was vague:

> There is a place, Tegea, in the level plains of Arcadia.
> There two winds blow, strong by necessity,
> And stroke and counterstroke, and misery lies upon misery;
> There the life-giving earth holds Agamemnon's son.
> After bringing him, you shall become master of Tegea.[9]

None of the Spartans had any idea what this meant, beyond that Orestes was buried somewhere in Tegea. But soon afterwards, a man named Lichas – one of the so-called *agathergoi* (literally 'good-doers'), former members of the elite royal bodyguard of knights who were sent on foreign errands by the authorities – stumbled across the answer while he was in Tegea on another matter. It happened that Lichas found himself at a blacksmith's workshop. When the two got to talking, the blacksmith boasted to Lichas about an ossuary he had found in his workshop when he was digging a well. It was seven Greek cubits long (3.15

metres), he claimed, and inside it were the remains of a human the same size as the coffin. These bones had to be the remains of an ancient demigod, the blacksmith reasoned, as no mere mortal could have been more than three metres tall.

After hearing the blacksmith's tale, Lichas realised that these must be Orestes' bones. He reasoned that the bellows were the 'two winds' from Apollo's prophecy; the blacksmith's hammer and anvil were the 'stroke and counterstroke'; and the forged iron represented the 'misery upon misery', because iron weapons cause pain to men. When Lichas reported his findings to the authorities, they hatched a plan to get the bones for Sparta. They pretended to exile Lichas, who then went to Tegea, and told the blacksmith a sob story about being banished by the Spartans. After some resistance – Sparta was, after all, an on-and-off enemy of Tegea – the blacksmith agreed to rent him a room above his workshop. As soon as the opportunity presented itself, Lichas sneaked into the workshop at night, dug up the grave, and took the bones back to Sparta.[10]

As far-fetched as this story sounds, it may contain an element of truth – but what Lichas, the blacksmith, and whoever originally buried the bones thought were giant human remains were probably the bones of Pleistocene-epoch megafauna. Tegea lies in the basin of a prehistoric lake where woolly mammoths, giraffids and giant rhinoceros have been discovered, and modern palaeontologists have demonstrated that the bones of a complete mammoth skeleton can be cleverly rearranged to look like a stupendously giant human. We can also be confident that ancient Greeks found other prehistoric skeletons around this time. The so-called 'Monster of Troy' vase, a Corinthian wine cup from around 550 BCE, shows Heracles tackling a white-headed monster that looks suspiciously like a fossilised skull emerging from an eroding rocky outcrop.

So Orestes' bones were probably the remains of a mammoth

that had been mistakenly identified as a giant hero, only to be rediscovered by the blacksmith. This was not an isolated event. At around this time, the Spartans also brought back the bones of Orestes' son Tisamenus from Achaea in the northern Peloponnese, reburying them near their mess halls,[11] and in the fifth century BCE, the Athenian general Cimon brought the bones of the Athenian hero Theseus back to Athens from the island of Scyros, where he had died in exile.[12] Tisamenus' bones and those of Theseus were presumably also those of misidentified fossilised megafauna.

* * *

Our sources suggest that reclaiming Orestes' bones changed everything for the superstitious Spartans, who thereafter always had the upper hand in their wars – indeed, by 545 BCE, Herodotus says they had 'overcome most of the Peloponnese'.[13] In reality, what changed for the Spartans was their foreign policy. Rather than try to 'overcome' their fellow Peloponnesians by conquering and enslaving them, the Spartans switched to what might be called 'aggressive diplomacy' – perhaps because they realised that they lacked the numbers to keep conquering them. Their new policy involved ousting 'tyrants' – a word the Greeks used to describe strong men who had seized control of *poleis* across Greece in the sixth century BCE – from neighbouring city-states and placing power in the hands of like-minded wealthy 'oligarchs' who owed their authority to Sparta.[14] By doing this, the Spartans created a network of neighbouring allies who would provide a buffer zone from outside threats such as Argos, leaving them free to deal with internal threats from the helots in Laconia and Messenia.

The Spartans soon had a network of Peloponnesian cities bound to them which included most of the Dorian

Peloponnesians: Corinth, Sicyon, Tegea, Mantinea, Elis and Megara. This network both boosted Sparta's power and influence and isolated Argos. By the time the Persians invaded Greece in 480 BCE, this had developed into a well-established alliance system that contemporary sources refer to as 'the Lacedaemonians and their allies'; modern scholars typically call it the 'Peloponnesian League' or the 'Spartan alliance'. In time, this alliance would grow to include a shifting set of allies in central and northern Greece, as well as the Aegean islands, the Ionian islands and Sicily. This network was the platform on which Sparta's rise to power was built.

The Spartans also used the mythical past to justify their claims to authority in the Peloponnese. By reclaiming the bones of Orestes and Tisamenus – son and grandson of Agamemnon – and keeping them in Sparta, they were effectively claiming that Agamemnon was really Spartan, not from Argos as he was in the myths. As Agamemnon was a descendant of Pelops, for whom the Peloponnese was named, this effectively gave the Spartans the 'right' to inherit Agamemnon's authority as leader of the Peloponnesians. Their message to the Argives and rest of the Peloponnese was clear: the Peloponnese was Sparta's backyard.

The Spartans also used their authority as the most powerful Dorian state in the Peloponnese to control one of the two Dorian 'votes' on the council that ran the oracle at Delphi. This council included representatives from the twelve different 'tribes' of Greeks who oversaw the affairs of Apollo's sanctuary: the Thessalians, Boeotians, Dorians, Ionians, Perrhaebians and Dolopians, Magnesians, Locrians, Ainians, Achaeans from Phthiotis, Malians, Phocians, and the Delphians themselves.[15] Each 'tribe' sent two sacred ambassadors to the twice-annual council meetings, with the Dorians sending one from Doris and one from the Peloponnese. Holding the Peloponnesian Dorian vote gave the Spartans prestige and influence over the activities at Apollo's sanctuary, which had considerable influence over Greek interstate relations.

*　*　*

A key figure in the development of the new Spartan diplomatic network was Chilon, who served as ephor in 556/5 BCE. He was said to have worked closely with King Anaxandridas of the Agiad royal house to develop this new policy of deposing tyrannical governments across Greece.[16] Chilon, who was also famous for his elegiac poetry, was recognised as one of the so-called 'Seven Sages' of the ancient world – a group that also included the philosopher and mathematician Thales of Miletus; the tyrant Pittacus of Mytilene; the sixth-century BCE poet and law-maker Bias of Priene; the Athenian poet, legislator and politician Solon; Cleobulus, the tyrant of Lindos on Rhodes; and Periander of Corinth, a sixth-century BCE tyrant, poet and philosopher.

Chilon was particularly noted for his brevity of speech. His reported sayings included 'Honour old age' and 'Obey the laws', but his best-known maxim was 'Know thyself' – although some claimed that Thales of Miletus had coined it first. The later historian Diodorus Siculus even claims that when Chilon travelled to Delphi he was sufficiently self-confident to dedicate his own wisdom as an offering to the god, erecting a column inscribed with three maxims: 'Know thyself'; 'Nothing overmuch'; and 'A pledge, and ruin is nigh'.[17] Chilon – like the lawgiver Lycurgus – was worshipped as a demigod at Sparta after his death. Even now, visitors to Sparti can see a relief in the museum bearing his name; this may have come from his sanctuary, where sacrifices would have been made and votive offerings deposited.[18]

Chilon's brevity of speech became normal Spartan practice,

which in turn is the origin of the English term 'laconic'. As his reputation shows, this was not regarded as a sign of intellectual poverty. Socrates observed, his admiration clear, that if you spoke to an ordinary Spartan, you would initially find him simple in words, 'But then he throws up valuable words short and terse like a javelin so that you will seem no better than a child.'[19]

Chilon's wisdom was famous beyond Classical Greece. Indeed, a sixth-century CE Byzantine silver spoon at the British Museum has the words 'Chilon, in hollow Lacedaemon' inscribed on the bowl, and 'Know thyself' on the neck. While many later painters who focused on Sparta chose Lycurgus as their subject, Chilon was also often depicted. An imaginary portrait (c. 1660) by the Italian late-Baroque painter and printmaker Luca Giordano depicts him as a medieval monk reading a manuscript, complete with tonsure rather than flowing Spartan locks. One of the odder examples of Chilon-themed art is a fresco from the Baths of the Seven Sages at the Roman port of Ostia which claims that 'cunning Chilon taught to fart silently'. Silence was a virtue in ancient Sparta; but not necessarily in the manner that the fresco painter suggested.

* * *

By around 545 BCE, Sparta's growing influence had caught the attention not only of the other Greeks in the Peloponnese but also of powerful states abroad. The most notable of these was Croesus, the all-powerful king of Lydia, who ruled most of the western regions of modern-day Turkey west of the Kizilirmak river. Croesus' vast kingdom was more than fifty times larger than Sparta and comprised numerous peoples, including Lydians, Phrygians, Mysians, Mariandynians, Chalybes, Paphlagonians, Thracians, Carians, and Greeks from the city-states of the coast of Asia Minor.[20] It was from the Lydians that the Greeks first got the idea of using gold and silver coinage – the types that Lycurgus was said to have banned centuries earlier.[21] Croesus is credited with issuing the first true gold coins with a standardised purity for general circulation, the so-called 'Croeseid' which bore an image of a lion and a bull. His wealth was legendary – hence the saying 'As rich as Croesus'.

At the time when Croesus spotted the rising power of the Spartans to the west, he was growing fearful of a rising power to the east: the Persian king Cyrus, who had recently overthrown his grandfather Astyages, the king of the Medes. Wishing to stop Cyrus from becoming more powerful, but afraid that the gods might not support such an endeavour, Croesus asked the oracle at Delphi: 'Shall Croesus make war on the Persians, and shall he make any army of men his ally?' In response, Apollo said that if he chose to make war on the Persians, he would 'destroy a mighty empire' and advised that he seek allies among the most powerful Greek states.[22]

Croesus investigated which Greek city-states were the most powerful. After learning that the Spartans were 'pre-eminent' among the Dorians, he sent envoys to them with the following message: 'Lacedaemonians, the oracle of the god advised me to make the Greek my friend, and having learned that *you* stand at the head of Greece, *you* are the ones to whom I make this invitation, wanting to become a friend and ally, without guile and without deceit.' The Spartans were delighted by the attention from Croesus, who had already supplied them with the gold to make a statue of Apollo. When the Spartans had tried to pay, Croesus insisted it was a gift.[23] The Spartans swiftly agreed to a sworn alliance that made them the Lydian king's 'co-fighters' and 'guest-friends'.

'Guest-friendship' in the ancient world – *xenia* in Greek – was an institutionalised relationship involving the exchange of gifts, which established generosity and brotherhood between the two parties. By making the Spartans his guest-friends, Croesus was effectively treating them as equals. Given his wealth and power, this was a significant moment in Spartan history, and one that the Spartans clearly recognised; to show their gratitude, they sent him a bronze bowl large enough to hold 300 amphoras of wine.

Croesus' ally King Amasis of Egypt also reached out to the Spartans at this time. Although Herodotus does not record a formal alliance between Sparta and Egypt, he does mention that Amasis sent the Spartans a magnificent gift – a linen breastplate with a large number of creatures woven into it and embellished with gold and cotton thread.[24] This present was clearly an attempt to court the Spartans into joining an alliance against Persia.

Yet what promised to be Sparta's triumphant arrival on the world stage turned out to be a disaster. Although Apollo warned Croesus he needed the Spartans as allies, the overconfident Lydian king ignored the god and invaded Persia without them. Cyrus marched out to meet him, and the pitched battle that followed ended in a stalemate. Croesus returned home and disbanded his army, thinking that he had time to gather allies for a new invasion the following spring. But Cyrus had other ideas, marching swiftly against Sardis, the Lydian capital.

Croesus gathered what forces he had available. But even though – as Herodotus puts it – there was no nation in Asia 'more valiant or warlike' than the Lydians, Croesus suffered a humiliating defeat, partly because his cavalry were spooked by the camels in Cyrus' army. Herodotus stresses that 'horses fear camels and can endure neither the sight nor the smell of them'; as soon as the horses being ridden by Croesus' cavalry-men encountered Cyrus' camels, they turned and fled.[25] Croesus took refuge in the city of Sardis, trusting that his allies would come to his rescue. But the citadel fell to the Persians before the allies could arrive. Indeed, by the time the Spartans had prepared their ships ready to send an army to Asia, another messenger came to tell them that Sardis had fallen, and Croesus taken prisoner. Just as Apollo had prophesied, Croesus had destroyed 'a mighty empire': his own. And defeat also brought the Greeks of Asia Minor under Persian control. Their plight would eventually draw the Spartans into action.

* * *

While later apologists absolved the Spartans of blame, explaining that they had never formalised their alliance with Croesus,[26] the blunt reality is that the Spartans were unable to help Croesus because they did not *yet* have mastery over the Peloponnese. At the time Croesus appealed for help, they were involved in a territorial dispute with Argos over the lands to the north and east of Laconia known as Thyrea. The Spartans had provoked the conflict, having seized the land from Argos and started to cultivate it themselves. Having a network of Peloponnesian allies clearly gave the Spartans the confidence to tangle with the Argives for the first time since the disaster at Hysiae in 669 BCE. As we know, the Spartans and the Argives decided to resolve their dispute by means of a duel between 300 men from each city – the 'Battle of the Champions'. Their decision seems to resemble something out of Greek myth, but more than a century later the Argives would make a clause that either side could challenge the other to a one-off battle for Thyrea a precondition of a fifty-year peace treaty between the two states. On that occasion the Spartans agreed, despite thinking the Argives' insistence on this clause had been 'complete folly'.[27]

As we have already seen, both sides claimed to have won the duel: the Argives had the greater number of survivors, while the Spartans thought they had been victorious because their survivor, Othryadas, had remained on the battlefield, stripped the bodies of the slain and used their arms to build a trophy. However, no one would dispute the fact that the Spartans won the subsequent pitched battle, which resulted in heavy casualties on both sides. Their victory secured control of Thyrea and proved to everyone that the Spartans were masters of the Peloponnese. Victory over Argos probably also won the Spartans the right to hold the 'Dorian' vote at Delphi.

The conquest of Thyrea was a pivotal event for the Spartans. Each year thereafter, they held a festival to celebrate their victory called the 'Parparonia' – Parparos being the site of the battle. The Spartans also began wearing what they called 'Thyreatic crowns' made from palm leaves, while celebrating the annual Gymnopaidiai religious festival in honour of Apollo.[28] A sixth-century BCE bronze figurine from Amyclae now displayed at the National Museum in Athens seems to depict a Spartan youth wearing one such crown.

We have already learned that it was only after the Battle of the Champions that the Spartans made it compulsory for Spartan men to wear their hair long, with Herodotus claiming that they had previously always kept it cut close.[29] Modern scholars have noted that Laconian vase paintings from before the middle of the sixth century BCE belie this assertion, but we could perhaps interpret Herodotus as meaning that the Spartan citizens now *all* began to wear their hair long. Plutarch criticised Herodotus for claiming that Othryadas committed suicide out of 'shame' at being the sole survivor, as he felt that the Spartan had done nothing wrong. But it may be that the Battle of the Champions was actually the first step in a process whereby Spartans became expected to fight to the death.

That might explain why the Spartans seem to have come to remember the incident differently. In popular legend,

Othryadas was reimagined as the Spartan general who miraculously revived after being left for dead and used broken spear shafts as crutches to haul himself about the battlefield, erecting a victory monument with wooden shields taken from the Argive dead. Not content with this token of Spartan victory, while he was dying Othryadas daubed a dedication in his own blood: 'To Zeus, Guardian of Trophies.'[30] This version of the story explains a later epigram sometimes attributed to the famous fifth-century BCE poet Simonides:

> We three hundred, Spartan fatherland, fighting with as many Inachidae [Argives] for Thyrea, not turning our necks, where we first planted our feet, and here quit our lives. The shield, covered with the gore of Othryadas, proclaims, 'Thyrea, Zeus, is of the Lacedaemonians.' But if any of the Argives escaped death, he was of the race of Adrastus. For Sparta, to not die, but flee, is death.

The reference to Adrastus, the mythical king of Argos, is a particularly pointed jibe; he was the only one of the so-called 'Seven Against Thebes' – seven mythic heroes who assisted Oedipus' son Polynices in a doomed attempt to take back the city of Thebes from his brother Eteocles – who did not fight to the death.

Over time, however, the significance of the Battle of the Champions faded. By the second century CE, the satirist Lucian could write: 'I was especially inclined to laugh at people who quarrelled about boundary lines ... when I looked toward the Peloponnese, and caught sight of Cynouria, I noted what a tiny region, no bigger than an Egyptian bean, had caused so many Argives and Spartans to fall in a single day.'[31] In Lucian's day, Thyrea was better known as the site of an estate owned by the wealthy second-century CE Athenian rhetorician and philanthropist, Herodes Atticus. Herodes, whose family claimed to be able to trace its ancestry back to the mythical heroes Ajax and Telamon, funded the Panathenaic stadium in Athens, the Odeon on the slope of the Athenian acropolis, and the stadium at Delphi. Herodes was clearly a Spartophile; as a youth, he even completed the Roman-period version of the Spartan upbringing, which, as we have already seen, was open to the sons of foreigners,[32] and funded the thermal baths at Thermopylae. The fact that a wealthy foreigner like Herodes had chosen to undertake the Spartan upbringing shows the enduring power of Sparta's reputation, even when its super-power status was long gone. How much more enticing would Sparta have been at the time of the Battle of the Champions, when the city-state was ascendant?

*   *   *

Although the Spartans had been unable to help Croesus against Cyrus, the Aeolian and Ionian Greeks who lived in Asia Minor recognised their growing power and sent ambassadors to Sparta to ask for their help against the Persians.[33] The Asian Greeks chose one of their number, a man named Pythennos from the city of Phocaea, to speak on their behalf. To ensure that as many Spartiates as possible would gather to listen to him, Pythennos donned a purple robe – a clear sign of his wealth and importance, which the Spartans would have well recognised – and when he felt his audience was big enough, he made a long speech begging for help.

Despite his best efforts, Pythennos' plea failed, and the Spartans refused to send military assistance to the Ionians. His failure could be a sign that the Spartans recognised that the task was currently beyond them – or it could suggest that they just weren't interested in helping. The Spartans may have been growing their power and influence in the Peloponnese, but that does not necessarily mean they were developing any sort of coherent strategy for regional domination. Nonetheless, they did resolve to warn Cyrus off. The sole Spartan ambassador, Lacrines, travelled to Croesus' former capital of Sardis and delivered a curt message to Cyrus, warning him not to harm any settlement on Greek soil, since the Lacedaemonians 'would not tolerate it'.[34]

The fact that a city-state with as few as 9,000 citizens dared to threaten Cyrus, whose growing kingdom now stretched from the Indian subcontinent to the Mediterranean shores, evinces the Spartans' great self-confidence. The Spartans would become notorious for sending solitary ambassadors to deliver blunt messages to foreign kings, who naturally saw the lack of pomp and ceremony as a sign of disrespect. When the third-century BCE Macedonian king Demetrius Poliorcetes, who was used to being flattered by the Greeks and was literally deified by the Athenians, complained that the Spartans had insulted him by sending just one man, the Spartan envoy asked the god-king, 'Is one-to-one not sufficient?'[35]

Cyrus was just as confused as Demetrius by the Spartans' lack of respect for a king of his status. In response, he asked some Greeks in his entourage 'who on earth the Lacedaemonians were – and how numerous they were – that they addressed him in this way'.

When the Greeks in Cyrus' entourage told the Persian king who the Spartans were, and presumably explained how few of them there were, he replied, 'I have never yet found occasion to fear the kind of men who have a place set apart in the middle of their city, where once assembled they deceive each other swearing oaths.' Cyrus was referring to the ancient Greek practice of each city-state having its own marketplace, which the Persians thought strange. Xenophon reports that because the Persians saw markets as hotbeds for deceit, they did everything they could to exclude hucksters and pedlars from where the royal palace and other government buildings were located.[36]

Herodotus stresses that Cyrus' jibe was insulting to all the Greeks, nonetheless it would have been particularly insulting to the Spartans. Although they were to develop a reputation for deceit and duplicity, the Spartans at this point had a well-deserved reputation for piety; the accusation that they were using oaths to cheat each other would have stung. But even worse, the Spartan citizens were decidedly non-mercantile. Accusing them of hanging around in a marketplace like low-status merchants would have been particularly galling to such gentlemen of leisure.

Cyrus finished his retort with an oath of his own: 'If I remain healthy, their tongues will be occupied with events at home rather than those in Ionia.' While Cyrus would not make good on his threat to invade Greece, he did conquer the Greeks of Asia Minor and succeed in making them his tribute-paying subjects. His successors, Darius and Xerxes, would make good on his oath to cause trouble for the Spartans.

*　　*　　*

The Spartans' inability to help Croesus and their refusal to help the Ionians showed that they were not yet willing or able to tackle a serious world power like Persia. But Sparta's policy of ousting tyrants would soon lead them back to the fringes of Asia. Civil strife on the island of Samos led citizens there who were hostile to the tyrant Polycrates to Laconia to beg the Spartans for assistance.[37] They may have hoped to draw on pre-existing connections with the Spartans. Archias, the grandson of one of the Spartans who would take part in the campaign to Samos, was a guest-friend of Samos, which suggests that the family already had close connections with the island. A bronze figurine of a crouching lion from around 550 BCE, dedicated to Hera at Samos, which bears an inscription that reads 'Eumnastos the Spartiate to Hera', shows that other Spartans were travelling to Samos at the time.

The Samians made a long and passionate speech, expecting that this would show the immensity of their need. But they had misjudged their audience. At the 'first sitting', as Herodotus puts it, the Spartan authorities pronounced that the Samians had spoken for so long that by the end of the speech they had forgotten what their supplicants had said at the beginning. It was blunt, rude and typical of the Spartans, who were notoriously intolerant of foreigners and their fondness for long speeches. Most notably, the fifth-century BCE Eurypontid king Agis, when asked his response to a speech by ambassadors from Perinthus, a Greek city on the Sea of Marmara, replied, 'What else except that you barely managed to stop talking while I remained silent?'[38]

Having been rebuffed for their prolixity, the Samians made a second attempt to persuade the Spartans to help. This time they tried to tailor their speech to their audience by holding up a grain sack and telling the Spartans: 'This sack needs filling with grain.' Being Spartan, the authorities could not resist telling the Samians that the word 'sack' was superfluous. After this additional moment of needless rudeness, the Spartans did agree to help; they equipped what Herodotus calls a 'great host' to send to Samos, in order to oust Polycrates. Although the Corinthians transported the army, the fact that Herodotus mentions only 'Lacedaemonian' soldiers suggests their invasion force consisted largely of Spartan citizens and *perioikoi*. The fact that they were essentially acting alone suggests that the Spartans arrogantly assumed that they were strong enough to oust Polycrates without help, which belies any attempts to paint them as having any sort of coherent imperial strategy.

The Spartan forces laid siege to Polycrates' citadel, and had soon breached the walls of a city tower next to the sea, prompting Polycrates himself to lead a great force to repel them. After some initial success, Polycrates' forces soon fell back, suffering many casualties in the process. But the Spartan counterattack failed to capture the citadel, as only two of their number – Archias and Lycopas – managed to fight their way inside the fortifications in pursuit of the fleeing Samians. Both were hacked down as they found themselves isolated from their peers. Herodotus opines that the Spartans would have prevailed if they had all been as brave as these two.

The Spartans besieged Polycrates in his citadel for forty days without success, before returning home in failure. The Samians later claimed that Polycrates had bought them off, only to cheat them by paying with gold-plated iron coins rather than solid gold. But even Herodotus, who is often easily convinced by tall stories, dismisses this as nonsense. The blunt reality is that the Spartans were not – and would never be – good at siege warfare. Clearly, they gave up because they knew that they would not be able to win.

Not long after the Spartans failed to oust Polycrates, he was eliminated by their mutual enemy, the Persians. To cut a long story short, Polycrates was lured to Asia, murdered and then crucified by Oroetes, a Persian nobleman. Oroetes served as viceroy of Sardis under Cyrus, and his sons Cambyses and Smerdis; he had hoped to curry favour with Smerdis by bringing Samos under Persian control.[39] But Smerdis was overthrown by a Persian nobleman named Darius, who had Oroetes executed for opposing him. Now Persian king, one of Darius' first royal acts was to send troops to Samos to drive out Polycrates' deputy Maeandrius and replace him with Polycrates' brother Syloson.

Maeandrius fled to Sparta for help. The Spartans appear to have offered him asylum, but they refused to give military assistance, clearly unwilling to risk another failure. However, when Maeandrius noticed how much the new Agiad king Cleomenes, who had succeeded his tyrant-ousting father Anaxandridas, admired his gold and silver drinking cups, he spotted an opportunity. Whenever Cleomenes called at his house, Maeandrius would arrange for his servants to take out the cups and clean them. Eventually Maeandrius offered them to Cleomenes as a gift – but his plan to bribe the king failed. The incorruptible Cleomenes went straight to the ephors and told them that the Samian 'stranger' should leave not only Sparta, but the Peloponnese. As Cleomenes saw it, Maeandrius might persuade him or another Spartan to do something 'bad'. The ephors listened, and expelled Maeandrius – the first recorded 'alien act', the Spartan practice of expelling a foreigner when they felt the need.[40]

This incident was emblematic of the next few decades in Spartan history: the Spartans would prove remarkably reluctant to involve themselves in events so far from home, and whatever actions they did take, the Agiad king Cleomenes was central to the story.

4

Royal Rivalries:
Cleomenes vs. Demaratus

520–490 BCE

Early fifth-century BCE Parian marble sculpture of a hoplite wearing a 'Corinthian' helmet with ram-shaped cheek-piece, found near the Spartan acropolis. Dubbed 'Leonidas' by its excavators, it more likely represents a mythical hero or a god.

The last decades of the sixth century BCE were crucial in shaping the course of Sparta's rise on the world stage. But squabbling between – and even within – the royal houses during this period had a habit of hampering the potential for unified Spartan action. The Agiad king, Cleomenes, who reigned from around 520 to 490 BCE, was keen to follow his father Anaxandridas' policy of ousting tyrants, and is also usually seen as adopting an anti-Persian policy. But Cleomenes was often opposed by his Eurypontid co-king, Demaratus, who would ultimately defect to the Persian cause and accompany Xerxes on his invasion of Greece in 481 BCE. Cleomenes was also opposed by his younger half-brother Dorieus – less for reasons to do with policy, and more because Dorieus could not bear his older brother being king. Just as today, finding a satisfactory role is often tricky for surplus princes. Nonetheless, Cleomenes was able to dominate Spartan affairs to the extent that his policies effectively became those of Sparta – and his opposition to Persia ultimately put Sparta on course for a showdown with the great superpower of the day.

Ironically, Cleomenes should not have become the Agiad king in the first place. He was only born because his father Anaxandridas had become a bigamist – contrary to Spartan law – at the behest of the ephors. This odd arrangement came about because he had failed to produce an heir with his first wife, who was his sister's daughter. The ephors ordered him to send his young wife away and marry another who could bear children, because they were not prepared to allow the Agiad line to die out. But Anaxandridas refused to abandon his young wife, adding that the ephors were giving him bad advice and turning someone who was 'blameless' into a scapegoat.[1]

Faced with Anaxandridas' stubborn refusal, the ephors and Elders told him that if he was determined to 'cling' to his wife, he could keep her, but he should marry another woman who could give him children. Anaxandridas accepted this compromise and took a new wife, who swiftly gave birth to Cleomenes – only for his first wife, previously seemingly infertile, to suddenly fall pregnant, too. Friends of the second wife claimed that this later pregnancy was a fake, and that she was planning to introduce a 'substitute' baby. Angry and confused at this suggestion, the ephors sat round her bed, watching closely as she gave birth to a son, Dorieus. Anaxandridas' first wife later bore two more children, Leonidas and Cleombrotus, who may or may not have been twins; by the time Herodotus visited Sparta, no one could remember for sure. But Anaxandridas' second wife had no further children. It is tempting to think that this shows he kept his first wife out of love, but the fact that she was his sister's daughter suggests that Anaxandridas' main reason for loyalty was likely financial. Unusually in ancient Greece, Spartan women could own land in their own right, and endogamy – meaning close-kin marriage – seems to have been common practice among Spartan royals, as it kept inherited wealth in the family.

When Anaxandridas died and the Spartans automatically made Cleomenes king because he was the eldest son, there was trouble. For some reason this perfectly natural decision came as a surprise to Dorieus; although he was the younger son, he felt that the normal rules of primogeniture should be overturned, and that he should have been chosen because he was known to be 'the first among all the young men of his age'.[2] This was probably more than just sibling rivalry. Dorieus had been through the rigours of a Spartan upbringing, which was presumably how he had proven himself to be superior to his peers. But the immediate heirs to each of the Spartan thrones were exempt from this upbringing,[3] meaning that Cleomenes would never have had the chance to prove his worth. Despite Dorieus' reputation, the throne automatically passed to Cleomenes as the elder son. Many aspects of Spartan society were unusual; in this regard at least, Sparta was following convention.

Furious at having been passed over for the Crown, Dorieus refused to be ruled by his brother and instead demanded to be given a company of men with whom he could set up a colony. Setting off 'in a bad temper', he belied his reputation for being one of the best of the best by neglecting to consult the oracle at Delphi before going to Libya, where he tried to colonise the best lands. His efforts ended in failure; two years later he was driven out of Africa, thanks to the combined efforts of local tribes and the Carthaginians. Carthage was a powerful city-state in what is now Tunisia, which was at the time carving out its own empire in North Africa, Sicily and Spain. The Carthaginians had no intention of allowing the Spartans to gain a foothold in what they deemed to be their backyard.

Undeterred, Dorieus tried again to found a colony, this time in what is now southern Italy. On this occasion he did consult Apollo first; but rather than asking where he should set up his colony, Dorieus only asked whether he would capture the land he was sailing to. Dorieus was initially successful, as the oracle promised, setting up a colony at Eryx. Yet soon afterwards he got himself killed, having become involved in a war between the Greek colonies of Croton and Sybaris. Herodotus reports that the Sybarites told him that Dorieus would not have died if he had stuck with Eryx – but he tried to do more than the oracle said he should.[4] Herodotus himself felt that Dorieus should have swallowed his pride and stayed in Sparta.

He had a point: as Cleomenes would eventually die without

producing a male heir, the throne would later pass to their younger brother Leonidas, who was to lead the Spartans at Thermopylae. Had Dorieus been more patient, he – and not Leonidas – might have been the hero whose actions are still inspiring people across the globe.

*   *   *

In a strange coincidence, Anaxandridas' fellow king Ariston was also unable to produce an heir, despite having been married twice. Refusing to accept responsibility for the problem – he was less enlightened than Anaxandridas, it would seem – Ariston decided to solve his problem by taking a third wife. The ephors didn't have to tell him to do this, as they had with Anaxandridas; Ariston made his own decision, opting to steal the wife of his best friend Agetus. His motive might have been more than producing an heir, for Agetus' wife happened to be the most beautiful woman in Sparta.

The backstory here tells us a lot about Spartan attitudes to women, physical appearance and the gods. Agetus' unnamed wife had once been so ugly that her parents gave strict instructions to her nurse that she should never show the baby to another soul. Realising that the girl was bound for a miserable life in image-obsessed Sparta, the nurse took matters into her own hands; every day she took the girl to the sanctuary at Therapne just south of Sparta, where Helen and Menelaus were said to have been buried,[5] and Helen was worshipped as a demigoddess. The nurse prayed to Helen, beseeching the beautiful deity to deliver the girl from her 'misshapenness'. One day a mysterious old woman appeared and insisted on looking at the girl. The maid relented, even though that meant going against the parents' orders, and the old woman touched the baby's face, declaring, 'You shall be the most beautiful woman of all

in Sparta.' From that day on, she was transformed.[6] The implication is that the mysterious old woman was the demigoddess
Helen in disguise.

As fanciful as this is to modern sensibilities, it would have
made perfect sense to Spartans at the time. They believed that
Helen and her brother Pollux were immortal children of Zeus,
who had 'seduced' their mother Leda, the wife of King Tynda-
reus of Sparta, while taking the form of a swan. Helen's brothers
Castor and Pollux were believed to reside at Therapne on alternate days, after Pollux convinced Zeus to allow him to share his
immortality with his mortal twin brother.[7] So the appearance
of Helen at Therapne would have come as no surprise to the
average Spartan.

'Chafed' by desire for Agetus' wife, Ariston came up with
a 'device' to dupe his friend. Promising Agetus that he would
give him anything that he 'owned' as a gift, Ariston asked his
friend for a similar present. They sealed the bargain with oaths,
which should have rung alarm bells – but Agetus did not see
the danger. Agetus asked for something inconsequential from
Ariston's possessions, which Ariston handed over without
fuss. But when it was Ariston's turn, he stunned his friend by
demanding his wife. Spartan women may have developed a
fearsome reputation for telling Spartan men what to do, but
Agetus' wife was still his 'property'. Agetus was enraged by this
deceitful trick, but nonetheless handed her over: conventional
Greek piety demanded that he keep his oath.

So, after sending his second wife away, Ariston took up his
third and was delighted when she fell pregnant – only for his
joy to evaporate when she gave birth prematurely. Ariston happened to be with the ephors when he was informed of the birth,
meaning there were witnesses to him 'counting on his fingers' the
number of months since he had married. After reaching only
seven, he swore out loud, 'He cannot be mine!' Later Ariston

came to regret his outburst and regarded the child, Demaratus, as his legitimate son, but this unguarded oath would come back to haunt Demaratus decades later when he made the mistake of crossing his co-king Cleomenes.

* * *

Now partly responsible for shaping Spartan foreign relations, Cleomenes continued his father's policy of expelling tyrants from Greek cities. This time the tyrant was as important as they come: Hippias, the son of Peisistratus – whose family had ruled the great city of Athens for two generations. Ousting Hippias would place the wealthy and powerful city of Athens in the hands of rich aristocrats who were loyal to Sparta, extending Sparta's network of allies beyond the Peloponnese.

But Cleomenes' intervention was not strictly politically necessary, as Athens was already well disposed to Sparta – in fact, Hippias was a Spartan guest-friend. The reason for intervening in Athenian affairs was typically Spartan: Apollo at Delphi told them to do it. The Spartans considered the matters of the gods more important than those of men,[8] so when Apollo told them to oust Hippias, they jumped right to it. The trouble was, Apollo didn't really want the Spartans to oust Hippias. Instead, the Alcmaeonidae, a noble Athenian family who had been banished by Hippias' father Peisistratus, had bribed the Pythian priestess to tell every Spartan delegation that visited Delphi to expel the tyrant.

Nonetheless, there were probably other reasons that the Spartans moved against their erstwhile friend. First, Hippias was also on good terms with Sparta's great rival Argos.[9] Such was the rivalry between the two long-term enemies that no third party could hope to remain friendly to one for any length of time without upsetting the other. Second, Hippias had recently married off his daughter to the son of Hippoclus, the tyrant of Lampacus, a Greek city in northern Asia Minor – and Hippoclus was understood to have influence with Darius, the Persian king.[10] The Spartans may well have feared that Hippias would 'Medise' – the term in ancient Greece for collaborating with the Persians. Having just seen the Persians subdue the Greeks of Asia Minor, the last thing the Spartans wanted was the Persians getting a foothold in what they regarded as their turf.

Although they were confident that they were doing the right thing, the Spartans' first attempt to expel Hippias was a disaster. They sent a force commanded by a Spartan named Anchimolius to Athens by sea, but when he landed his forces at the bay of Phaleron, south of Athens, they were attacked by 1,000 horsemen sent by Hippias' Thessalian allies. Many of the Spartans were killed in the assault, including Anchimolius; the remnants of his army fled to their ships before sailing home.[11]

Anchimolius is the first of many Spartan commanders we will see falling in the front line – perhaps seeking to ensure that they would not suffer the shame of surviving defeat. The fact that Herodotus describes seeing his tomb on Athenian soil, at the nearby temple of Heracles at Cynosarges, suggests that his reputation survived intact. Nor do the rank-and-file who fled seem to have suffered any punishment for their shameful retreat. This might imply that the Spartans were not yet imposing special penalties on cowards.

The next time the Spartans attempted to oust Hippias, they put together a much larger force. Cleomenes led this mission himself, and attacked by land. The Spartan force was again intercepted by the Thessalian cavalry, but this time it was the Thessalians who were routed; forty were slain and the rest fled, leaving Hippias to face the Spartans alone. Cleomenes marched into Athens, prompting those who were opposed to the

Peisistratid family to rise up. Faced with both invading Spartans and hostile Athenians, Hippias and his supporters dug in on the Athenian acropolis and prepared to withstand a siege.

Although they had plenty of food and water, Hippias and his followers did not hold out for long. The Spartans managed to capture the children of the Peisistratids when they tried to sneak them out of the citadel. Cleomenes issued Hippias with a blunt ultimatum: he would return the children safe if the Peisistratids left Athens within five days. Hippias accepted the deal, and the long Peisistratid tyranny in Athens ended.[12] For Cleomenes and the Spartans, the mission was a complete success.

Had the story ended there, the liberation of Athens would probably have fostered long-term goodwill between the two city-states. But what Cleomenes did next set Sparta and Athens on the path to a rivalry that would shape the course of Spartan history – with Athens constituting the single greatest stumbling block to Spartan dominance.

The removal of the Peisistratids left a power vacuum, and when the other noble families in Athens began squabbling among themselves, Cleomenes didn't have the sense to leave well alone. Instead, he intervened to support his Athenian guest-friend Isagoras against Cleisthenes, the leader of the Alcmaeonid family.[13] Despite his later reputation as the founder of Athenian democracy, Cleisthenes' father Megacles had once been Peisistratus' son-in-law, and his grandfather Cleisthenes had been the tyrant of Sicyon. So Cleomenes would have had good reason not to allow Cleisthenes to get too powerful. Allegedly, Cleomenes was keen to involve himself in Athenian affairs because he was on terms of 'too great familiarity' with Isagoras' wife – but it is more likely that he simply saw an opportunity to enhance his personal influence over Athenian affairs.

Cleomenes sent a herald to the Athenians and demanded that they expel the 'accursed' Alcmaeonidae – according to an old story, the Alcmaeonidae had sacrilegiously killed the supporters of an earlier would-be tyrant, Cylon, who had tried to seize power in Athens after winning at the Olympic Games in 640 BCE.[14] Cleisthenes left voluntarily, and had Cleomenes stopped even there, his reputation would probably have survived unscathed. Instead, he banished 700 other prominent Athenian families, clearing the way for Isagoras and his supporters to control Athens.

Even then, Cleomenes might have got away with an unblemished reputation and ensured Athens was a compliant Spartan ally, but he pushed things too far when he tried to dissolve the Athenian council and put the city-state under the control of his guest-friend and 300 of his partisans. This was exactly the sort of narrow government that the Spartans liked their allies to have; given his personal connections with Isagoras, Athens would have been beholden to Cleomenes. But it was too much for the other Athenians, who banded together and refused to comply. Cleomenes, Isagoras and their followers seized control of the Athenian acropolis to try to force through the regime change, only to find themselves under siege by the rest of the Athenians. So Cleomenes, who had previously besieged Hippias on the acropolis while liberating the Athenians, ended up being besieged there himself.

This was the occasion on which Cleomenes barged his way into the temple of Athena, even though it was unlawful for a Dorian to enter the sacred precinct, blithely telling the priestess that it was all right because he was actually an Achaean. Cleomenes' witty one-liner was even cleverer in the original Greek. By telling the priestess that he was 'not Dorian', his actual words were 'not Dorieus', which in the original Greek could mean both 'not of Doris' or 'not [the person named] Dorieus'. In other words, Cleomenes basically told the priestess that he was not his brother.

After a two-day siege, Cleomenes agreed to a truce that allowed him to leave Athens safely with Isagoras and the few Spartans who were with them. Isagoras' Athenian followers, however, were abandoned, and ended up being bound and executed. The Athenian playwright Aristophanes would later mock Cleomenes in his comedy *Lysistrata*, with the chorus recalling how 'for all the Spartan spirit in his nostrils, he left without his weapons ... wearing a short cloak on his back, hungry, filthy, unshaven, unwashed'.[15]

Cleomenes' overzealous support of Isagoras was not only an embarrassment for him; he had cost Sparta dearly. Sparta could have had the ongoing goodwill of Greece's other great power; instead, Athens became a near-permanent thorn in Sparta's side. After Isagoras' rival Cleisthenes returned, he set out a series of political reforms that put Athens on the path to full democracy, including equality of speech and before the law, in many ways more real than Spartan equality. And as we shall see, the citizens of democratic Athens were almost always hostile to aristocratic Sparta.

*　　*　　*

One might think that Cleomenes would have learned from this disastrous turn of events to leave Athens well alone, but feeling 'deeply injured' by what had happened,[16] in around 504 BCE he gathered an army from all over the Peloponnese, aiming to install Isagoras as Athens' sole ruler. Placing Athens in the hands of a strongman loyal to Sparta would have made sense if the Spartans were hoping to extend their influence beyond the Peloponnese, but it was a significant departure from their long-term policy of ousting tyrants. This may explain why

Cleomenes kept his plans secret from both his co-king Dema-ratus and Sparta's allies. At this point in history, Spartan kings had the power to gather an army and lead it wherever they wished – but that didn't mean they had to tell the army where they were going. It was only when he had led his army to the edge of Athenian territory and the Athenians marched out to face him that Cleomenes was forced to reveal that they would be joining up with armies from Thebes, Athens' northern neigh-bour, and Chalcis, a city on the island of Euboea to Athens' east; their plan, he announced, was to install Isagoras as 'tyrant' of Athens.

The fact that the Spartans, who had hitherto been so hostile to tyranny, were suddenly aiming to install a tyrant in Athens did not sit well with the Corinthians – so they immediately went home. Although like all the Spartans' allies they were bound by oaths 'to follow the Spartans whithersoever they might lead', the Corinthians may have exploited the fact that their oaths did not explicitly include the wording 'to fight alongside' them. Such careful and self-serving interpretations of oaths were common in ancient Greece. Ironically, the Spartans also developed a rep-utation for such sneakiness. Cleomenes reportedly made a truce with Argos for 'seven days', and then attacked on the third night, arguing that the word 'night' had not been included in their agreement.[17] A Spartan named Leucippus founded a colony at Metapontum near Taras, duping the Tarentines into agreeing to let him stay for 'day and night'; the Tarentines thought this meant *a* day and *a* night, but Leucippus successfully argued that this meant he could stay forever.[18] The Spartans may well have appreciated the Corinthians' clever thinking. At the very least, they do not seem to have held their allies' withdrawal against them.

When the Corinthians left, Demaratus, Cleomenes' co-king and the joint leader of the expedition, did too. This must have come as a surprise to Cleomenes, as there had been no previous indication that Demaratus was hostile to him. When the rest of the allies saw both that the Spartan kings were in disagreement and that the Corinthian troops had gone home, they likewise departed. With his co-king and allies gone, Cleomenes felt he had no choice but to return home himself, leaving the Thebans and the Chalcidians to fight the Athenians alone. The Athenians emerged victorious. After thumping the Thebans – capturing 700 prisoners in the process – they crossed over to Euboea, where they routed the Chalcidians, taking even more prisoners. The Athenians then stole some of the prime lands in Chalcis, occupying them with 4,000 colonists.[19]

To say Cleomenes' campaign was a fiasco is an understatement. But the result in Sparta was the passing of a law forbidding both kings to go out together with the army – his co-king, Demaratus, seems to have been held partly responsible for the failure.

The Spartans watched as newly liberated Athens grew stronger, and after a few years, they decided to try to reinstall Hippias as tyrant. They reasoned that the Athenians were clearly not willing to 'obey' them; putting a tyranny in place would make them weak and ultimately ready to serve a 'master'. But to justify the change in policy to their allies, they fell back on the story that the Alcmaeonidae had bribed the priestess at Delphi. As the oracle that had previously ordered them to expel Hippias had been false, and Hippias was their 'friend', it was only right that they put Hippias back in his rightful place as tyrant. They also complained that the Athenians had been ungrateful for the 'freedom' the Spartans had given them, even daring to cast out the Spartans and their king.

The Spartans' allies – who had mostly benefited greatly from their policy of expelling tyrants – were initially shy about revealing their unhappiness at this policy reversal. But when

Socles, the Corinthian representative, made a long and passionate speech criticising tyranny – which, as he pointed out, the Spartans had never tried themselves – the other allies began to beg the Spartans not to meddle with the internal affairs of another Greek state.

Hippias, who was himself present for the discussion, swore that the Corinthians would one day miss the Peisistratids. He was proved right when, some seventy-five years later, they begged the Spartans to lead them to war against democratic Athens. Nonetheless, when the Spartans saw that their allies were uniting against them, they were forced to back down,[20] in what must have been a significant blow to their reputation.

It is entirely possible that the Corinthians were motivated by the chance to get one over on the Spartans. Although they were formal allies, they may have wanted to ensure that Sparta did not get too powerful as a result of intervening in Athenian affairs.

*   *   *

Their setbacks against the Athenians notwithstanding, by the winter of 499 BCE the Spartans' status as the strongest military force in mainland Greece was such that Aristagoras, tyrant of the Greek city of Miletus in Asia Minor, came to Laconia to beg for help against the Persians.[21] He had hitherto been collaborating with the Persians, but a plan he had hatched to expand his power and theirs by attacking the Aegean island of Naxos had gone awry.[22] Fearing the displeasure of the Persian king Darius, Aristagoras stirred up a revolt against them.

He was received at Sparta by Cleomenes. Knowing that he would have to work hard to convince the arrogant and secretive Spartans to help, Aristagoras began with flattery, telling Cleomenes that it was no surprise that he had come to them, because they were the 'best' in warfare. By contrast, he said, the Persian 'barbarians' were 'without virtue' and fought with bows and short spears. Even more ridiculous – to Greek eyes, at least – they wore trousers and peaked caps on their heads when they went into battle. All this, Aristagoras insisted, showed that they would be 'easy to overcome'. To sweeten the deal, he added that the Persians were rich beyond Cleomenes' wildest dreams; all their wealth could be Sparta's if he agreed to help.

Aristagoras then revealed his trump card: an engraved bronze tablet depicting the whole world, including the seas and rivers. He showed Cleomenes where the Lydians, Ionians, Phrygians, Cappadocians, Syrians, Cilicians, Cypriots, Armenians and Cissians lived, before finally pointing out the Persian heartland, where Darius kept the 'storehouses of his wealth'. The Spartans were wasting their time and resources fighting over small strips of land against their fellow Greeks who lacked gold and silver, he said, when they could easily rule the whole of Asia. Cleomenes was clearly interested, but told Aristagoras that he needed time to think, and asked him to come back two days later.

Aristagoras had so far done well in leading Cleomenes on about how easy the task of tackling the Persians would be. But when the two men met again, the Spartan king asked the question Aristagoras must have been dreading: how many days' journey was it from the Aegean Sea to Persia? Aristagoras made the mistake of answering honestly, revealing that it would take three months to march to the Persian capital at Susa.

Cleomenes cut him off in mid-explanation: 'Milesian stranger, leave Sparta by sunset. There is no argument good enough to persuade the Lacedaemonians if you want to lead them three months' journey from the sea.' The Spartans may have had ambitions for regional domination, but there was no way they were going to risk sending an army that far away from home and for that long – just think what havoc the helots and the Argives could wreak in their absence.[23].

In one last throw of the dice, Aristagoras went to see Cleomenes at home, where he knelt at the king's feet and begged assistance as a suppliant. Cleomenes' young daughter Gorgo, aged eight or nine at the time, was in the room, so Aristagoras asked for her to be removed. But Cleomenes refused, telling him not to be put off by the presence of a little girl. Stymied, Aristagoras showed why he wanted privacy by offering Cleomenes a bribe of 60,000 drachmas. When the Spartan king declined this – and subsequent – offers, Aristagoras continued to keep increasing the stakes until he reached a staggering sum of 300,000 drachmas, roughly equivalent to £30 million or $45 million today. At this point Gorgo cried out, 'Father, the little foreigner will corrupt you if you do not go away and leave him.' Delighted by his daughter's 'advice', Cleomenes left the room immediately.

Gorgo's intervention not only protected her father's reputation; it also changed the course of history. Realising he would not persuade the Spartans to support his cause, Aristagoras went to Athens to try his luck there.[24]

* * *

This was not the only choice comment Gorgo made about the visiting Milesian tyrant. When she saw Aristagoras having his shoes placed on his feet by one of his slaves, she cried out, 'Father! The foreigner doesn't have hands!' Gorgo seems to have been entirely unafraid to speak her mind; some six sayings of hers have been preserved by Plutarch. By far the most famous was her blunt response to an Athenian woman who asked, 'Why are you Spartan women the only ones who can rule men?' Gorgo replied, 'Because we alone give birth to men.'[25] It has even been suggested by some modern scholars that Gorgo herself might have been the source of some of Herodotus' stories about her and other Spartans.

Gorgo was not the only Spartan woman noted for speaking her mind. All of Sparta's women were notorious in antiquity for telling men – and not just Spartans – what to do. Plutarch claimed that 'the men in Sparta were always obedient to their wives',[26] and Aristotle complained that during the period of Sparta's 'empire', many Spartan affairs were 'managed' by women.[27] Not known for his enlightened attitude to women, Aristotle even went so far as to complain that militaristic men like the Spartans were 'men dominated by women'.

Much of the excitement about the strength of Sparta's women stems from the fact that there are some forty preserved sayings by them – around 10 per cent of the sayings recorded by all Spartans. The vast majority are judgements by Spartan mothers on how their sons fared in combat. One particularly frightening Spartan mother went so far as to hitch up her dress to expose herself to her cowardly sons, before calling them 'bad slaves' and inviting them to 'crawl back in' where they came from. Other Spartan mothers were equally blunt. When one Spartan made the mistake of glorifying his brother's death in combat, their mother asked, 'Isn't it a disgrace not to have joined him?' When another Spartan lad made the mistake of telling his mother that everyone in his company had been killed, she screamed, 'So they sent you to announce the bad news to us?' – before bashing his brains in with a broken rooftile.[28]

On learning that their sons had been killed in combat, many Spartan mothers appear to have been remarkably accepting of the fact. When one was asked if she was sad her son had lost his life, she replied, 'No, by the Twin Gods. I brought him into the world to die on behalf of Sparta.' Another Spartan mother handed her son his shield, telling him, 'Your father kept this safe for you; so either keep this safe, or don't exist.'[29] Dropping one's shield was a sign of cowardice throughout Greece, so this essentially meant that the Spartiate should either return home still bearing his shield, or not come back at all. This was broadly the same message conveyed by what might be the most iconic saying by a Spartan woman, the mother who exhorted her son to come back either carrying his shield or carried on it like a stretcher: 'With this, or on this,' she says with appropriate Spartan brevity. (This line was so good that Frank Miller gave it to Gorgo when she bids farewell to Leonidas in his graphic novel 300.)

In recent years, Classical scholars have been critical of the historicity of this latter saying, on the grounds that Spartans who fell in battle were not brought home for burial, but instead interred near where they had died. However, scholars who reject this saying are perhaps being too literal in their interpretation; after all, Xenophon tells us that a group of Spartan soldiers called 'shield bearers' carried the wounded and dead from the battlefield back to the camp using shields as stretchers.[30] Thus, we might rescue the saying by understanding it as meaning '[Return to camp] with this, or on this'.

The Spartan decision to avoid getting involved in what became known as the Ionian Revolt (499–493 BCE) turned out to be wise, at least in the short term. After failing to convince Cleomenes to help, Aristagoras tried his luck with the Athenians, convincing them to send twenty warships. In a wonderful observation about the difference between kingship and democracy, Herodotus observed wryly that it must be easier to persuade many men than one, because Aristagoras had been unable to deceive Cleomenes but had succeeded in deceiving 30,000 Athenians.[31]

The Athenians' intervention earned them the wrath of Darius, who was reportedly so angered by their involvement in the Ionian insurrection against him that he resolved to punish them. To ensure that he didn't forget, he even ordered a slave to remind him three times at every mealtime thereafter to 'remember the Athenians'.[32]

Staying out of the Ionian Revolt allowed the Spartans to concentrate on troubles closer to home – particularly ongoing tension with their old Peloponnesian rival Argos. Indeed, it may even have been trouble with Argos that drove the decision not to get involved in the Ionian Revolt in the first place. When Cleomenes consulted Apollo at Delphi about how to handle Argos, he was told that if he went to war, he would capture 'Argos'. Confident that Apollo was promising the conquest of Sparta's bitter rival, Cleomenes led an army of Spartiates to the point where the Erasinos river served as a border between the two city-states, before making a sacrifice to the god of the river. But when he inspected the liver of the sacrificial victim, the signs were unfavourable. Accordingly, he withdrew to the Thyrea, sacrificed a bull at the edge of the sea and then took his army by ship to the territory of Tiryns, near the modern tourist spot of Nafplio.[33] Cleomenes' actions may seem odd, but the Spartans were particularly sensitive to omens from the gods, not least Poseidon.

Cleomenes then led his army to Sepeia, around 100 kilometres north-east of Sparta. The Argives marched out to face him, but they were anxious – they had received an oracle pronouncing that 'the female will defeat the male'. They thought this meant that the Spartans would defeat them, since in Greek *Sparta* is a feminine noun and *Argos* a masculine one. But as they were convinced that they would not be beaten by the Spartans in an open battle, they were on the lookout for a Spartan trick. Fearing an ambush, they left only a narrow no-man's-land between the two armies so they could watch the Spartans' every move. Whenever the Spartan herald signalled anything to his peers, such as taking a meal or standing down for the night, the Argives did the exact same thing,[34] thinking this would prevent them from being tricked. This went on for several days, with neither side willing to make the first move.

When Cleomenes realised what was happening, he gave his men a secret order: when the Spartan herald announced that they should have their lunch, they would instead take up their arms and attack. The plan worked, and the Argives swiftly found themselves under an unexpected and fearsome assault. Herodotus says that the Spartans killed 'many' Argives in this attack.[35] Exactly how many is not clear, but the Argives would later claim that 6,000 of their men were killed, citing this as the reason why they were unable to help defend Greece against Xerxes more than a decade later.[36]

The Argive survivors took refuge in a nearby grove of trees that was sacred to the demigod Argos. This led to a stalemate; Cleomenes was unwilling to risk sending his men into a woodland where their numerical superiority would be negated by the trees, but the Argives had no way of escaping without being slaughtered. To break the deadlock, Cleomenes came up with a despicable trick, luring out some of the leading Argive fighters by announcing that he had received the standard 200 drachmas per head ransom money from their relatives. The truth was that no ransom had been received; Cleomenes had them put to death after they revealed the names of other Argives hiding in the grove. Fifty more Argives were drawn out in this way, with the Spartans killing them one by one. Eventually, the Argives who remained in the grove grew suspicious. One of them climbed to the top of the trees and saw what was happening to those being 'ransomed', after which those who remained refused to leave.[37] So Cleomenes ordered his helots to pile firewood around the grove and to burn the whole thing down; the remaining Argives were burned alive.

The city of Argos now seemed to lie open to Cleomenes, but he did not take it. Just as he was about to launch an assault, he asked to which god the grove was sacred. When he was told it was Argos, Cleomenes groaned, 'Apollo of prophecy, how grossly you have deceived me when you said I would capture Argos!' He had come to understand too late that when Apollo had promised that he would capture 'Argos', the god had been referring not to the city, but the demigod's grove.[38]

Cleomenes returned home to Sparta, but along the way he took 1,000 hoplites to the sanctuary of Hera known as the Argive Heraion, and made a sacrifice to the goddess, patron of the city of Argos. There Cleomenes committed another act of sacrilege, ordering his helots to beat up Hera's priest when he tried to stop Cleomenes from sacrificing there because it was unholy for a foreigner to do so. Over the course of his reign, Cleomenes developed a reputation for sacrilegious acts. He reportedly desecrated the remains of the Athenian noble family of the Alcmaeonidae; he cut down a wood at Eleusis that was sacred to the goddesses Demeter and Persephone;[39] and he was even said to have dug up the corpse of the Argive demigod Anthes, reportedly flaying its skin to make parchment on which oracles could be transcribed.[40]

When Cleomenes arrived home in Sparta, his enemies criticised him for failing to capture the city of Argos. In response, Cleomenes claimed that while he had been sacrificing to Hera, he had asked the goddess whether Apollo's prophecy had been fulfilled by the destruction of the grove or whether he could still capture the city. According to Cleomenes, a flame shot from the breast of Hera's cult statue, a sign that the oracle had already been fulfilled. As Cleomenes saw it, if a flame had shot from her head, he would have known that he could take the city and the grove. As odd as this story sounds, 'empyromancy' – the art of divination by means of observing fire – was normal ancient Greek practice, and Cleomenes was a priest himself.

The Spartans reportedly found Cleomenes' story entirely credible and let the matter drop. It is likely, however, that the real reason Cleomenes stopped short of destroying Argos was that it was better to keep a weakened Argos as a threat to ensure that other Peloponnesian groups – especially the Corinthians, who had recently proved quite truculent – needed Sparta's protection.

For a long time, Argos was only a minor threat to Sparta, because after the battle it fell into severe civil strife.[41] The crushing defeat freed the cities of Mycenae and Tiryns from Argive control; both would join the Spartans in fighting against Xerxes' Persia.[42] It was clear that even without destroying the city, Cleomenes' victory over the Argives had bolstered Sparta's power and influence.

*　　*　　*

The next major events in Spartan history demonstrate that Cleomenes and the Spartans were fully aware of the threat the Persians represented to their power – indeed, to their very existence. Keen to test whether the Greeks beyond Asia were prepared to resist him, the Persian king Darius sent envoys to each of the city-states, demanding that they give 'earth and water' – tokens of submission. In addition, he gave orders for ships of war and transportation to be built, based on the assumption that many Greeks would resist him.[43]

While many Greek city-states did offer such tokens, the Spartans and the Athenians were not among them. The Spartans threw the Persian ambassadors down a well, telling them they would have all the earth and water they wanted there. The

Athenians, meanwhile, threw their Persians into the so-called 'pit' where they dispatched criminals.[44] This story is the inspiration for the famous sequence in Zack Snyder's film *300*, when Leonidas shouts 'This is Sparta!' before kicking Xerxes' jewel-covered envoy down a well. Although this well-known scene has spawned countless internet memes, in reality Leonidas was not king at the time Darius sent his demands: Cleomenes and Demaratus were the co-kings who would have been part of that fateful decision.

The island of Aegina was among the city-states that offered Darius tokens of submission. The potential 'Medism' of Aegina was a great danger to all the other Greeks, including the Spartans. Aegina – which was so close to Athens that the fifth-century BCE Athenian statesman Pericles called it the 'stye in the eye' of Athens' port, Piraeus[45] – boasted a powerful navy. If Darius were able to use the island as a base in any future invasion of Greece, it would leave all the Greeks vulnerable.

So when the Athenians learned that the Aeginetans had offered earth and water to Darius, they denounced them to the Spartans as traitors, accusing them of plotting to join the Persians in attacking Athens. Perhaps keen to curry favour with the Athenians after his recent difficulties with them, Cleomenes went in person to Aegina to arrest the ringleaders responsible. Unfortunately for him, his Eurypontid counterpart Demaratus wrote 'instructions' to a prominent Aeginetan named Crius, advising him to allege that Cleomenes had no authority to act against Aegina, and that he was only intervening because he had taken a bribe from the Athenians.[46] Quite why Demaratus did this is not clear. Perhaps he was merely trying to stymie Cleomenes' influence, or it may be that he was hoping to thwart Cleomenes' anti-Persian endeavours altogether.

Emboldened by Demaratus' letter, Crius convinced his fellow Aeginetans to resist Cleomenes' demands. When Cleomenes

found himself being abused by Crius, he asked the Aeginetan for his name, which meant 'ram' in Greek. Cleomenes shot
back, 'Well, Mr Ram, you'd better have your horns coated with
bronze, because big trouble is coming your way.'[47] This was no
empty threat: Cleomenes was determined to have his revenge
upon Demaratus – and on Crius, too. When he got to Sparta,
he went straight to Demaratus' cousin Leotychidas and made a
pact with him: Cleomenes would help make Leotychidas king
in place of Demaratus, after which Leotychidas would help him
deal with the Aeginetans.[48]

It helped that Leotychidas already hated Demaratus,
because his cousin had carried off his intended bride, quite literally, in a real-life version of the odd Spartan ritual whereby
brides were 'taken by force'.[49] Vengeful, he immediately brought
a lawsuit against his cousin, swearing 'that Demaratus was not
rightful king of Sparta, since he was not the true son of Ariston',
producing as witnesses the ephors who had been sitting with
Ariston when he realised that Demaratus could not be his
son. Although the ephors were prepared to swear that this
was the case, their testimony was not enough for the Spartans, who – quite naturally – referred the matter to the oracle
at Delphi. When Apollo himself pronounced that Demaratus
was not Ariston's son, the Spartans made Leotychidas king in
his place.[50] Spartan foreign policy was thus left essentially in
Cleomenes' hands.

*   *   *

Demaratus lived as an ordinary Spartan citizen for some time
after he was deposed, during which time he even managed to
get himself elected to a magistracy – a sign that he retained the
respect of many of his former subjects. But everything changed
when Leotychidas publicly insulted him while they were both

watching a performance at the Gymnopaidiai festival. When Leotychidas – who, as the Eurypontid king, would have been sitting in the front row of the theatre – spotted Demaratus, he sent a servant to ask the deposed king what it was like to hold elected office after having previously occupied a position of such power. With a certain style, Demaratus jibed that Leotychidas obviously wouldn't know, having never been sufficiently respected to hold an elected office. He added the threat that Leotychidas' insult would bring 'either a myriad blessings or a myriad evils upon Sparta'.[51]

Demaratus covered his head with his cloak – a sign of shame or anger – and left the theatre. When he got home, he sacrificed an ox to Zeus and sent for his mother. When she arrived, Demaratus placed the bloody ox entrails in her hands and demanded that she tell him the truth about who his father was. He complained that it was rumoured that Ariston had no 'seed', that Leotychidas had told the court that Agetus was his father, and that other Spartans told him that his real father was in fact a helot mule driver. 'In the name of the god,' Demaratus implored, 'speak the truth.'

Demaratus' mother responded to her son's questions by telling a strange story. On the third night after Ariston brought her home, he had lain with her and given her the garlands he was wearing, before leaving the room. Shortly afterwards, he came back in and asked where she had got the garlands. She insisted that he had given them to her, but he denied it – so, to make him believe her, she swore an oath to that effect. Seeing that his wife was willing to invoke the gods as witnesses to the appearance of this mystery 'phantom', Ariston guessed that she must have been visited by the Spartan demigod Astrabacus; the garlands had come from his sacred precinct, located at the doors to Ariston's courtyard. (Quite why there was a sanctuary dedicated to the great-grandson of Agis – the progenitor of the Agiad royal house – at the gates of the house of the Eurypontid king is unclear.) Ariston consulted the official Spartan seers, who confirmed his suspicion that Astrabacus had indeed lain with his wife while disguised as Ariston. Demaratus' mother insisted that his father was either Astrabacus or Ariston, because she had conceived that night. She dismissed Ariston's opinion as based on ignorance, adding that women often gave birth prematurely. She added a glorious curse: 'May Leotychidas' wife, and the wives of others who say these things, give birth to children fathered by mule-drivers.'[52] The fact that the ancient Greek word for a mule's saddle is *astrabē* suggests that some sort of pun with Astrabacus' name is involved here.

Having learned this about his past, Demaratus resolved to leave Sparta. He pretended to go north-east to the oracle at Delphi to ask the truth about his father, but instead went north-west to Elis. The Spartans suspected that he was trying to run away and sent a posse of men to bring him back. Demaratus then crossed to the island of Zacynthus; when the Spartans got there, the Zacynthians refused to hand him over. Demaratus' ultimate destination probably explains the Spartans' pursuit of him; he went to Persia, where Darius treated him with great honour, and even gave him two Greek cities to rule in Asia Minor.

Life at the Persian court, however, did not always run smoothly. Many years later, Darius' grandson Darius II offered Demaratus a gift, only for him to infuriate the Persian king by requesting permission to ride through Sardis wearing his tiara upright, as only Persian kings did. Darius' cousin Mithropaustus reportedly grabbed the ornament from Demaratus' head, declaring, 'This tiara does not have a brain to cover.'[53]

*   *   *

With Demaratus eliminated, Cleomenes returned to Aegina with the newly crowned Leotychidas. Seeing that the two Spartan kings were united, the Aeginetans allowed the Spartans to take their leading citizens to Athens as hostages; the threat of execution would ensure Aegina's loyalty to the anti-Persian cause. But not long after this, it emerged that Cleomenes had, in fact, bribed the oracle at Delphi to proclaim that Demaratus was illegitimate. The story went that he had won over an influential Delphian named Cobon, who 'persuaded' the priestess to say what he wanted to be said. Cobon was banished, and the priestess deposed.

With yet another of his sacrilegious actions exposed, Cleomenes fled Sparta for Arcadia, where he tried to stir up trouble by making the Arcadians swear oaths of loyalty to him personally rather than to his city-state. When news of this reached the Spartans, they panicked and restored Cleomenes to the kingship. Soon after his return from exile, however, a 'mad sickness' fell upon him, causing him to strike any Spartan whom he happened to meet in the face with his staff. His 'relatives' – most likely his daughter Gorgo and his half-brother Leonidas, who were by now married – had little choice but to bind him in the stocks and keep him under guard.

Given the age gap between Leonidas and Gorgo, Leonidas had either lost a wife or (perhaps more likely) delayed marrying until Gorgo came of age so that the wealth of the two families could be combined. As we have seen, Spartan women inherited land in their own right, and it is hard to overstate just how significant such female landownership was. For one point of comparison, women were not able to own property in Britain until the Married Women's Property Act of 1870, and only in 1926 were they allowed to hold property on the same terms as men. Had Gorgo married into another Spartan family, the property she inherited would have been lost to the Agiads forever. Her marriage to her uncle ensured that the Agiad wealth stayed in the family.

Cleomenes was later found dead, his legs and abdomen cut to ribbons with a knife. The official story was that he had been left alone with only a helot to guard him, and he bullied the helot into giving him a knife by threatening to harm him if he was ever released. After getting hold of the 'iron', Cleomenes started slashing himself, working upwards from the shin to the thigh, to his hip and sides, making long cuts to his flesh. Finally, he cut his belly into strips, dealing himself a fatal blow in the process.[54]

Exactly what happened to Cleomenes has intrigued scholars ever since. Herodotus' account includes an Argives claim that he was driven mad because he had sacrilegiously burned the sacred grove at Argos.[55] The Spartans themselves claimed that he went mad after picking up the habit of drinking neat wine from Scythian ambassadors; a stronger mix was from then on known as a 'Scythian cup'.[56] It has even been suggested that Cleomenes might have been hallucinating due to withdrawal after he stopped drinking while he was imprisoned. Herodotus suspected that Cleomenes had been punished by the gods for what he did to Demaratus. However, some modern commentators have speculated that Gorgo and Leonidas might have somehow been involved, as both profited from Cleomenes' supposedly accidental death.

Despite the grisly circumstances surrounding Cleomenes' madness and suicide, he would no doubt have received great honours after his death. When a Spartan king died, horsemen were sent throughout Laconia to proclaim the king's passing, and women went about the city of Sparta beating cauldrons. One free man and woman from each household were required to wear mourning clothes, with heavy fines issued for violations of this rule. A set number of *perioikoi* and helots from around

Lakonike were required to travel to Sparta to mourn; literally thousands of people descended on the city for the official mourning period.[57]

* * *

Cleomenes' death changed the state of both internal and external politics for the Spartans. When the Aeginetans learned he was dead, they sent messengers to Sparta denouncing Leotychidas for helping Cleomenes take the hostages to Athens. Clearly angry at Leotychidas for his role in deposing Demaratus, the Spartans convened a court that decided he had treated the Aeginetans harshly, and sentenced him to be handed over to them in compensation for the hostage-taking. Leotychidas was only spared at the last moment, when a Spartan called Theasides intervened. He warned the Aeginetans that while the Spartans might be getting carried away with themselves because of their 'fury' at Leotychidas, they might later come to their senses and blame the Aeginetans for what they had done in their anger. Rather than keeping Leotychidas as a hostage, the Aeginetans agreed to take him with them to Athens to get their hostages back.[58]

On meeting with the Athenians, Leotychidas stressed that they had been given the hostages 'on trust'. To convince them to hand them back, he told a story from Sparta's past. A Spartiate named Glaucus, he said, had been known for his sense of justice and trustworthiness. Because of this, a wealthy Milesian had entrusted him with a large sum of silver, on the understanding that he would return the money to his relatives when they asked for it. When, many years later, the Milesian's sons travelled to Sparta and presented Glaucus with tokens proving the money belonged to them, Glaucus claimed to have no memory of the matter. He then travelled to Delphi to ask Apollo if he might steal the money by swearing a false oath. Apollo's reply was blunt: Glaucus could take the money by swearing a false oath, but if he did, the son of the oath-god Horkos, who had 'no name, no hands, and no feet', would not rest until he had in his handless grasp a perjurer's family and house. When Glaucus heard this message, he asked for Apollo's forgiveness, only for the priestess to reply that 'to tempt the god and to do the deed had the same effect'. Leotychidas finished his story by warning the Athenians that although Glaucus did eventually give the money back, he had no living descendant in Sparta and no household bore his name.

Leotychidas stressed the key point: when a deposit has been left with you on trust, you should give it back. Still, the Athenians refused to listen, and the Aeginetan hostages remained in Athens.[59] The fact that the Athenians ignored this warning from the Spartan king shows that at this time, the threat from Sparta was deemed to be limited.

*　*　*

Not long after this, the Spartans missed an opportunity to demonstrate their military might when Darius sent an amphibious expedition to Greece, with orders (as the Greeks told it) to enslave the Athenians and Eretrians as punishment for their helping the Ionians in their revolt – and to bring the 'slaves' to him.

The Persians started with Eretria on the island of Euboea. After a brief siege they captured the city and destroyed it.[60] They then sailed across the Euboean gulf and landed on the Athenian eastern seaboard at Marathon, where 10,000 Athenian hoplites were there to repel them, along with 1,000 from their ally, Plataea.

The Athenians were sufficiently afraid of the Persian forces that they also sent a messenger to the Spartans to ask for their help. The messenger, a professional 'day runner' called Pheidippides, ran all the way from Athens to Sparta – a distance of 246 kilometres – in just a day and a half. When Pheidippides arrived, he begged the Spartan authorities not to let Athens 'meet with slavery at the hands of the barbarian'.[61] This was not empty rhetoric; as Herodotus reports, the Persians had already enslaved the Eretrians.

The Spartans resolved to help the Athenians, but said that they could not do so yet: it was only the ninth day of the month, and they could not leave Sparta until the full moon. This is sometimes thought to mean that the Spartans were celebrating the Carneia festival, but Herodotus is unclear about which religious festival prevented the Spartans from leaving. Plutarch later harangued Herodotus for his 'malice' towards the Spartans,[62] claiming that they must have had another reason for not coming straight away. For his part, Plato claims that the Spartans were prevented from helping by 'the war against the Messenians'.[63] It was around this time that Cleomenes was said to be plotting with the Arcadians, and it has been suggested that his subversive activities might have included collaborating with the helots. If any of that were true, of course, the Spartans would certainly never have told Pheidippides that they were too busy dealing with a slave rebellion or a plot by a renegade king to help.

After a quick rest, Pheidippides had to run all the way back to Athens to report the bad news that the Spartans would not be coming to help anytime soon, leaving the Athenians to face the Persians at the Battle of Marathon with just the Plataeans for support. Nonetheless, the Athenians emerged victorious; only 192 Athenians and 11 Plataeans died in the fighting, compared with 6,400 Persians. Later legend had it that Pheidippides ran all the way back to the city – a distance of 42 kilometres – to announce the victory, only to drop dead after uttering the words 'We win'. (The modern Olympic marathon, first held in Athens in 1896, is based on this story.) Had they been there, the Spartans would have undoubtedly appreciated Pheidippides' brevity.

Thus, Spartan religious sensibilities – or internal problems – prevented them from participating in the first Greek victory over the Persians, a battle that Herodotus describes as the first occasion on which any Greeks had 'endured the sight of Median dress and the men wearing it'. Until Marathon, the very word 'Median' had been a source of fear in Greece.[64] The Battle of Marathon has been remembered as a pivotal point in the course of world history; indeed, the philosopher and economist John Stuart Mill would famously describe it as 'more important than the Battle of Hastings', 'even as an event in English history'.[65] Isaac Asimov went further still, claiming that, 'If the Athenians had lost at Marathon ... Greece might have never gone on to develop the peak of its civilisation, a peak whose fruits we moderns have inherited.'[66] Nonetheless, Marathon was far less significant for Darius, who after all by now ruled over 14 million people and around 2,000 times more land than Athens – lands which one of his own documents describes as 'this kingship, large, beautiful with men and with horses'. As Robert Graves' poem 'The Persian Version' puts it: 'Truth-loving Persians do not dwell upon / The trivial skirmish fought near Marathon.'[67]

To their credit, the Spartans did not dismiss the Athenian victory at Marathon as a small affair. Once the full moon had passed, two thousand Spartan hoplites – likely an advance force – dashed to Athens. They were so eager to get to the battlefield in time that they covered a distance of nearly 300 kilometres in just two days and a night. Although they arrived too late to participate in the battle, the Spartans were so 'anxious' to see the notorious Persians that they insisted on surveying the battlefield with their own eyes.[68]

One can well imagine them peering closely at the bodies of the Persian dead, marvelling at the tiaras on their heads, their colourful sleeved tunics, and – most astoundingly to Greek eyes – the trousers on their legs. The Spartans would also have looked in wonder at their bows and arrows, and the fact that instead of bronze shields they carried wickerwork ones.[69] A century later, the Agiad king Agesilaus would embolden his troops by stripping Persian captives naked to reveal their pale bodies that were never exposed to the sun.[70] Having learned what they needed to on the battlefield, the Spartans praised the Athenians for their achievement – and then went home.[71] But it would not be long until they were facing the Persians themselves – as the undisputed leaders of the Panhellenic forces against a truly massive Persian invading force, led by Darius' son Xerxes. The Spartans' efforts against the Persians would become the stuff of legends, and it was this that would in large part forge their reputation as the best soldiers on earth.[72]

5

Xerxes' Invasion: The Spartans Liberate Greece?

481–479 BCE

Glazed brick relief panel (*c.* 510 BCE), depicting a Persian soldier from Susa. Part of a larger frieze perhaps representing the royal bodyguards known as the 'Immortals'.

The Spartans' leadership of a small coalition of Greek *poleis* who chose to resist when Darius' son Xerxes invaded mainland Greece in 481 BCE is arguably the most significant event in Sparta's history. As far as the Greeks were concerned, Xerxes' invasion presented them with a stark choice: resist, or face enslavement. The thirty city-states who chose to defy Xerxes naturally turned to the Spartans, famed for ousting tyrants, to lead them in this fight for freedom. Nonetheless, the Messenians might have found a certain irony in the choice of the Spartans, who themselves had enslaved their fellow Greeks, as leaders in this war for liberty.

The magnitude of the Spartans' task can be seen in Xerxes' official documents, which boldly proclaim, 'I am Xerxes, the great king, king of kings, king of countries containing all kinds of men, king on this great earth far and wide.' Another official document lists Xerxes' many foreign subjects, announcing, 'I ruled them, they bore me tribute, what was said to them by me, that they did.' Included in this list are the 'Yaunâ who live by the sea' and the 'Yaunâ who live across the sea'. The former are the Ionians, the Greeks of Asia Minor who contributed ships to Xerxes' fleet, while the latter must be the Macedonians and other northern Greeks who had recently submitted to the Persians. If Xerxes had got his way, the Spartans and the other Greeks in Europe would have joined the Ionians in paying tribute, and the world we live in today would look very different.

It was fitting that the Spartans learned of this threat to their existence from the exiled king Demaratus, who after opposing

Cleomenes' anti-Persian policy had recently become part of Xerxes' entourage. When Demaratus learned that Xerxes had resolved to personally lead a campaign to conquer Greece, he decided to send word to the Spartans. Anxious that his message might be intercepted on its way out of Persia, he took a wax-covered writing tablet, scraped away the wax, and gouged his doom-laden message into the wood underneath. Demaratus then poured fresh wax onto the tablet, so that it would appear blank if intercepted by the Persian 'way-wardens', who operated as a kind of secret police. When the Spartan authorities received this seemingly blank tablet, they were baffled. But Gorgo, wife of the Agiad king Leonidas, guessed what Demaratus had done, and ordered the Spartan men to scrape away the wax to reveal the message written on the wood.[1]

Demaratus' message must have been almost beyond the Spartans' comprehension. Xerxes, who ruled over 14 million people – roughly 12 per cent of the world's population at that point – had assembled a force of 800,000 infantry, cavalry, camel-riders and chariot drivers, comprising individuals from more than forty nations including Persians, Medes, Cissians, Assyrians, Bactrians and Scythians. Xerxes had also assembled a fleet of 1,207 warships from Phoenicia, Syria, Egypt, Cyprus and Asia Minor. Herodotus carefully calculated his force as totalling 2,317,610 men. Modern estimates are more in the range of between 100,000 and 300,000 men; these figures are essentially guesswork, and, while much lower than Herodotus' numbers, they may still be too high.

Whereas their Greek opponents fought as hoplites in a phalanx, the Persians used long bows and reed arrows – a style of fighting that was well suited to an open battle on the flat plains of Asia. Accordingly, in Aeschylus' tragedy *The Persians*, the Persian queen Atossa asks the chorus of Persian elders whether the Greeks fought with 'bow-stretching arrows' and receives the reply, 'They have lances for fighting close and shields that serve for armour.'[2] But perhaps the most memorable illustration of this difference between the Greek and Persian fighting styles is Dienekes' famous retort to the warning that there were so many archers in Xerxes' army that their arrows would darken the sky: 'Good, we'll fight in the shade.'[3]

*   *   *

The Greek sources paint a portrait of Xerxes as young, easily led, wilful, inconsistent, overconfident and prone to dramatic shows of strength. He famously built a pontoon bridge across the seven *stadia*-wide Hellespont (around 1,300 metres) and cut a massive canal through the Mount Athos peninsula. When Xerxes' bridge was destroyed by a storm, the king was reportedly so angry with the waters that he ordered his men to punish the straits with 300 lashes and place a yoke of fetters in the waters to bind them.[4] Buried within the Greek stories, however, a more balanced view can be seen, with Xerxes pouring a libation into the sea from a golden phial, praying to the sun that no accidents should befall him to prevent his subjugation of Europe. After making this prayer, he cast the golden vessel into the Hellespont, along with a golden bowl and a Persian sword.[5] Without Xerxes' side of the story, we will obviously never know what the Persian king was really like.

Once his army had crossed into Europe, Xerxes summoned Demaratus and asked him whether the Greeks would dare face him. Wary of the king's notorious temper, Demaratus asked Xerxes whether he wanted to be told the truth, or simply what he wanted to hear. When Xerxes insisted that he wanted to know the truth, Demaratus told him that the Spartans would never accept his proposals, and that they would challenge him in battle even if all the other Greeks surrendered. Xerxes scoffed at this, but Demaratus was resolute, insisting that the Spartans would fight against Xerxes' army even if they numbered only a thousand.[6]

At this, Xerxes challenged Demaratus, pointing out that he claimed to be the Spartan king, and that if he really was king of such brave fighters, he should be willing to fight against ten or even twenty Persians. After all, Xerxes insisted, his own bodyguards would each be willing to fight three Greeks. Demaratus did not take the bait, accepting that he did not want to fight ten, two, or even one man. But with some guts, he jibed that if he was compelled to fight someone, he'd like it to be one of those Persians who claimed to be a match for three Greeks. Given that Demaratus had been exempt from the rigorous Spartan upbringing, this might suggest that their heirs to the throne were still expected to undertake some kind of physical training.

To explain why the Spartans were such formidable fighters, Demaratus delivered what might be the most famous line in all of Greek literature about the Spartans:

> The Spartans are free, but not wholly free: for *nomos* [law or custom] is their master, and they stand in awe of it yet more than your men do you. They do what it orders: and it always orders the same, not to flee from battle before any multitude of men but, remaining at their place in the line of battle, to conquer or die.[7]

Unable to believe that the Spartans would fight his men to the death, Xerxes simply laughed again. But soon, Demaratus would be vindicated.

*   *   *

When Xerxes reached Macedonia, he sent demands for earth and water from the Greeks. But he did not bother asking the Spartans and Athenians, because – as we have already seen – they had previously sacrilegiously murdered messengers sent by his father Darius.[8] Despite their reputation for piety, the Spartans had not been at all concerned by this religious crime at the time. But around the time that Xerxes was making his preparations, the Spartans started receiving bad omens from the gods. Although the Athenians reported no such problems, the Spartans interpreted them as a sign of the gods' displeasure at their sacrilegious killing.

The ephors called for volunteers to sacrifice their lives to atone for the atrocity, and two 'wealthy and noble Spartans' called Sperthias and Bulis answered the call. Having crossed to Asia, they were entertained by Hydarnes, the Persian general in charge of the Asian coast. Hydarnes told them that if they were prepared to accept Xerxes as their ruler, they would surely hold high office in a Persian-ruled Greece. But Sperthias and Bulis responded rudely, telling the Persian general that he was giving them bad advice because he understood only half of the truth. As a subject of Xerxes, Hydarnes only knew how to be a slave. Had he experienced 'sweet freedom', Hydarnes would advise them not only to fight against Xerxes, but to do so with spears and battle-axes.[9]

When Sperthias and Bulis eventually arrived at Xerxes' court at Susa, they caused more offence by refusing to perform *proskynesis* (literally 'kissing towards' in ancient Greek) – a common ritual in the Near East whereby visitors to the king would greet him with a kiss, a bow, kneeling or full-on prostration, according to their rank. Although the Spartans had a reputation for being rude to foreigners, Sperthias and Bulis were not just being difficult; Greeks only ever prostrated themselves before the gods, and felt that it would be sacrilege to do so before a mortal.

Sperthias and Bulis were not the only foreigners to feel this way. In the Book of Esther in the Hebrew Bible, Mordecai, a Jewish resident of the Persian city of Susa, refuses to kneel before Haman, an official of the Persian king 'Ahasuerus',[10] who is commonly identified as Xerxes. Mordecai's refusal to follow Persian court protocol angers Haman so much that he resolves to kill not just Mordecai, but all the Jewish exiles throughout the Persian kingdom. Fortunately, Mordecai's former ward Esther is now the Persian queen; she intervenes to save her people, and Haman winds up hanging from gallows he set up in order to execute Mordecai.

The story of Sperthias and Bulis is a little different. Having 'fought off' the demand to prostrate themselves, Sperthias and Bulis then addressed Xerxes boldly: 'King of the Medes, the Lacedaemonians have sent us to pay the penalty for the heralds who were murdered in Sparta.' But Xerxes refused to kill them, saying that he would not be 'like the Spartans', who had broken a code common to all humans.[11] Xerxes probably also realised that it would be better not to release the overly superstitious Spartans from their guilt. Herodotus stresses that their sons, Anesterius and Nicolas, were both killed on diplomatic journeys to Persia, and sees this as a sign that the wrath of the gods was only averted for a time by their fathers' offer to sacrifice themselves. Ultimately, the gods took their revenge on their sons.

The Greeks received other inauspicious omens about their chances against the Persians. When the Athenians asked Apollo at Delphi for his advice, they received a blunt message: 'Wretched ones, why do you sit here? Flee and begone to the remotest ends of earth!' The Athenians were so dispirited at this that they begged Apollo to take pity on them and give them a better answer. This time, the god offered them a glimmer of hope, telling them that 'a wall of wood' would provide a stronghold for them and their children, and that 'on another day you shall face them, Divine Salamis – you shall slay many children of women'. The Athenian statesman Themistocles convinced his fellow citizens that Apollo's answer meant they would defeat the Persians near the island of Salamis with their navy – a metaphorical wooden wall. The Spartans fared slightly better than the Athenians: Apollo told them that either a Spartan king would die, or the city of Sparta would be sacked.[12]

* * *

The other Greeks chose the Spartans to be their leaders on both land and sea. Sparta's reputation for military excellence was undoubtedly partly behind this decision, but the fact that most of the Greek states who were fighting against the Persians were members of the Peloponnesian League may have been the main factor. These Greek states were bound by oaths to follow the Spartans wherever they led; for them, Sparta was the recognised leader, and had been for half a century. The other Greeks who were willing to fight against the Persians, like the Athenians, would have been hard pressed to push their own claims for leadership against such a well-established network.

The only major Peloponnesian *polis* not known to have participated in the war was Sparta's bitter rival Argos; they refused to help unless the Spartans gave them an equal share in the leadership. The Spartans indicated that they would be prepared to give the Argive general an equal vote to each of their kings; as they put it, Sparta had two kings, while Argos had only one. But as this would have given the Spartans a two-thirds majority over any major decision, the Argives opted to remain neutral. Nonetheless, the other Greeks felt that the Argives were only demanding a share in the leadership because they knew the

Spartans would refuse, giving them an excuse to do nothing.[13] As we have already seen, the Argives had another compelling reason for not getting involved: the extraordinarily heavy casualties inflicted upon them by Cleomenes at the Battle of Sepeia.

The Spartans also led a delegation to the island of Sicily, home to many Greek colonies, to ask for help from Gelon, the powerful tyrant of Syracuse. Their ambassador Syagrus told Gelon that 'the Lacedaemonians and their allies' had sent them to ask him for his aid, and went on to warn him that the Greeks of Sicily would surely be next on Xerxes' hit list. Gelon was seemingly obliging, offering to send a numerically pleasing 200 triremes, 20,000 hoplites, 2,000 cavalry, 2,000 archers and 2,000 light-armed troops to Greece to help. But there was a catch: he would only supply them if he were given sole command. At this, Syagrus lost his temper, telling Gelon that the great Achaean hero Agamemnon would cry in despair if the Syracusans took the leadership of the Greeks from the Spartiates; bluntly rejecting his offer, he declared: 'If you are too proud to take orders, then don't help us.'

In the face of this stark Spartan response, Gelon refused to allow his anger to get the better of him. 'My Spartiate friend,' he replied, 'When insults descend on a man his anger tends to rise; but all the obvious arrogance in your speech won't persuade me to be rude in return.' He then calmly asked for command of the Greek fleet. At this, the unnamed Athenian representative lost his temper, telling Gelon that the Athenians were prepared to suffer the Spartans having command of the fleet for the greater good, but if Gelon – or the Spartans, for that matter – thought that Athens would accept any other *polis* being put in charge of the fleet, they had better think again. Gelon then put the Athenian in his place too, wryly observing that the Greeks seemed to have a lot of officers but not many men.

Thus far, the narrative would seem to suggest that Spartan

and Athenian arrogance was costing the Greeks potentially game-changing help against Xerxes. But even if Gelon had wanted to send help (and after the event the Syracusans insisted that he really did intend to send help), he would not have been able to, because the Carthaginians launched a massive invasion of Sicily at the same time as Xerxes invaded.[14] When the Persian army arrived in mainland Greece, Gelon was far too busy to offer any help.

* * *

Having got nowhere with securing the support of the Argives or Gelon, the Spartan-led Greek forces first attempted to stop Xerxes' forces at the vale of Tempe, a ravine between Mount Olympus and Mount Ossa in northern Greece. Tempe at least seemed to be a good place to negate Xerxes' overwhelming numerical advantage – at its narrowest point the valley is only 25 metres wide, with cliffs nearly 500 metres high looming above. (The rift was said to have been created by the god Poseidon striking the earth with his trident, and Herodotus says that anyone who sees the valley will agree that Poseidon – the god of earthquakes – must have made it.)[15] The Spartan commander-in-chief, Euaenetus – a senior army officer, but not a royal – brought 10,000 hoplites with him. If they fought with their shields close together, 150 ranks of 60 men would have been able to block the Persians' passage. Xerxes' lightly armoured troops would have had no hope of forcing their way through.

However, when Euaenetus learned from Alexander I, the king of Macedon and one of Xerxes' vassals, that the Persians could take many routes that would allow them to circumvent his position, he realised that he had no hope of holding the Persians back, and withdrew south with his 10,000 hoplites.[16] The fact that many of the locals – including the Thessalians

– had already given Xerxes tokens of submission might have been connected to his decision to withdraw.[17]

The Spartans resolved next to face Xerxes at Thermopylae (literally, the 'Hot Gates' because of the thermal springs there), a narrow passage in Malia on the main route between northern and central Greece. This time, a Spartan king would be in command: Cleomenes' half-brother Leonidas, who had only recently ascended to the throne. To emphasise Leonidas' importance, Herodotus gives him his full genealogy – all the way back to the demigod Heracles and his father Zeus. The presence of a divinely descended Spartan king at the front line suggests that this time the Spartans really were committed to the fight. Yet Leonidas brought with him just 300 Spartiates, a force so small that the primary sources tend to paint him as leading something akin to a suicide squad. Not only does Herodotus tell us that the Spartans received the oracle foretelling that Sparta would fall unless one of their kings died, he also notes that all the Spartans sent to Thermopylae, including Leonidas, had living sons who would effectively replace them.[18] Later sources suggest that before departing, Leonidas instructed his wife Gorgo to marry a good man and bear good children, which implies that he did not expect to return home.[19] Even more dramatically, according to Diodorus, when the ephors told Leonidas that 1,000 hoplites were not enough, he replied, 'For holding the pass they are too few, but for their task they are many.' When asked what he meant, Leonidas said they were going 'to die for the freedom of all.'[20]

It is more likely that Leonidas and his men were an advance guard, tasked with holding Xerxes back until reinforcements could arrive. Thermopylae appeared to be an even better defensive position than Tempe. At its narrowest, the path was less than 20 metres wide, with sheer cliffs on one side and marshy bog to the other. It was so narrow that if the 300 Spartan hoplites accompanying the Spartan king Leonidas fought with their shields close together, barely thirty of them could have blocked the Persians' passage. If they lined up in the standard Greek hoplite phalanx, which had eight ranks of men, with the long spears of the first two ranks projecting outwards like jousting lances, Xerxes' men would have been unable to reach their opponents. Better still, unlike in Tempe, where the pass led out to open sea, the island of Euboea lay close to Thermopylae, creating a narrow strait where the smaller Greek force could hold up Xerxes' massive fleet. Leonidas had good reason to think that he could stymie the Persian advance for a long time with minimal manpower.

Nonetheless, Leonidas had far fewer allied troops at his disposal than the 10,000 hoplites Euanetus had taken to Tempe – just 2,680 other Peloponnesians, 1,100 Boeotians, 1,000 Phocians, and the Locrians, whom Diodorus numbers at 1,000, as well as an indeterminate number of helots. The Locrians seem to have sent all their available men, but in every other case these numbers were far less than these *poleis* could have supplied. Herodotus suggests that this was because Xerxes' invasion coincided with the Carneia, a pan-Dorian religious festival during which the Spartans and many of the other Peloponnesians were forbidden to fight.[21] In Sparta, the festival was 'a representation of military training': there were nine large tents where the men took their meals, and 'all actions … taken in response to the military herald's commands'.[22] The main reason there were comparatively few hoplites at Thermopylae, however, was that the marines from the Greek maritime powers like Athens, Corinth, Megara and Aegina were on board their warships, ready to fight Xerxes' men at sea in an allied Greek fleet. At Tempe, conversely, the thousands of hoplite marines had disembarked and were ready to fight the Persians on the ground, as there was nowhere near the pass where Euanetus' fleet could safely confront Xerxes' armada.

Despite their strong defensive position, Xerxes assumed the Greeks would simply retreat when they realised the futility of their task. When they didn't, he sent a spy to find out why. The Spartans happened to be on guard at the time, and the spy was amazed to see that some of them were wrestling naked while others were sitting around, combing their hair. When Xerxes learned what the spy had seen, he summoned Demaratus and demanded to know what this odd behaviour meant. Demaratus told him that it meant the Spartans were going to fight; it was customary for them to 'adorn their heads' when they were about to risk their lives. He added that Xerxes could take him 'as a liar' if it turned out not to be true.

While, as Herodotus puts it, Xerxes simply 'could not understand' what Demaratus had said,[23] the fact that Leonidas and his men were spending their time exercising prior to the battle at Thermopylae does not surprise modern experts. After all, we have already seen how important sport was to the Spartan way of life. Moreover, Xenophon explains that it was mandated by Spartan law that hoplites should maintain their gymnastic exercises twice every day – in the morning and the evening – for the duration of military campaigns, in order to enhance their physical impressiveness, and make them look superior to other men. The only proviso was that no running was allowed outside the military camp, to prevent any Spartan hoplite from straying too far from his weapons.[24]

This law about exercising while on campaign was taken so seriously in Sparta that the fourth-century BCE commander Thibron was killed while campaigning in Asia when he was surprised by the sudden arrival of Persian forces while practising throwing the discus. (Xenophon nevertheless criticises Thibron for having acted in an overconfident and undisciplined manner.)[25] Perhaps the most noteworthy event relating to exercising during times of war befell Isadas, the son of the fourth-century BCE officer Phoebidas. When the Thebans launched a surprise attack on Sparta in 362 BCE, he rushed straight from the gymnasium; stark naked and covered in oil, he grabbed a spear in one hand and a sword in the other, before pushing his way to the front of the Spartan lines. There, Isadas struck down everyone who came up against him, without receiving so much as a scratch to his body. Plutarch surmises that the enemy must have thought he was a god fighting amongst them. After the fighting was over, the ephors gave him a crown for valour – and a 1,000-drachma fine (£100,000 or $150,000 today), for risking his body by not wearing armour.[26]

*   *   *

Xerxes waited four whole days for the Greeks to flee. When they didn't, he grew angry at what he perceived as their 'folly and shamelessness'. So he sent the Medes and Cissians against the Spartans, with orders to take them prisoner and bring them to him. Xerxes' men bore down upon Leonidas and his troops, but as they lacked body armour, were using flimsy shields made from wickerwork, and carried spears that were far shorter than those used by the Greeks, they were not up to the task. Many Medes and Cissians fell; when others attacked in turn, they fell in just the same way. Herodotus reports that the Spartans fought so well against these contingents that they made it clear to everyone, especially Xerxes, that he had in his army 'many people, but few men'.[27]

After the Medes and Cissians failed, Xerxes went for his big guns. The so-called 'Immortals' were an elite unit of 10,000 picked men who were so named because there were always 10,000 of them; they were immediately replaced when they fell. Since the Immortals were equipped with largely the same arms as the Medes and Cissians, however, they fared no better.[28] The narrowness of the pass enabled Leonidas to eke out his small numbers by arranging the different contingents so that they fought in relays. The Greeks killed so many of Xerxes' men that Diodorus claims 'the entire area about the passes was strewn with dead bodies.'[29] Xerxes is even said to have jumped from his seat three times in fear for his army.[30] Unable to gain any ground, the Persians withdrew; Leonidas and his men had won the day, hands down.

The second day went in much the same way as the first, with the Spartans and the other Greeks able to resist everything that Xerxes threw at them. As we saw earlier, Diodorus claims that the Spartan troops refused to rest, with the older and younger soldiers desperate to outperform each other in battle. As he rhapsodised: 'Who could be distinguished more than those men who were not equal even to the thousandth part of the enemy, yet dared to pit their manly excellence against the unbelievable multitudes?'[31] The Spartans employed special tactics that Herodotus claimed were 'worthy of mention', showing themselves to be particularly skilled fighters. One such technique involved feigning retreat and luring the Persians into wild pursuit; then the Spartans 'would turn about to face the barbarians, and ... throw down countless Persians.'[32] During such manoeuvres, 'a few of the Spartans themselves were also slain' – validating Demaratus' claims that the Spartans would be prepared to sacrifice themselves. Unable to gain any foothold, the Persians withdrew at the end of a second miserable day.

We should probably be slightly cynical about such accounts glorifying the Spartans' military prowess. Many modern scholars ask what happened to all the Persian archers – the ones that had threatened to leave the Spartans fighting in the shade. Furthermore, could the Spartans and their fellow Greeks really have fought so long without breaks in high summer, with each day providing around fourteen hours of daylight? If they did, the toll on their bodies would have been considerable. In his best-selling novel *Gates of Fire*, Stephen Pressfield does a fine job of exploring what might have happened if the fighting really did last all day long on both days, with the Spartans becoming increasingly battered, with slash wounds, stab wounds, pulled muscles, and Dienekes even losing an eye. Given that matches in modern contact sports, whether ice hockey, rugby or soccer, run for only sixty, eighty or ninety minutes and tend to leave players physically exhausted, some academics question how realistic this might be. Others have pointed out that Herodotus really only describes six Persian assaults over the course of two days of fighting. If the fighting really went so badly for Xerxes' men, there must have been long pauses while the Persians backed off and considered what tactic to try next. But we should probably not be too cynical; the adrenaline rush from fighting for your life means that soldiers are often capable of unimaginable feats of endurance in the heat of battle.

Just as it must have seemed that Leonidas and his men were going to succeed in holding the Persians at bay, a local Trachinian named Ephialtes told Xerxes about the existence of a goat track that would allow him to circumvent their position. Leonidas had only learned about this path after he arrived at Thermopylae, and he gave the local Phocians the task of defending it. It probably seemed a good idea to exploit their local knowledge in this way, but it was a decision that would prove fatal. A price was later put on Ephialtes' head by the Amphictyonic Council that oversaw the affairs of Delphi; although he was murdered by a fellow Trachinian for private reasons, the Spartans rewarded his killer anyway.[33]

Once Ephialtes (whose name, appropriately, means 'nightmare' in both ancient and modern Greek) had offered him this golden opportunity to end the stalemate, Xerxes acted swiftly, ordering Ephialtes to lead his general Hydarnes and the Immortals along the path. When the Phocians who were guarding the path heard their approach, they put on their armour and prepared to fight. Hydarnes was terrified that the Phocians were Spartans. When Ephialtes assured him that they were not – quite how he could tell is unclear, unless the Spartans were already emblazoning the letter *lambda* for 'Lacedaemon' on their shields – the Persians launched a volley of arrows at them, forcing them to withdraw to higher ground. Although the Phocians had intended to fight to the death, the Persians were able to simply sweep past.[34]

Leonidas learned that Hydarnes and the Immortals were approaching before it was too late. Some said he was warned by deserters, others that Leonidas' seer foretold that death was coming at dawn, having examined the sacrificial victims. Whatever the case, Leonidas made a choice that would turn him and his men into legends. Having dismissed most of his forces, he opted to remain at his post for long enough to allow them to withdraw safely. Although there were other less glorious versions of the story of Thermopylae, Herodotus stresses that he believes the truth is that Leonidas chose to stay and fight to the death, in order to gain 'glory'.[35] The word Herodotus uses – *kleos* – is the type of honour that drove the heroes of Homer's epic poems to either achieve great things or die trying.

On what turned out to be the final morning of the battle, Leonidas and his remaining Spartan troops took the fight to the Persians. They were accompanied by the hoplites from Thespiae, who insisted that 'they would stay and die' with them. The hoplites from Thebes also remained. Although Herodotus claims that Leonidas detained them as hostages to ensure that Thebes did not defect to the Persians,[36] it seems unlikely that he would have forced potential traitors to fight alongside him; modern scholars tend to think that the Thebans who fought at Thermopylae were genuine freedom fighters whose sacrifice ultimately went unacknowledged because the other Thebans Medised and later fought on the wrong side. Indeed, Plutarch later accuses Herodotus of badmouthing the Thebans because they refused to pay him when he travelled to Thebes to give lectures.[37]

Advancing into a wider – and therefore less safe – part of the pass, the Spartans fought with such gusto that Herodotus describes them as 'in a frenzy', while the Persians reportedly had to be driven on with whips to face the onslaught.[38] Many of the Persians were pushed into the sea where they drowned, while many more were trampled alive. Diodorus claims the Spartans were able to 'perform heroic and incredible deeds' because they were prepared to die.[39] One such Spartan was Eurytus, who was suffering from an eye problem which was so bad that he had to be led by hand to the fighting by his helot attendant (modern explanations for Eurytus' condition have ranged from conjunctivitis caused by the dust to a psychiatric disorder triggered by combat stress). Having plunged into the melee, the sightless Eurytus was soon killed.

By the time Hydarnes and the Immortals appeared behind them, Leonidas and many of his men had been killed in the fighting. They took many brave Persians down with them in the process, including two of Xerxes' half-brothers – Abrocomes and Hyperanthes – a sign that Xerxes was still committing crack troops to the fight. Herodotus reports that the fighting over Leonidas' body was particularly fierce, with the Spartans managing to hurl the Persians back four times with 'much shoving'.[40]

When the Immortals appeared behind them, the remaining Spartans and Thespians withdrew to a small bluff to make their final stand for glory, losing touch with the Thebans, who surrendered; Xerxes would later have the Theban captives branded like cattle as a token of slavery. By now, most of the Spartans and Thespians had lost their spears, leaving them to fight with swords or knives. Some of them fought on with just their bare hands and teeth, while the Persians bore down on them on all sides. As we saw earlier, even without their weapons, the Spartans proved such formidable opponents that the Persians preferred to bury them in a hail of missiles.

Few modern scholars accept the bizarre story told by Diodorus of Leonidas launching a last-ditch night attack on Xerxes' pavilion, at which the Persians panicked – with Xerxes escaping only by fleeing cowardly into the night.[41] Like Herodotus, Diodorus has the Persians shoot the Spartans down with arrows and javelins, rather than take them on man-to-man. Modern scholars also doubt Diodorus' claim that Leonidas ordered his men to prepare their breakfast quickly because they would soon be dining in Hades (in the film *300* this line is adapted slightly, so that Leonidas roars 'Spartans! Tonight – we dine – in Hell!').[42] Like *molōn labe*, this one-liner must be a later invention; it was far too good for Herodotus to have overlooked it had it been known in his day.

Although Thermopylae was a humiliating defeat for the Spartans, over time it came to be remembered as a moral victory. Xerxes was so angry at his humiliation that he cut off Leonidas' head and impaled it on a pike.[43] He also engaged in an elaborate charade, leaving all the Spartans unburied for all to see, while hiding hordes of his own dead so that no one would see just how many Persians had been killed by so few Spartans.[44] The Spartans themselves stubbornly insisted that Leonidas had 'won', but that his followers were 'insufficient for the whole destruction of the Medes'.[45] After the battle, the Spartans set up a stone stele recording an epigram which is often attributed to Simonides of Ceos: 'Stranger, go tell the Spartans, that here, obedient to their orders, we lie.'[46] An epigram that Simonides actually wrote for the Spartans seems even more glorifying: 'The earth covers the glorious men who died here with you, Leonidas, O king of wide Sparta, having faced in battle the might of the very many arrows, swift horses, and Medes.'[47]

The Spartans also seem to have ensured that the two survivors – Pantites and Aristodemus – did not have an opportunity to discredit this official story. Pantites had been sent away as a messenger, but when he returned to Sparta he was so 'dishonoured' by the other Spartans that he hanged himself, unable to cope with the shame. Aristodemus had an eye affliction, just like Eurytus, but chose to return home rather than join Eurytus in death. Back in Sparta he was also reviled as a 'coward'; no Spartan would so much as speak to him. The following summer at the Battle of Plataea, he effectively committed suicide, rushing out from the Spartan ranks like a berserker and dying after achieving 'great deeds'.[48]

Around a hundred years after the fighting, Isocrates called Thermopylae 'a victory for the soul' because none of the Spartans had left their post.[49] Later still, Diodorus would even claim that the Spartans who fought at Thermopylae 'were more responsible for the common freedom of the Greeks' than those who fought in subsequent victories over the Persians, for 'when the deeds of these men were remembered, the Persians were panic-stricken, whereas the Greeks were driven to similar courageous exploits.'[50] But such hyperbolic claims cannot conceal the fact that Leonidas' men had only been able to hold Xerxes' advance up for a week, and they were slaughtered after less than three days of fighting.

*   *   *

Fortunately for the Spartans and their allies, the defence of Greece was not dependent on their holding Xerxes back at the

'Hot Gates'. While Leonidas and his men were fighting at Thermopylae, the Spartan admiral Eurybiades was doing his best to hold off Xerxes' armada at Artemisium with his own fleet of 271 triremes. As at Thermopylae, the Spartan contribution was tiny – just ten warships. Unlike at Thermopylae, however, where the Spartans' tiny contribution of 300 hoplites was a token force, the ten triremes they sent to support that army at Thermopylae probably represented the majority of their warships. The Athenian admiral Themistocles single-handedly commanded 127 triremes: almost half of the entire Greek fleet. The fact that the Athenians were able to bring so many ships was the consequence of one of the most prescient decisions Europe's first democratic state ever made. When the Athenians discovered a particularly rich seam of silver at their mines in Laurium in 483 BCE, they had initially agreed to divide the cash equally among the citizens – only for Themistocles to persuade the people to spend the money on 200 triremes. Themistocles saved Greece by doing so, compelling the hitherto land-oriented Athenians to become 'men of the sea'.[51] Nonetheless, it was insisted Eurybiades be the overall commander; the other Greeks made it clear that they would break up the fleet and desert unless 'the Laconian' was in charge.[52]

The Greeks were reportedly so reluctant to fight at Artemisium that the local Euboeans had to resort to bribery to keep them there. Themistocles allegedly received 30 talents, the equivalent of £18 million or $27 million in modern money, as an incentive; he gave five to Eurybiades (half what Aristagoras initially offered Cleomenes to convince him to join the Ionian revolt) and three to Adeimantus, the Corinthian admiral whose forty triremes represented the second-largest contingent after the Athenians'. This might well be nonsense – but the notion that Eurybiades took a bribe fits a pattern that appears throughout our sources: the Spartans tended to covet gold and silver.

As our sources treat the Battle of Artemisium as a minor footnote in comparison to both the land battle at Thermopylae and the subsequent decisive contest at sea at Salamis, it is difficult to say much about this naval encounter with any certainty. We can, however, glean that there were two inconclusive engagements between the fleets, which cost both sides many ships and men.[53] How the fighting worked is unclear – partly because authors like Herodotus had no real understanding of naval warfare. Modern experts think that 'normal' Greek naval tactics involved the ships of both sides lining up against each other in two lines, bow to bow, with each ship then trying to row quickly into the gaps between the enemy ships, before wheeling around and striking their opponents in the side. Such tactics obviously involved great skill, and such manoeuvres would have been extremely difficult if the fighting took place in narrow waters. The choice to engage at the narrow straits between Euboea and the mainland – like the pass at Thermopylae – was clearly intended to negate the Persians' superior numbers. It seems to have worked after a fashion at Artemisium, but when Leonidas failed to hold Thermopylae, Eurybiades was forced to flee south.

The defeat at Thermopylae left the Greek mainland open to the Persians. The Athenians sailed home and collected their women, children, elderly and infirm, before moving them to the island of Aegina and the city of Troezen in the Peloponnese. The Persians captured Athens, razed its walls, and burned the temples to the ground. Xerxes had succeeded where his father Darius had failed. Sparta's attempt to defend Greece was not going well.

*   *   *

Eurybiades gathered the fleet at the island of Salamis, south of Athens. Themistocles argued that the Greeks should try to stop Xerxes' armada there, in the narrow straits, but the Spartans and other Peloponnesians were unconvinced. They favoured withdrawing to the Peloponnese and hiding behind a wall they were building across the Isthmus of Corinth. The fleet – including the Athenian ships – would fall back to support the army at the wall. Not only would this strategy mean abandoning the whole of central Greece to Xerxes, it also imperilled the Peloponnese, as Xerxes could move his troops behind the defenders by sea. Themistocles tried to make this clear to Eurybiades, but the Corinthian admiral told him to hold his tongue – after all, he had no city to represent. Themistocles replied that he represented the most powerful Greek city; as long as the Athenians had two hundred fully manned warships, he said, no Greek city would be able to repel them.[54]

The disagreement grew so intense that Eurybiades tried to strike Themistocles with his staff. (Spartan citizens – particularly those in positions of authority – usually carried a wooden staff; although the literary sources are vague about what they looked like, a limestone relief from the sanctuary of Artemis Orthia shows a long-haired man holding a chest-high, T-shaped example.) When Eurybiades threatened Themistocles, the Athenian admiral responded boldly: 'Strike but listen!'[55]

Themistocles seems to have made a convincing case; with a combination of fear and flattery, he was able to persuade Eurybiades that it would be better to fight at Salamis. If they did so, he said, the Greeks could keep Xerxes away from the Peloponnese altogether. 'If you stay here, you will be a good man,' he added, but: 'If not, you will ruin Greece.' The implication was that the Athenians would take all their men and ships and found a new city in Italy. The thought of facing hundreds of Xerxes' warships without the Athenians' ships that made up more than half his fleet was too much for Eurybiades, so he 'decided' to stay at Salamis and fight. Subsequent legends had it that Themistocles made sure the battle took place by sending Xerxes a message warning him that the Greeks were about to flee, implying that he would lose his opportunity to crush them if he didn't act quickly.[56]

No matter how the decision to fight at Salamis came about, for the Greeks it turned out to be the right one. Our sources – Herodotus, Diodorus, Plutarch, and even Aeschylus' play *The Persians* – all fail to give much detail regarding what happened in the fighting. When they do, they either provide stories of individuals undertaking brave actions, or odd personal moments. A good example is Herodotus' lengthy description of the antics of the Aeginetan ship captain Polycritus. He was the son of Crius, who had earlier collaborated with Demaratus to stymie Cleomenes' attempts to ensure Aegina did not Medise, and been taken to Athens as hostage. When Polycritus spotted Themistocles' ship passing by his own, he started hurling abuse at the Athenian admiral for the fact that the Athenians had doubted the Aeginetans' resolve to fight the Persians.[57]

Another excellent example of how far off topic Herodotus goes is his fixation on the achievements of Artemisia, the queen of his homeland Halicarnassus. Herodotus turns her into one of Xerxes' key advisors, has the Athenians place a price of 10,000 drachmas (£1 million or $1.5 million today) on her head because they were enraged that a woman would dare attack their city,[58] and claims that when Xerxes spotted her fighting bravely, he cried aloud, 'My men have turned into women, and my women into men!'[59]

Putting all these vignettes aside, the crucial fact about the Battle of Salamis is that Xerxes' fleet was destroyed. The defeat prompted the Persian king to return home. Yet the Greek victory did little in the short term to free the Greeks of

Persian interference. Xerxes left his cousin Mardonius behind to complete the conquest of Greece without him. Mardonius asked for 300,000 troops, and promised Xerxes that he would make him master of all Greece. To make it clear how strong his position was, Mardonius occupied Athens for a second time. Herodotus says that he hoped to light signal flares across the Aegean to inform Xerxes – now safely back in Asia – that he had taken Athens again. He was disappointed to find, however, that no Athenians had returned home, rendering his recapture of Athens an entirely symbolic gesture. The Greeks may have won the Battle of Salamis, but much of Greece remained very much in Persian hands.

As the commander-in-chief at Salamis, Eurybiades was able to claim responsibility for the naval victory, but everyone knew that the Athenians were really responsible. Nonetheless, Themistocles missed out on the credit. When they held a vote to decide who the best fighters were, the other Greek naval commanders – who were mostly Dorian – voted to give the prize to the Dorian Aeginetans, and each voted for himself as the best admiral. Themistocles had to make do with second prize; Herodotus stresses that there were only single votes in the competition for the best admiral, but Themistocles outstripped everyone else in the vote for who was the second best.[60]

The Spartans, however, so often arrogant and hostile towards foreigners, went out of their way to formally recognise Themistocles' starring role in the fighting at Salamis. They invited him to Sparta, where he and Eurybiades were presented with olive crowns. They also gave Themistocles the finest chariot in Sparta – an enormous honour, given how seriously chariot racing was taken in Sparta – and the elite royal bodyguard of knights escorted him to the border with Tegea when he departed. Themistocles was the only foreigner ever to be given such an escort.[61] Nonetheless, one might speculate whether the reason behind this was partly a keenness to ensure that the visiting Athenian general didn't see or speak to anyone the Spartans didn't want him to on his way home.

*   *   *

Although Eurybiades and Themistocles had worked well together at Salamis, relations between the Spartans and the Athenians remained tense. When Mardonius, now the Persian commander-in-chief, sent the Macedonian king Alexander to try to persuade the Athenians to change sides, the Spartans sent envoys desperately begging them not to join the Persians; they went so far as to offer to house and feed Athens' women and children until the war was over. The Athenians rebuked this offer, telling the Spartans bluntly that they were all Greeks, speaking the same language, sharing the same blood, religious practices and way of life.[62] Even more bluntly, they told the Spartans to stop worrying about whether they were going to change sides, and to send an army to liberate Athens as soon as they possibly could.

Despite the Spartans' apparent fears about the Athenians' commitment to the cause, they appear to have done little to prepare to drive the Persians out of central Greece. Instead, they focused on building a wall across the Isthmus to keep the Persians out of the Peloponnese. Eventually the Athenians grew impatient, and sent a delegation to Sparta to find out what was taking so long. When the ambassadors arrived, the Spartans rudely put them off, for day after day, as they were busy celebrating the Hyacinthia festival. After the Spartans had stalled for nine days, the Athenian ambassadors finally cracked and threatened to do a deal with the Persians. It was all well and good, they said, for the Spartans to celebrate their religious holiday, but they were treating the Athenians badly; why shouldn't they make common cause with the Persians instead? This threat finally got the Spartans to act. But even then, the Spartan response was bizarrely rude. The ephors told the Athenians that, 'As far as we know, our army is at Orestheum [a town in northern Laconia], marching against the foreigners.' Naturally, the Athenians had no idea what they meant. When they asked for clarification, the ephors smugly said that an army of 5,000 Spartiates, 5,000 *perioikoi*, and 35,000 helots 'armed for war', had been sent out against the Persians, under the command of two senior royals: Pausanias, Leonidas' nephew, who was acting as regent for Leonidas' son Pleistarchus; and his cousin Euryanax, the son of Dorieus.[63] Understandably, the Athenians were stunned – and thrilled – at this rapid turn of events. The Spartans were finally going to try to lead the Greeks to victory – and freedom.

Herodotus claims that this Spartan volte-face had only occurred the day before, after a Tegean named Chileus persuaded the ephors that they could not defeat the Persians without Athenian help and so should act.[64] That said, it is extremely unlikely that the Spartans could have mobilised such a large force so quickly. The whole episode, with all its delays and secrets, suggests that the Spartans were trying to mask their preparations from both the helot population at home and their Argive enemies abroad. By gathering their forces in secret, they were able to minimise the threat from within, and – just as important – force their way through the Argolid before the Argives were aware that they were coming. Although the Argives claimed that they had not Medised, it is entirely possible that they may have tried to stop them, if they had realised the Spartans were sending out an army. Nonetheless, the Spartans' manner and tone betrays a casual disregard for the Athenians' feelings. The disdain that the Spartans showed towards their allies over the centuries would not hold them in good stead during future crises.

*   *   *

Pausanias and Euryanax led their troops to the Isthmus, where they were joined by nearly 30,000 hoplites from Tegea, Corinth, Potidaea, Orchomenos, Sicyon, Epidaurus, Troezen, Lepreum, Mycenae, Tiryns, Phlius, Hermione, Eretria, Styria, Chalcis, Ambracia, Leucas, Anactoria, Cephallenia, Aegina, Megara, Plataea and Athens. Altogether, there were 38,700 heavily armed hoplites – probably the largest army the ancient Greeks would ever pull together – in addition to 35,000 helots armed as light-armed troops, and another 34,500 light-armed troops from the other states.[65] According to later sources, the Spartans made all the other Greeks swear an oath binding them to fight to the death, to obey any orders given by their generals, to bury the dead where they fell, and to dedicate a tenth of the property of the Greeks who had sided with the Persians to the god Apollo.[66] Modern scholars often doubt this story for the reason that Herodotus doesn't mention the oath – but he does report that Demaratus told Xerxes that they would indeed gather at the Isthmus and bind their allies with an oath, after which Xerxes should expect to face fiercer fighting even than that at Thermopylae. Characteristically, Xerxes chose to ignore Demaratus' warning.[67]

Pausanias and Euryanax led their army to Plataea in Boeotia, where Mardonius was awaiting them with his own massive army. As they did with Xerxes' original invasion force, the Greek sources tend to exaggerate wildly: Herodotus says there were 300,000 men, while Diodorus reports that there were as many as 500,000.[68] Modern estimates are usually closer to 100,000, but even that may be too high. Mardonius' forces comprised Persians, Medes, Sacae, Bactrians, Indians, Greeks from Asia, and a few men from each nation in Xerxes' kingdom chosen for their excellence at fighting. As these included marines from the Egyptian fleet who carried spears and 'hollow shields, with great rims,'[69] it seems likely that Mardonius chose men whose arms and armour were best suited to fighting against Greek hoplites.

While Mardonius was selecting his troops, the Spartans happened to send a single herald – as was customary for them – to Xerxes, to demand retribution for the death of Leonidas. The herald reportedly declaimed: 'King of the Medes, the Lacedaemonians and the Heraclids from Sparta demand justice, because you killed their king when he was defending Greece.' At this, Xerxes laughed, and pointed at Mardonius. 'Here is Mardonius,' he said, 'who shall give satisfaction to those as befits.'[70] Mardonius did indeed give the Spartans satisfaction in the fighting at Plataea – just not in the way that either he or Xerxes would have imagined.

Yet it takes Herodotus quite some time to get to the drama. He begins his account of the battle with an odd story about the Athenians and Spartans exchanging positions in the line prior to the commencement of battle. As the Athenians told the story to Herodotus, Pausanias was so afraid of the Persians that he asked them to change sides; as he explained, the Athenians knew the 'Medes', having fought against them at Marathon, whereas 'no single Spartan' had ever encountered them. The Athenians quite naturally agreed, they said, because they had been thinking the same thing – they just didn't want to offend the Spartans by suggesting it. But the swap achieved nothing; when the Boeotians spotted that the Spartans and Athenians had exchanged positions, they warned Mardonius, who moved his Persian troops so that they were once more facing the Spartans. Seeing that the Persians had moved, the Spartans and Athenians swapped back yet again. When he saw that the Spartans had moved again – as he saw it, out of fear – Mardonius jeered that he had previously believed that the Spartans would never flee, but would either kill or be killed. 'But now I know that this is not true,' he continued. 'We've seen you changing places with the Athenians. This is not the act of brave men; we have been deceived by you!'[71] Nonetheless, the idea of hundreds of thousands of fighting men swapping positions several times in the build-up to battle defies credibility. At best, what really happened was confused by later tradition; at worst, this whole sequence is a fantasy.

Not long after this, Pausanias gave orders for the whole Greek army to withdraw to a more favourable position. But as Herodotus describes it, things went very wrong, and only the Greeks that were lined up in the centre moved. The Spartans ended up staying where they were, because one of Pausanias' senior officers, Amompharetus, the commander of the *lochos* from the Spartan village of Pitana, refused to retreat. The Athenians also stayed in position – partly because of confusion in the ranks, and partly out of long-term prejudice against the Spartans, people who 'said one thing and thought another'.[72]

When the Athenians sent a rider to see what the Spartans were really thinking, he arrived as Pausanias and Euryanax were engaged in a heated argument with Amompharetus. The two royals were remonstrating with the senior officer, warning him that staying where they were would endanger all the Spartans. But Amompharetus refused to listen; just as the Athenian rider arrived, he picked up a rock and hurled it at Pausanias' feet, declaring: 'This is my vote against fleeing from the foreigners.' Completely exasperated, Pausanias told Amompharetus that he was crazy – and he told the Athenian messenger to notify his superiors of the trouble the Spartans were in.

Some modern scholars argue that this story is hard to believe; after all, the Spartiates did not vote with rocks like Athenian jurors did in the law courts, but by shouting. Other scholars focus on Amompharetus' insubordination – a sign, they say, either that the story is an exaggeration because a Spartan would never dare be that insubordinate, or that the Spartans really weren't nearly as rule-abiding as Demaratus had suggested they were. Another idea is that Amompharetus' force was actually a rear guard, ordered to remain behind to protect the entire army during a retreat. It's possible that Amompharetus had seen what happened to the men who withdrew at Thermopylae and was not willing to risk the same thing happening to him. The fact that Pantites had been sent away from Thermopylae by Leonidas had not spared him from dishonour after the battle; we have already seen that he was driven to suicide. Perhaps Amompharetus feared that Pausanias' orders would not cut it back home in Sparta, and he was not prepared to risk being shamed as a coward for withdrawing, hence his description of the order to fall back as akin to fleeing.

Whatever the reason for the delay, the next morning Pausanias stopped haggling with Amompharetus and led the Spartans and the Tegeans (who had been waiting patiently for the Spartans to get their act together) to the hills, a couple of kilometres from their original position. Initially, Amompharetus could not believe that Pausanias would choose to leave him and his men. Eventually, however, he started to follow – perhaps because Pausanias had cannily waited at the halfway point for Amompharetus to swallow his pride.

At the precise moment that Amompharetus and his men joined with the rest of the Spartans and the Tegeans, Mardonius attacked. Harried by the Persian cavalry, and with arrows and other missiles raining down on them, the Spartans waited patiently while Pausanias made sacrifices to the gods to ensure that the omens for a battle were good. One Spartan named Callicrates, who was also said to be the most handsome man in the entire Greek army, was cut down by a Persian arrow through the ribs while he was sitting calmly waiting for Pausanias to give the order to attack. As he fell, Callicrates told his comrades that he did not mind dying for Greece – but he did mind dying before he had shown his prowess in combat.[73]

Despite his repeated sacrifices, Pausanias could not get the right omens. It was taking so long that some modern scholars speculate that the Spartan general was using the sacrifices as an excuse to delay attacking for strategic reasons. Other Spartan commanders did exactly that. In the early fourth century BCE, the Eurypontid king Agesilaus refused to lead an attack on the Persians in Asia because the liver of the sacrificial victim lacked a lobe. This bad omen from the gods showed him that it was not the right time to mount an attack. The fact that he was facing the Persian forces on a wide, flat plain without cavalry support might also have influenced his decision – to attack at this point would have been almost suicidal. Clearly, Agesilaus used the bad omens as an excuse, and perhaps even invented the bad omen in the first place. Pausanias may have been doing something similar.

As Herodotus tells it, Pausanias eventually grew so desperate that he turned his gaze towards Hera's temple at Plataea, which was visible in the distance, and prayed for the goddess's assistance. While he was praying, the Tegeans grew tired of waiting and launched an attack. Almost immediately – surely too much of a coincidence to be true – the omens proved favourable, and Pausanias gave the order for the Spartans to join in the fighting. With the combined weight of 11,500 heavily armed hoplites bearing down on them, the Persians swiftly abandoned their bows and formed a wall with their wicker bucklers. The fighting was reportedly fierce on both sides.[74] Herodotus stresses that the Persians were neither weaker nor less brave than the Spartans; rather, they were let down by their lack of armour, and the fact that they were 'unskilled' compared to their Spartan counterparts. Unlike the Spartans, who well understood the need to maintain cohesion and fight in a tight unit, the Persians would time and again rush out singly, or in small groups, hurling themselves at the shield wall of Spartans, and so perish. However, Plutarch took issue with Herodotus' claims that the Persians fought bravely, doubting that the men who had needed to be urged on with whips while Xerxes was watching would all of a sudden fight bravely when he wasn't there.[75]

When Mardonius fell – struck down by a Spartan named Arimnestos – the Persians' resolve broke. They fled to a fort near Thebes, where the Tegeans set about besieging them. Seeing that all was lost, the Persian noble Artabazus fled back to Asia via the Hellespont, taking 40,000 men with him. But the other Persians in the fortress resisted stoutly, partly because – as Herodotus puts it – the Spartans had 'no skill' in assaulting walls.[76] But when the stalwart Athenians arrived (having routed the Boeotians, who fought against their fellow Greeks, and with too much gusto for later generations to forget), they scaled the walls and tore them down, allowing the Tegeans and Spartans to pile inside. What followed was a bloodbath, with only 3,000 Persians surviving. Herodotus concludes simply, 'Pausanias, the son of Cleombrotus, and grandson of Anaxandridas, won the most glorious victory known to us.'[77]

After the battle, Pausanias marched against Thebes and demanded that those who had taken the Persian side surrender. When the Thebans refused to hand them over, Pausanias laid waste to their fields and launched an assault on their city walls. Eventually the leading Medisers offered to surrender themselves for trial. They were reportedly confident they would beat the charges by bribery, but Pausanias sent them to Corinth – where he had them put to death. But the Spartans never extracted the tithe they swore to offer to Apollo. When Alexander the Great destroyed Thebes in 334 BCE, many Greeks believed that the Thebans were finally being punished for their collaboration during the 'Median War'.[78]

There is some dispute among our sources as to the extent of Greek casualties in the fighting. Herodotus says only 91 Spartiates, 16 Tegeans and 52 Athenians died,[79] but Plutarch reports that that an additional 1,201 other Greeks perished at Plataea,[80] while Diodorus numbers the Greek casualties at 'more than 10,000'.[81] The Spartans constructed three tumuli (burial mounds) over their dead: one for the 'Irens', one for the other Spartiates, and one for the helots. This would suggest that none of the *perioikoi* were killed in the fighting. But it may be that the *perioikoi* lined up in the phalanx behind the massed ranks of Spartiates, and never really faced the Persians. If the Spartiates insisted on lining up in front of the *perioikoi*, it would not only show the strength of the Spartan in-group, but also the overwhelming confidence – if not arrogance – of the Spartiates.

The Tegeans and Athenians made their own tumuli for their citizens who fell at Plataea, as did the Megarians and Phliasians for their men who had been killed in earlier skirmishes. Herodotus claims that the 'other Greeks' made tumuli that were nothing but empty barrows set up after the fighting, to cover their shame at not having participated in the battle.

As after Salamis, there was some dispute among the Greeks as to who were the bravest fighters. Herodotus agreed with those who suggested Aristodemus, who had tried to make up for the stigma of surviving Thermopylae by charging out from the ranks of Spartiates and hurling himself on the main of the Persian forces. Herodotus stresses that Aristodemus achieved 'great deeds', but the Spartans themselves felt otherwise, arguing that Posidonius, Philocyon and Amompharetus were all braver than Aristodemus, because they had not wanted to die.[82] The message the Spartans seem to have been trying to convey by refusing to honour Aristodemus was that being brave did not mean sacrificing your life because you wanted to die, but doing so even when you wanted to live.

After the battle, an Aeginetan named Lampon tried to curry favour with Pausanias, urging him to avenge his uncle Leonidas by cutting off Mardonius' head and setting it on a pole – just as Xerxes had done. But Pausanias told Lampon that what he proposed was an act fit only for a 'barbarian': 'It is enough if I please the Spartans by doing and speaking well.'[83] He also caused a stir when he summoned the other generals to a special feast, having been stunned by the opulence of Mardonius' tent, and ordered the bakers and the cooks to prepare a dinner such as they were accustomed to do for the Persian. Once a typical Persian feast had been laid out on the magnificent golden and silver couches and tables, Pausanias ordered his own cooks to prepare a 'Laconian dinner'. When the other Greeks arrived for the feast, Pausanias announced: 'Men of Greece, I have brought you here because I desired to show you the foolishness of the leader of the Medes who, with such provisions for life as you see, came here to take away from us our possessions which are so pitiful'.[84]

Pausanias' mockery of the Persians' luxury is sometimes seen as the actions of a typically austere Spartan. But the story might just betray the first signs that Pausanias wanted more than what the Spartan lifestyle offered – a problem that would increasingly afflict Sparta over the following century.

* * *

In Asia – reportedly on the very same day as the Battle of Plataea – the Eurypontid king Leotychidas defeated the remnants of the Persian fleet at Cape Mycale, near the island of Samos. The fact that the Spartans committed a king to command the fleet is sometimes seen as a sign that the victory at Salamis had suddenly convinced them of the importance of naval warfare.

However, this would be the only time in Spartan history that a Spartan king took command at sea. In the end, it was no naval battle anyway. Tigranes, the Persian who was commanding the three hundred warships, beached his ships at the first sight of the Greek fleet. Leotychidas then beached his own ships, before leading his hoplite marines against the Persians. On the beach, Tigranes' 60,000 marines proved no match for the Greeks; they were routed and fled for the camp where they made a defiant stand. In Herodotus' account, the Spartans set off at a run to try to get around behind their position, while the Athenians launched a brutal frontal assault as they wanted the victory to be theirs.[85] Diodorus, on the other hand, merely refers to a great slaughter of the Persians by all the Greeks, including the Spartans.[86] After news of Leotychidas' victory reached Xerxes, he fled to Ecbatana in central Asia. The Persian king would offer no threat to the Greeks of Europe for the rest of his reign. But the Greeks of Asia would still need protecting from the threat of Persian domination.

With the war in Europe over, the Spartans dedicated the so-called 'Serpent Column', an eight-metre-tall three-headed snake made of bronze, which sat atop a golden tripod, on a marble pedestal near the temple of Apollo at Delphi. The original now stands at the Hippodrome of ancient Constantinople in Istanbul, while a fragment of one of the bronze heads is in that city's Museum of Antiquities. Pausanias had the words 'Pausanias, leader of the Greeks, when he destroyed the army of the Medes, dedicated this monument to Phoebus [Apollo]' inscribed on the monument, but the ephors excised Pausanias' self-aggrandising couplet, replacing it with the words 'Those who fought the war', followed by the names of the states who helped repel the Persians.[87] These are recorded on the coils of the snake. Sparta, Athens and then Corinth – in that order – had pride of place at the head of the list.

The Spartans erected more monuments to commemorate their central role in defeating Xerxes' forces – most notably the 'Persian Stoa', built using the spoils from the war.[88] This was by far the most prominent building in the Spartan marketplace, with white marble statues depicting the defeated Persians – including Mardonius and Artemisia – supporting the roof.[89] The first-century BCE Roman architect and engineer Vitruvius later claimed that the Spartans hoped that the sight of the colonnade would ensure that their enemies would fear their bravery, while rousing their fellow citizens to match their endeavours in fighting for 'freedom'. But leading the Greeks to victory over a kingdom that covered millions of square miles had encouraged many of the 5,000 or so Spartiates who fought at Plataea to dream of more than just freedom fighting; for some, the lure of the world beyond mainland Greece would prove enticing indeed.

6

Sparta During the 'Fifty Years':
Isolationist and Isolated

479–431 BCE

Marble stele (*c.* 450–432 BCE). Found at Cape Taenarum, the Greek inscription records the consecration of a slave, perhaps a helot, named Kleogenes to the service of the god Poseidon.

L eading the triumph over the Persians ought to have put the Spartans in a position of undisputed dominance in the Greek-speaking world. Despite the hiccup that was the defeat at Thermopylae, Sparta was universally recognised as having led the Greeks to victory. It was Eurybiades – not Themistocles – who commanded the fleet at Salamis; Pausanias and the Spartans had taken on the bulk of the Persian army at Plataea and prevailed; and Leotychidas' victory at Mycale ended any threat of the Persians returning to the Greek mainland. At the time, the idea that Sparta would not become the undisputed hegemon of mainland Greece would have been unthinkable.

But almost as soon as the war was over, the Spartans adopted an isolationist policy not unlike the United States after the First World War, leaving the Athenians to take control of the continuing war against the Persians. It was not the Spartans but the Athenians who used the war as a springboard towards hegemonic power in the fifty years between the Persian Wars and the Peloponnesian War (431–404 BCE): the so-called *pentakontaëtia* (literally, 'fifty-year period'). As Sparta was still the supreme land power in mainland Greece, however, the Athenians' dominance was largely maritime – meaning that there were effectively two heavyweights in Greece.

Our main contemporary source for this period is the Athenian historian Thucydides (c. 460-400 BCE), who wrote an unfinished narrative history of the Peloponnesian War, but also provided sketchy details of events of the *pentakontaëtia*. Thucydides saw active service in the Peloponnesian War, while serving as an Athenian general. He wrote his *History* after he was exiled from Athens in 424 BCE for his part in losing the Athenian colony of Amphipolis to the Spartan general Brasidas, as we will see later.

Thucydides set out to improve on Herodotus' approach to writing history, claiming that the war he was intending to describe was more important than the Persian War, and observing that he could be more accurate because he wasn't describing 'very old' events. When outlinling his methodology, Thucydides stresses that he will improve on earlier writers who have not been as 'painstaking' as him and readily accept the first story that comes along rather than digging for the truth. He singles out two sloppy observations made by his predecessors, which are both clearly directed at Herodotus: that the Spartan kings had two votes on the council of Elders, and that there was a *lochos* from Pitana in the Spartan army.[1] The former criticism is unfair; Herodotus claims that Spartan kings could vote by proxy, rather than have two votes – the latter may reflect that Spartan military practice changed over time. After all, what Thucydides confidently reports as the truth about the organisation of Spartan armies in his day is contradicted by his successor Xenophon.

Rather than reporting different accounts from different sources, playing them off against each other as Herodotus does, Thucydides reports only what he believes to be the truth, promising not to jeopardise the accuracy of his narrative by focusing on events in the distant past that have essentially been reduced to myth. He also stresses that he will recount speeches that he heard himself, and cover events that he experienced in person.[2] This means that modern scholars often treat Thucydides as the first modern 'scientific' historian, with Herodotus seen as more akin to a journalist. The irony of that line of thought is that Herodotus is the one who follows modern historical practice in carefully citing his sources before giving his own judgement, whereas it is Thucydides who acts like a journalist, never really revealing his sources and presenting his own view without allowing us to ever see the evidence. The reality is that we have to be much more careful with Thucydides' opinions than modern scholars have often thought.

An excellent example of the dangers in following Thucydides blindly is his tendency to paint the transfer of leadership of the war against the Persians from Sparta to Athens as a pragmatic compromise between the two states. Thucydides goes so far as to suggest that the Spartans wanted to be rid of leading the war against the Persians, and willingly handed control to the Athenians because they were satisfied with the competency and secure in their friendship.³ Building on this line of thought, Plutarch says the Spartans showed 'lofty wisdom' in choosing to prioritise their 'ancient customs' above having sway over the whole of Greece.⁴ But the truth is that the transfer of hegemony from Sparta to Athens was not quite as harmonious as the sources paint it.

*　*　*

The Spartans had managed to irk the Athenians even before the dust from the Battle of Mycale had settled. When the Greeks assembled at the island of Samos, they debated how they might best protect the Greeks of Asia Minor. The Peloponnesians – which must have included the Spartans – argued that it was impossible to safeguard them completely from Persian encroachment; they argued that they should forcibly 'depopulate the marketplaces' of the Greek *poleis* who had Medised – Thessaly and Thebes, but potentially even Argos – and transport the Greeks of Asia there. Understandably, the Asian Greeks were horrified by the suggestion that they should give up their homes and move to the Greek mainland.

Athens – the mother city of the Ionian cities – argued vociferously against the proposal, forcing the Peloponnesians to back down. Instead, the Samians, Chians, Lesbians and all the other islanders were brought into the anti-Persian alliance, and bound by oaths 'to remain faithful and not desert their allies'.[5] This ensured that the war against the Persians would continue in order to protect the Asian Greeks.

This compromise papered over the cracks in the alliance, but relations were further undermined when the Spartans tried to prevent the Athenians from rebuilding their walls – on the dubious argument that it would be dangerous for any city north of the Isthmus to have walls that could be used by the Persians if they returned.[6] Themistocles convinced the Athenians to rebuild their fortifications as fast as possible; the column drums recycled from the old temple of Athena can still be seen in the hurriedly rebuilt north wall of the Acropolis. Themistocles himself went to Sparta as an ambassador, only to lie through his teeth, telling the Spartans that no building work was taking place and urging them to send ambassadors to Athens to see for themselves. When the Spartans sent ambassadors to Athens to check, the Athenians stopped them from leaving – at Themistocles' suggestion – to allow them to restore their fortifications enough to make it impossible for the Spartans to use force to prevent them from completing their work. It is safe to say that Themistocles was not nearly as popular in Sparta when he left in 478 BCE as he had been when he received his olive crown and military escort after the Battle of Salamis.

While all this was going on, the Agiad regent Pausanias led an allied naval force to Cyprus and then to the Hellespont, with the aim of liberating these regions from Persian control.[7] These activities were far more significant than the brief mention by Thucydides in his history might seem to imply. As during the war against Xerxes, the allied force operated under Spartan leadership, but with the other Greek states contributing ships, men and their own senior officers. Initially the campaign went well for Pausanias, who – along with his Spartan countrymen – was held in high esteem because of the victory at Plataea. We can see how well they were regarded in the surviving fragments of the elegy Simonides wrote to commemorate Plataea:

> From the Eurotas and from Sparta's town they marched,
> accompanied by Zeus' horsemaster sons,
> the Tyndarid Heroes, and by Menelaus' strength,
> those doughty captains of their fathers' folk,
> led forth by great Cleombrotus' most noble son, Pausanias.[8]

Despite Thucydides' claims that the Spartans weren't interested in continuing the war, Pausanias seems to have been leading from the front, and the Spartans were clearly taking their role as leaders of the Greeks seriously.

However, we have already seen that Pausanias tried to claim the glory for the victory at Plataea for himself – and once he was free from the shackles of the stifling communal lifestyle at home, he appears to have become the first of many Spartans to be swayed by the delights of the outside world. When he was in Byzantium everything unravelled spectacularly; Pausanias was accused of treating his Greek subordinates with violence and disrespect, ensuring that the Spartans received preferential access to bedding, fodder and drinking water, dishing out harsh punishments like floggings, and making men stand all day with an iron anchor on their shoulders. Plutarch even claims that the Spartan rowers – who definitely would not have been Spartiates, but more likely *perioikoi* or even freed helots – would drive their fellow Greeks away from the springs with whips to ensure that they themselves gained first access to water at the end of a hard day of fighting or training. When the Athenian general

Aristides resolved to 'admonish' him for disrespecting his allies, Pausanias refused to listen.[9]

*   *   *

Pausanias was not the only Spartan hero from the Persian War to disgrace himself at around this time. King Leotychidas – victor over the Persian forces at Mycale, no less – was dispatched to Thessaly with a large 'Lacedaemonian' army. The Spartans' plan may have been to fulfil their sworn obligations to punish the Greeks who had collaborated with the Persians. A string of victories offered Leotychidas the chance to make the whole country – once the homeland of the great heroes Achilles and Jason – subject to Sparta.[10] But Leotychidas succumbed to greed while on the cusp of greatness. He was caught in the act of accepting silver – literally sitting on a Persian 'sleeve' filled with silver coins inside his own army's camp while at the same time ostensibly on a mission to tithe the Thessalians for collaboration. The Spartan king, who was only king in the first place because Cleomenes bribed the officials at Delphi, was swiftly tried – and banished. His house was razed to the ground, and he went into exile in nearby Tegea.[11] Leotychidas was succeeded by his grandson Archidamus; his son Zeuxidamas (the new king's father) had already died.

Pausanias too allegedly turned traitor to the Greek cause when he captured Byzantium from the Persians. The story went that he caught several notable Persians and turned them over to Gongylus of Eretria. Officially, Gongylus, whom Pausanias made 'tyrant' of Byzantium, was tasked with keeping these men under guard, but Pausanias secretly ordered Gongylus to allow the Persians to escape. Thucydides even quotes – apparently verbatim – the text of a letter Pausanias gave to Gongylus to give to Xerxes. It began: 'Pausanias, the hegemon of Sparta, wanting to gratify you, sends back to you these men whom he captured by spear.' The letter went on to demand the hand of Xerxes' daughter in marriage, in return for which Pausanias would make Sparta – and the rest of Greece – subordinate to the Persian king. Another tradition had it that Pausanias wrote to Darius' cousin Megabates asking for the hand of his daughter in marriage, thus sealing a dodgy deal that would make him the 'tyrant' of Greece.[12] Although Herodotus reports this alternative version, he makes it clear that he doesn't believe it to be true.

In the face of Pausanias' arrogance, the Athenian generals embarked on a charm offensive, with Aristides and Cimon doing everything they could to treat their allies with 'gentleness and humanity'. As a result, various Greek captains and generals went to Aristides and tried to persuade him to take over the leadership, but the Athenian was unwilling to risk crossing the Spartans unless the allies 'did something big'. So two Ionian captains, Uliades of Samos and Antagoras of Chios, came up with a plan and rammed Pausanias' trireme off Byzantium. Pausanias reportedly lost his temper and threatened to punish them. They abused him, telling him that he should be grateful that he was still held in awe because of the horde that fought with him at Plataea. It was only his reputation, they said – built on the backs of those men – that stopped them from punishing him as he deserved. While this incident was clearly 'big', Plutarch is vague about how this led to the Athenians taking control.[13] Presumably it was only an indirect cause for the Athenians seizing the initiative from the Spartans.

When news of Pausanias' arrogant – not to mention potentially treasonous – behaviour reached Sparta, he was recalled home to face charges, and a new general, Dorcis, was sent to replace him. The other Greeks refused to accept Dorcis as leader, however. Although Thucydides claims that this prompted the

Spartans to stop sending generals and willingly allow the Athenians to continue the 'Median War' without them,[14] Diodorus reveals that the Spartans so resented losing the command that they briefly considered fighting the Athenians for control. Some of the older Spartans even recalled an oracle they had once received from Delphi that warned against the 'lame kingship', insisting that losing the maritime half of their dual hegemony would render them lame. But when a meeting of the Elders was held to debate the matter, a descendant of Heracles named Hetoemaridas managed to convince the others that they should leave the leadership of the sea to Athens.[15]

The Spartans' confused response to Pausanias and the Athenians suggests that there they did not have a coherent policy. Some Spartans clearly wanted to focus on events close to home in the Peloponnese, and they may have been the driving force behind the earlier push to relocate the Asian Greeks closer to home. Others seem to have been keen to continue Sparta's influence abroad, and even to extend it into Asia.

This latter group may have included Pausanias, the supposedly treasonous regent. It has been suggested that his alleged Medising was actually part of a policy intended to benefit Sparta by extending his personal ties to Persian nobles, not unlike how the Spartans had been guest-friends with Croesus or how Pausanias' uncle Cleomenes had been the guest-friend of Athenian noblemen, and the later fourth-century BCE king Agesilaus would make guest-friend ties with Persian noblemen while trying to conquer western Asia Minor. By magnanimously releasing captured Persians and making marriage ties to their nobles, Pausanias might have been trying to forge connections to help facilitate peace and security for the Asian Greeks. But those Spartans who wanted to focus on the Peloponnese were able to paint his diplomatic activities in the worst possible light.

Nonetheless, Pausanias was acquitted of what Thucydides

calls the worst of the charges,[16] and returned to Byzantium as a private citizen. He even commandeered a warship from the allied city of Hermione, perhaps utilising guest-friendship ties with its senior citizens. According to our sources, Pausanias travelled to Byzantium, 'ostensibly' to take part in the war against the Persians, but 'in reality' to continue his plotting with the Persian king.[17] When he got there, Pausanias received a letter from Xerxes (hand-delivered by his trusted general Artabazus) promising gold, silver, foot-soldiers and whatever else he might need to help him make Greece a Persian possession. Pausanias started wandering the streets of Byzantium wearing Median dress (presumably including the dreaded trousers), accompanied by a bodyguard consisting of Medes and Egyptians, and even having Persian meals provided for him. Anyone who had heard Herodotus' story of how Pausanias had mocked the opulence of Mardonius' feasts after the Battle of Plataea would have appreciated the irony of that news.

One other story was even more sensational: Pausanias was said to have been so arrogant that he summoned a well-born Byzantine girl named Cleonice, in order to 'disgrace her'. Her terrified parents relented, only insisting that Pausanias' attendants remove the lights to preserve a semblance of their daughter's dignity. But the girl stumbled against the oil lamp's metal stand as she entered Pausanias' quarters where he was sleeping. Startled by the noise and believing himself under attack, Pausanias drew a Persian dagger he kept under his pillow – a sure sign of paranoia – and stabbed the girl with it.[18] The accidental killing of Cleonice inspired both Jacques-Louis David's painting *La Mort de Cléonice* (1825) and Lord Byron's *Manfred* from a decade earlier:

> the Spartan monarch drew
> From the Byzantine maid's unsleeping spirit

An answer and his destiny – he slew
That which he loved, unknowing what he slew,
And died unpardon'd'[19]

Plutarch reports that the Athenian general Cimon drove Pausanias from Byzantium before he was again recalled to Sparta, this time charged with Medism; the ephors sent Pausanias a warning using a special Spartan coded message stick called a *skytalē*; the message made it clear that the Spartiates would declare war against him if he did not return home. Once he was back in Sparta, Pausanias was briefly imprisoned but managed to wangle his release by offering to stand trial. But he continued to be held in suspicion because of his arrogance, his imitation of the 'barbarians', and his refusal to behave as the equal of the other Spartans with him. Some Spartans recalled how he had arrogantly attempted to have his name inscribed on the tripod at Delphi celebrating the allied victory at Plataea. Pausanias was even accused of plotting with the helots, promising them freedom if they joined him in an uprising.[20] It has even been suggested that he was aiming to try to solve Sparta's manpower problems by offering them citizenship. If the Spartans had opened up citizenship to the helots, they would have got far closer to putting together an army of 30,000 hoplites, the size that Aristotle believed Lakonike was capable of supporting. But it may well be that plotting with the helots was – like Medism – a convenient pretext to help eliminate a troublesome royal.

Even with the allegations mounting against him, the ephors were slow to act against Pausanias; they did not trust the word of helots, and it was Spartan custom not to take any irrevocable action against a Spartiate without indisputable proof.[21] In the end, the proof they needed was delivered by Pausanias' ex-lover, a man from the Macedonian city of Argilus. Pausanias had sent him to Xerxes' general Artabazus, bearing a letter. Noticing that

Pausanias' previous messengers to Artabazus had not returned, he picked open the seal and read the message, which ended with an instruction to kill him. Enraged at the betrayal, Pausanias' ex took the treasonous letter to the Spartan ephors, who finally decided to act.[22]

Realising the game was up, Pausanias sought sanctuary in the temple of Athena on the Spartan acropolis. Unwilling either to violate divine law or to allow him to escape, the ephors were initially unsure how to handle things. But when Pausanias' mother Theano silently placed a brick in front of the entrance to the temple,[23] they knew what to do. They sealed him inside, removed the roof so they could monitor him, and waited. When he was about to expire, they dragged him out – still breathing – so that he wouldn't die inside the sacred precinct. Although they initially intended to throw his body into the Kaiadas gorge where they disposed of criminals, the Spartans buried him nearby – a fortunate decision, for soon afterwards they received an oracle from Delphi, ordering them to move his remains to the forecourt of Athena's temple and to erect two bronze statues to honour him.[24]

Later legend had it that the famous poet Simonides of Ceos and Pausanias had been feasting together when the general asked the poet to say something wise. Simonides replied, 'Remember that you are a man.' At the time Pausanias felt insulted, but stuck inside Athena's temple, he remembered Simonides' wise words. 'O Cean foreigner,' he cried out. 'Your speech had much worth, though I ignorantly undervalued it!'[25] Yet it may well be that many of the stories about Pausanias' arrogance and treason were confected after the event, part of a deliberate policy to blacken his name. It has even been argued that the excising of Pausanias' self-glorifying couplet from the Serpent Column happened only after he was dead, a petty act sponsored by the stay-at-home Spartans who opposed his expansionist policies.

* * *

The Spartan withdrawal from the war against the Persians left the Athenians as the undisputed leaders of the allies. With the Spartans and other Peloponnesians out of the way, the Athenians, Aegean islanders and the Greeks of Asia forged a new alliance system, which modern scholars refer to as the 'Delian League', as the league's treasury was housed on the island of Delos, the birthplace of the god Apollo, whom all the Ionians, including the Athenians, claimed as an ancestor.[26] The members of the new league swore a fresh oath binding them to fight together against the Persians, dropping iron ingots into the sea while they swore to convey that their pact was permanent. The Athenians provided leadership and the lion's share of the fleet, while the other allies contributed ships, manpower and money, according to their means.

Over time, the less powerful allies increasingly contributed money rather than ships or men. As a result, the Athenians were able to use the league's treasury to build more and more warships, and to gain more and more fighting experience. As they honed their skills, their allies became comparatively weak, while the Athenians came increasingly to think of their financial 'contribution' (the so-called *phoros*) as 'tribute', akin to the taxes that subjects paid to the Persian king. This became even more obvious in 454 BCE, when the Athenians moved the treasury to Athens for 'safe keeping'. By the beginning of the conflict with Sparta now known as the Peloponnesian War, Pericles boasted that they had an annual income of 600 talents (£360 million or $540 million in today's money), and that the treasury on the Acropolis contained 600,000 talents of silver (£360 billion or $540 billion).[27]

If the allies objected, there was not much they could do about it. Their oaths were permanent, and Athens was now far

View of the Eurotas valley from the site of the 'Menelaion'.

The modern town of Sparti, with the snow-capped peaks of Mount Taygetus looming above.

Bronze statuette of
a running or dancing
Spartan girl, hitching
up her tunic to expose
her thigh, found at
the sanctuary of Zeus,
Dodona, Greece
(*c.* 530–500 BCE).

Bronze statuette of a long-haired Spartan warrior (*c.* 510–500 BCE), showing the long, thin cloak of his uniform.

View of the Roman-period theatre from the Spartan acropolis.

Johan Tobias Sergel, *Othryades the Spartan, Dying* (terracotta, *c.* 1778).

Bronze figurine of a reclining banqueter, dish in hand, from the tripod-support of a bronze bowl (*c.* 530–500 BCE), probably made in Laconia, and found at the sanctuary of Zeus at Dodona, Greece.

Interior, Laconian wine cup, by the 'Rider Painter' (*c.* 550–530 BCE), depicting a nude, long-haired Spartan youth astride a horse.

Bronze shield-blazon in the form of a Gorgon's head (*gorgoneion*), from the sanctuary of Athena Chalkioikos in Sparta (*c.* 530–520 BCE).

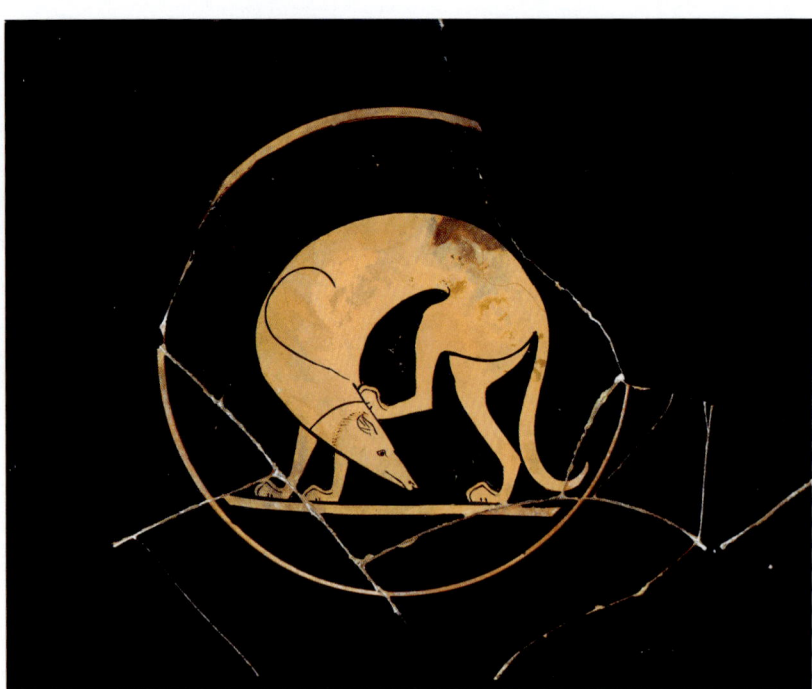

Interior, Attic red-figure wine cup, by the 'Euergides Painter' (fifth century BCE), depicting a Laconian hunting hound.

Interior, Laconian
wine cup, by either the
'Naucratis Painter' or
'Hunt Painter'
(*c.* 555 BCE), depicting
two long-haired Spartans
(a youth following his
bearded mentor) in a
hunting scene.

Fifth-century BCE silver
ossuary and gold crown,
thought to be from the tomb
of Brasidas in Amphipolis.

Blue marble relief (*c.* 525–500 BCE), depicting the 'Twin Gods' Castor and Pollux.

Sixth-century BCE gold 'stater' coin minted by the Lydian king Croesus (obverse),
depicting an open-jawed lion and the head of a bull.

too powerful to resist. The Naxians tried to leave the league quite early in its history, only for the Athenians to besiege them and compel them to remain in it. The Naxians were merely the first of many to try – and fail – to leave the league. When rebels 'rejoined' they were forced to swear oaths of obedience to the Athenians. Numerous Athenian inscriptions recording these new deals have been preserved. One from 447 BCE shows that the citizens from the *polis* of Colophon in Asia Minor were forced to swear, 'I will do as much good as I can for the Athenian people, I will not rebel against the Athenians in word or deed, neither of my own volition or by persuasion,'[28] while two from either 446 or 424 BCE have the citizens of Chalicis and Eretria on the island of Euboea swear to be 'the best and truest possible' allies to the Athenians.[29] The taking of oaths by Athens' newly conquered subjects was not administered by ambassadors, as was normal in ancient Greek interstate relations, but rather by roving bands of officials sent out by the Athenians called 'oath commissioners'. The Athenians so tightly controlled the reintegrated members of the league that Thucydides even talks of them being 'enslaved' by Athens.[30] Very soon, all the Greeks came to see the Delian League as the Athenian Empire.

In 469 BCE, not long after Naxos' failed rebellion, the Athenian general Cimon led the league's forces to a massive victory over the Persians on land and on sea at the Battle of Eurymedon River.[31] His expedition, which culminated in a victory that has been likened to the Battle of Salamis and the Battle of Plataea combined, might have been prompted by a need to show the members of the league that it was still needed. But the victory was so decisive that it probably did the opposite, effectively showing that the league had served its purpose. Any members who had hopes of freedom would, however, need an outside benefactor. The obvious candidate was the leader they had already rejected – Sparta. This would have given the Spartans an opportunity to regain their standing in the Aegean. By the time the smaller members of the Delian League had decided to seek help against Athens, however, the Spartans had problems of their own.

*   *   *

We do not have many details regarding Sparta's affairs in the 470s and 460s BCE, after they lost the leadership of the war against the Persians. What we do know is that they had significant problems with their Peloponnesian allies, and particularly the Arcadians to the north. The biggest troublemakers were their most long-term allies, the Tegeans. This might have come as a surprise to the Spartans, since the Tegeans had not long before fought alongside them at Plataea. It may be, however, that the Tegeans had grown tired of following the Spartans wherever they went, and were already sufficiently frustrated with them to have tetchily reminded them of their previous victories over Sparta on the battlefield at Plataea. The brewing trouble with Tegea may have been the reason why the isolationist Spartans were so resistant to the idea of continuing the war against Persia. The fact that Argos was on the rise was probably crucial – and may be what tempted the Tegeans away from the Spartan cause.

Exactly what happened is not clear: the crucial events fall in the chronological void between the narratives of Herodotus and Thucydides. We do know about a great Spartan victory over the Tegeans and Argives, and another against all the Arcadian *poleis* – except Mantinea – at the Arcadian town of Dipaea a few years later.[32] Even if Isocrates' claims that the Spartans were so outnumbered at the Battle of Dipaea that they had to fight in a single line is an exaggeration,[33] they must have been fighting without help for this to be considered even vaguely plausible. That they were fighting alone shows the weakness of Sparta's alliance system. In this period they were so distracted by their 'own wars' that they were unable to prevent Argos from sacking Mycenae and selling the population into slavery.[34] All these events show that the Spartan hold over the Peloponnese was far weaker than it would need to be if they were to succeed in dominating the whole of Greece – let alone the wider region.

Nonetheless, by 465 BCE the Spartans' fortunes were sufficiently recovered that Thucydides claims they entered into a 'secret' pact with Athens' powerful ally Thasos.[35] The Thasians would have made good allies – their island was rich in timber and precious metals, and they were also exploiting gold mines in the region of Mount Pangaeus, which would much later bankroll Philip of Macedon's conquest of the Greeks. The substance of this supposed pact was that if the Thasians rebelled, the Spartans would help them, which it was assumed would also prompt other Athenian subjects to rebel. Given Sparta's obvious weakness at the time, however, if any author other than Thucydides wrote of the secret deal, their claims would be dismissed as complete fantasy. Whether or not it was real, the deal led to nothing; just as the Thasians rebelled, Sparta was struck by what Thucydides calls the 'great earthquake'.[36] Clearly a shattering event, it tore several peaks from Mount Taygetus, destroying all but five houses in Sparta[37] and killing tens of thousands of people in Lakonike.[38] Modern archaeoseismologists have calculated that the earthquake would have measured around 7.2 magnitude, more than enough to demolish even a well-built ancient city.

With the city of Sparta in ruins, the helots of Laconia and Messenia – as well as the *perioikoi* from Thouria and Aethrae in Messenia – seized the opportunity to rebel. According to Plutarch, the Eurypontid king Archidamus recognised the potential danger posed by the helots and ordered the trumpeter to sound the alarm to indicate that an enemy was attacking. Archidamus thus put off the helots who thought that they would be able to capture the city undefended. However, Polyaenus, who would later compile a collection of military 'stratagems' for the Roman emperors Marcus Aurelius and Lucius Verus, claims that Archidamus was not afraid of the helots. The 'trumpet' call, he suggests, was designed to get the Spartiates outside, where they would be safe from the collapsing buildings. Polyaenus' story seems to fit with the fact that many Spartans were said to be killed by aftershocks and collapsing walls.[39]

At some point in the early stages of the helot rebellion, Arimnestos – the slayer of Mardonius at Plataea – led 300 Spartans against 'all the Messenians', only to die along with all his men on the Stenyklaros plain. It may be that he was overconfident at the thought of going into battle against untrained runaway slaves. Even so, the loss of one of the heroes of Plataea and perhaps 10 per cent of their fighting men must have terrified the Spartans.

Nonetheless, the rebellious helots were never going to stand up against the might of the full Spartan army. Once the Spartans mobilised, they drove the Messenian helots into retreat. The survivors dug in on Mount Ithome, and a ten-year siege followed. As in Pausanias' stories relating to the earlier Messenian Wars, the Spartans struggled to dislodge the helots from Ithome, meaning that they were soon forced to beg for help from their allies. But help proved thin on the ground – the only Dorian allies we know definitely assisted were the Mantineans and the Aeginetans.[40] There is no explicit evidence of help from the Corinthians, the other Arcadians, the Megarians or the Eleans. Indeed, things were so desperate that the Spartans were forced to call on the Plataeans[41] and the Athenians – invoking the sworn alliance from the Persian Wars almost twenty years after the war had ended. This would be comparable to the Soviet Union invoking the fact that they were formal allies during the Second World War to call on the United States for military assistance during the Cold War. The fact that the Spartans did this shows how truly desperate – and isolated – they were. The gratitude they would later show the Aeginetans, including giving lands in Thyrea to refugees after the Athenians expelled them from their homeland,[42] also shows the depth of their plight.

Understandably, the Athenians were not particularly inclined to help the Spartans. But Cimon, who was so well-disposed to the Spartans that he named his eldest son Lacedaemonius, convinced them not to abandon their former 'yoke partner',[43] which suggests that he was willing to treat the alliance against Xerxes as still valid. The comic dramatist Aristophanes later mocked the Spartans, reminding them how their ambassador Pericleidas had come to Athens as a suppliant, 'ashen faced in his red robes, begging for an army'.[44] But after they'd come to help, the Spartans began to worry that the Messenians might tempt them to bring about a 'revolution', so they sent the Athenians away, telling them their services were no longer needed.[45] The snubbed Athenians returned home raging against the Athenian 'Laconisers' (the ancient Greek term for Spartophiles), especially Cimon, who was exiled for ten years soon afterwards. The Athenians then made alliances with Argos and Thessaly, who had either been neutral or on the wrong side during the Persian Wars – a clear indication that the old alliance against the Persians was over. After decades of growing hostility, Sparta and Athens were now enemies. To gain supremacy in the region, the Spartans would not only have to recover control of the Peloponnese but also overcome the wealthy and powerful Athenians.

* * *

The earthquake and subsequent helot rebellions were not the only blows the Spartans suffered at this time. Around 460 BCE Sparta's long-term ally Megara defected to the Athenians after the Spartans sided with Corinth over a boundary dispute between the neighbouring *poleis*. The Megarians accepted an Athenian garrison within their city and built long walls linking their city to the port of Nisaea. Although this gave the Athenians a foothold on the Isthmus while also antagonising the Corinthians, Sparta was still not prepared to act.[46]

The Spartans were effectively being attacked on all sides: they were trying to deal with a Messenian rebellion to the west, the Arcadians to the north-west were openly hostile, and their old enemy Argos in the north-east was now allied to Athens. Their inability to respond to these threats indicates just how weak they were; they could not devote the manpower required to deal with external threats while the Messenian rebellion was ongoing. It made Sparta look weak – hence the growing defections and rebellions – but they had no real options.

In 457 BCE, an event finally forced the Spartans to act. Oddly, it was not the Athenians who provoked them, but the Phocians in central Greece who attacked Doris, the Spartans' ancestral home. Failure to defend the Dorian metropolis would have likely ended any claims the Spartans had to lead the Peloponnesian Dorians and jeopardised their control of the Dorian 'vote' on the Amphictyonic Council. So the Spartans sent a force of 1,500 hoplites to defend the motherland. Nicomedes, acting as regent for his nephew, the Agiad king Pleistoanax, was in command of this paltry force, which was presumably all the men the Spartans could spare, but the strength of the Dorian ties can be seen in the fact that they were soon joined by 10,000 Peloponnesian allies. With the route through the Isthmus effectively blocked by the Megarians, Nicomedes had no choice but to transport his army to central Greece by sea. Once there, he inflicted a heavy defeat on the Phocians and compelled them to liberate the Dorians.[47]

Having set off for home, Nicomedes found that the Athenians had moved their fleet into the Corinthian gulf to block his return: an obviously hostile act. Scared by the strength of the Athenian navy, and wary of the land route past Athens and Megara, he waited in Boeotia to see what the Athenians intended to do. While he waited, Nicomedes reportedly engaged in 'secret' negotiations with the 'oligarchs', a small number of wealthy Athenians hostile to democracy. The Athenians marched out with all their available citizen hoplites, some 13,000, to meet the Spartans in battle near the Boeotian city of Tanagra. They were joined by 1,000 Argives and horsemen from Thessaly. Cimon turned up in his armour wanting to help, only to be rebuffed by the generals on account of his pro-Spartan sympathies. Ever the patriot, Cimon urged his friends to fight 'mightily' to prove their patriotism. Later sources claim that they formed themselves into a single unit of 100 men, set up Cimon's helmet and shield alongside them in the ranks, and fought to the death to a man. If true, this would have been a sacrifice that the Spartans would have appreciated. We know for certain that the Spartans emerged victorious from the battle, with both sides suffering heavy casualties.[48] Although this was probably the first significant pitched battle between the Spartans and the Athenians, our sources are frustratingly thin on details, confirming only that this was a major defeat for Athens.

The Spartans later used the spoils taken from the enemy to set up a dedication at Olympia:

The temple has a golden dish from Tanagra,
The Lacedaemonians and their allies put up the gift,
One tenth from the Argives and the Athenians
And the Ionians for their victory in the war.[49]

Nicomedes was unable, however, to capitalise on his victory by marching on Athens. Instead, he led his army home by land through the Megarid, cutting down the Megarians' fruit trees in a show of strength. The fact that the Spartans represented just 15 per cent or so of the allied army might explain Nicomedes' caution. That there were so few Spartiates in their army would have been obvious to allies and enemies alike, and the problem would only get worse. If the Spartans had genuine hopes of regional domination, they would need to find a solution – and fast.

*　*　*

Ironically, victory at Tanagra led to further problems for Sparta. Defeat appears to have prompted the Athenians to complete the so-called 'Long Walls'. These were two parallel walls, six kilometres long and four metres thick, and roughly 180 metres apart, that linked the city to the fortified harbour of Piraeus, where the fleet was docked. There was a third 'Phaleric' wall to the east, keeping the whole bay of Phaleron safe from attack by land. Athens' naval might, combined with these fortifications, now made the Athenians almost invulnerable to attack. A mere sixty-two days later, they attacked and defeated the Boeotians in a pitched battle near the city of Oenophyta. The Athenians' victory brought both Boeotia and Phocis under their control. Shortly afterwards, the Spartans suffered another significant blow when the island of Aegina – whose citizens had just helped them against the rebelling Messenians – succumbed to Athens. The demise of Athens' great naval rival left the Aegean Sea at their mercy, and the jubilant Athenians celebrated by raiding the Spartan harbour at Gytheion and burning the dockyards. Around this time, Athens also made alliances with the Achaeans and Troezen in the Peloponnese; Sparta's sphere of influence was dwindling as Athens' power continued to grow.

Nonetheless, as had already happened many times, the fortunes of Greek *poleis* changed swiftly. The Spartans eventually managed to dislodge the Messenian rebels from Ithome. After ten long years, the helots were allowed to leave – on the condition that they left the Peloponnese and never returned. This happened after the Spartans received a face-saving oracle from Apollo simply stating, 'Let go the suppliant of Zeus Ithomata.'[50] The Athenians gave the Messenians land at Naupactus, on the northern side of the Corinthian gulf. They could see the Peloponnese from there, but the agreement stated that they would be enslaved if they returned.[51] A bronze spear-butt dedicated to Zeus at Olympia around this time bears the inscription, 'Dedicated by the Messenians, taken from the Spartans.'

The decade-long helot insurrection must have left the Spartans with considerable psychological scars. Indeed, Plutarch argues that the brutal helot killing known as the *krypteia* was only established at this time.[52] He thought Lycurgus had been too enlightened to have created such a barbaric practice, but it would be naive to think that the Spartans only now started to brutalise the helots. Nonetheless, Thucydides' claim that 'considerations of security against the helots were always paramount'[53] may have applied particularly in this period, as the Spartans struggled to handle the existential threat that the helots suddenly represented. It is possible that the notorious story of the massacre of 2,000 helots arose then; the Spartans' paranoia at the time would explain why they resorted to such a horrific atrocity. It would also explain why they were so slow to act against the Athenians in the years that followed – the risk of overcommitting manpower too far from home was suddenly very real.

With things finally starting to look more positive for the Spartans, they received a further boost when the Athenians overreached in trying to assist the Egyptians in a rebellion against the Persians. The Athenians claimed that the Persians were so desperate that their king Darius II offered the Spartans a massive cash incentive to attack Athens.[54] Yet again, Thucydides seems to know far too much about the Spartans' supposedly 'secret' diplomacy – but in the end the bribe wasn't needed. The Persians crushed the Egyptian rebellion, and the Athenians lost the best part of fifty triremes and thousands of men. Soon the Athenians faced rebellions by their own allies. Although Thucydides is vague about the details, we know that they felt so vulnerable at this time that they moved the treasury of their league from Delos to Athens for safe keeping.[55] They had earlier benefited from the Spartans' overreaching; now it was the Spartans who were about to profit from Athenian over-expansion.

Rather than allow the tensions to slide into full-on warfare, however, in 451 BCE the Spartans and the Athenians agreed to what modern scholars usually call the so-called 'Five Years' Truce'. The Athenians needed time to lick their wounds after the Egyptian disaster, and the Spartans needed to recover from the helot rebellion and to restore their authority in the Peloponnese. Indeed, immediately after making the truce with Athens, the Spartans negotiated a thirty-year truce with Argos.[56] In agreeing to this treaty, the Argives, it seems, accepted that they were not strong enough to fight the Spartans for leadership of the Dorians or the Peloponnesians. Sparta's more reluctant Peloponnesian allies will have taken note. Even better for the Spartans, while the Athenians might be allies of Argos, when the shorter truce between Sparta and Athens ended they could not expect the Argives to help them fight the Spartans if a full-scale war did start.

By 449 BCE, the Spartans were feeling strong enough to send a force across the Corinthian gulf to liberate the sanctuary of Delphi from the control of Athens' allies in Phocis. By currying favour with the Delphian government, they may have been trying to gain privileged access to the sanctuary for consulting Apollo. However, almost as soon as the Spartans had returned home, the Athenians sent a force to restore Delphi to Phocian control.[57] This piece of tit-for-tat action not only shows the hostility of the Spartans and the Athenians towards each other, but also the fact that neither side was prepared to do anything that jeopardised the peace treaty.

Things changed again in 447 BCE, when the Boeotians shook off the Athenian shackles and, as Thucydides puts it, 'lived again under their own laws'.[58] With Athens obviously weakened, Sparta apparently on the rise, and the Five Years' Truce about to lapse, the Megarians and the Euboeans took the opportunity to rebel against Athenian control. When the Athenian general Pericles led a force to Euboea in 446 BCE, the Spartans seized the moment to launch a full-scale attack. This time, Pleistoanax was old enough to lead the army – his first major campaign as the Agiad king. News of the Spartan offensive forced Pericles to return from Euboea. As the Spartans broke into Athenian territory, ravaging Eleusis and the Thriasian plain west of Athens, Pericles lined up his army against Pleistoanax's massive force, but Plutarch claims they were afraid to fight hoplites who were 'so many, so brave, and so eager for battle'.[59] The Spartans would have felt that a half-century-long grudge was about to be resolved – and in their favour. Even better, Pausanias' son was about to avenge his father's humiliation by defeating the Athenians on their home soil. As an added bonus for the Spartans, Pericles was the grand-nephew of Cleisthenes, so they would also get their revenge on the Alcmaeonid family. The path to glory for Sparta had probably never seemed more open.

Yet just as the conflict between Sparta and Athens seemed set to reach a climax, it fizzled out into nothing. Pericles somehow convinced Pleistoanax and his advisor Cleandridas to withdraw, proposing they negotiate a long-term peace treaty between the two cities. The subsequent 'Thirty Years' Peace' – a favourable deal for Sparta – required the Athenians to surrender Nisaea and Pagae to Megara, confirmed that Megara, Troezen, Achaea and Boeotia were Spartan allies, and undid the Athenian alliance with Argos. From now on, Athens could establish only friendly relations, not a full-on military alliance, with Argos.[60]

Not everyone in Sparta was happy with the deal. Rumours soon circulated that Pericles had bribed Cleandridas and Pleistoanax; it was even reported that Pericles included an unexplained fee of ten talents – £6 million or $9 million in today's money – in his official accounts for his year as general, labelled 'necessary expenditure'. Normally in Athens, a general's accounts were audited carefully by the council. Indeed, one general – Paches – reportedly committed suicide in the council chamber when he realised how badly the council's audit of his year in office was going against him. But the normally careful Athenians were said to have signed off Pericles' accounts without questioning the unexplained payment.[61]

The angry Spartans imposed a fine on Pleistoanax that was so large he couldn't pay it, forcing him into exile in Arcadia, where he was sufficiently scared of reprisals from Sparta that he built half his house on land sacred to Zeus: if anyone came to attack him, he could have sought sanctuary in that half of the house. The fact that Pleistoanax felt the need to do this shows the fragility of his position. For the next two decades Sparta effectively had only one king, his Eurypontid colleague Archidamus. As for Cleandridas, he saw the writing on the wall and did not bother to face trial; he was condemned to death *in absentia*. His son Gylippus would also later succumb to greed; Plutarch suggests that the family's 'love of silver' was congenital.[62]

Modern scholars, however, are usually less quick to condemn Pleistoanax. As the son of the disgraced regent Pausanias – a man whose own downfall was the result of allegations of treachery and greed – he would have had to have been daft to do anything that was not above board. Peace was obviously in Sparta's medium-term interests, and given that the Spartans were notoriously risk averse, it appears that when Pericles offered them a way out of the fighting, Pleistoanax and Cleandridas grabbed the opportunity with both hands. Their later condemnation is likely the result of in-fighting; Spartan 'hawks' likely seized upon – and perhaps even actively spread – the rumours of Pericles' bribes, in order to oust a king and his advisor who were less committed to war.

* * *

The Spartans who wanted war with Athens would eventually get their way, and a series of crises soon drove them to the brink. The first arose in 433 BCE, when the Athenians intervened in a dispute between Corinth and their former colony, the island of Corcyra (now Corfu). A small Athenian flotilla commanded by Cimon's son Lacedaemonius attacked the Corinthian fleet as they were on the cusp of defeating the Corcyraeans. Their intervention did not prevent a Corinthian victory, but it did stop them landing troops on the island. The angry Corinthians accused the Athenians of violating the peace treaty with Sparta, but also feared that they themselves had already violated the Thirty Years' Peace by attacking Lacedaemonius' ships. Thucydides regarded this escalation in tension as the 'first cause' of the Peloponnesian War.[63]

Not long after this came the second cause, when the Athenians provoked the Corinthians by moving against another Corinthian colony – this time the city of Potidaea in northern Greece. Although Potidaea was a tribute-paying 'member' of the Delian League, it was sufficiently close to Corinth that magistrates were sent out from Corinth to Potidaea to govern the city. When the Athenians issued demands that the Potidaeans demolish their city walls, send hostages to Athens and depose the Corinthian magistrates, the Corinthians snapped. They encouraged the Potidaeans to revolt from Athens and even unofficially sent foot-soldiers to help.[64] A third provocation came when the Athenians accused the Megarians of cultivating sacred lands on their border and issued a proclamation – the so-called 'Megarian decree' – banning them from trading in Athens, or with any other member of the Delian League.[65]

As a result of these provocations, representatives were invited to Sparta from all over Greece, including Athens, to attend a peace conference. The Athenians, and the Spartans opposed to war with Athens, who included the Eurypontid king Archidamus, hoped the conference would resolve the tensions. But the meeting swiftly degenerated into a pile-on, with the Corinthians, Megarians and even tribute-paying members of the Delian League demanding that the Spartans take action against the 'tyranny' of Athenian imperialism.

The Corinthians told the assembled allies that the Athenians were people 'inclined to go abroad' in search of gain, while the Spartans were 'stay-at-home' people, afraid of losing what they had by moving away. They then harangued the Spartans for their slowness to act and accused them of neglecting their allies in the face of Athenian aggression. The Spartans, they said, had allowed the Athenians to rebuild their walls after the 'Median War', to build the 'Long Walls' and to 'enslave' other Greeks. The Corinthians then threatened the Spartans, who were obviously anxious about violating the oaths of the peace, warning them that not defending their allies would be a violation of the oaths that they had exchanged, and that abandoning them to Athens might just compel them to seek a new protector.[66]

The Corinthians finished by urging the Spartans not to allow the prestige of the Peloponnese, enjoyed by their ancestors, to suffer. Their message was clear: the Spartans may be the rightful successors of Agamemnon, but if they did not get their act together and lead them to war against the Athenians, the Corinthians would seek the protection of Argos. Their stance highlights how hard it was for the Spartans to project their power with small numbers of men in a rapidly changing world. Unless they led the Dorians to war against the Athenians, the concept of Spartan hegemony would be under threat. In this febrile atmosphere, the Athenian ambassador had one last chance to stop the war. His argument needed to be good. But it wasn't good enough, partly because he made the mistake many ambassadors to Sparta made: he talked for too long.

During his long speech, the Athenian ambassador stressed that the Athenians had fought bravely against the Persians, even claiming that they fought single-handed at Marathon, and that their exploits at Salamis saved the Peloponnese because the Persians had immediately withdrawn most of their army. He also pointed out that the Athenians were arranging the affairs of their allies just as the Spartans did with their own, and that it was only natural for them to accept an empire when it fell into their lap. He also warned the Spartans not to act precipitously, and suggested that they should put their dispute to arbitration, even invoking the gods who had witnessed their exchange of oaths. But the Athenian had spoken for so long it was unclear to the Spartans exactly why he thought that this point was so significant.

When he had finally finished, the Spartans sent everyone

away and discussed matters among themselves, during which the Eurypontid king Archidamus made an almost equally long speech, stressing that the Spartans were not ready for war and should not feel ashamed about the Corinthians' accusing them of weakness. Archidamus concluded by reminding the Spartans that they were the toughest fighters in Greece because of the fierceness of their training. Many of his subjects might have felt that was a bit rich coming from a man who had been exempt from the communal upbringing.

Finally, it was the ephor Sthenelaidas' turn to speak. 'I do not understand these long speeches,' he began, perhaps intending to criticise both the Athenians and Archidamus. Sthenelaidas then noted that the Athenians had said a lot in praise of themselves, but nothing to deny their injustices against the Spartans and the other Peloponnesians. In fact, he suggested, the fact that they had previously 'behaved well against the Persians' made things worse. As far as he was concerned, the Athenians deserved punishment because they had stopped doing good things and were now doing bad things. He then said that the Athenians should not be telling the Spartans that they should deliberate about whether to go to war, when they had treated them unjustly. Sthenelaidas finished with what he intended to be a killer punchline: 'Vote for war, Spartans, as the honour of Sparta demands. Do not allow the further aggrandisement of Athens, or betray our allies, but with the gods on our side, let us advance against the unjust.'

Sthenelaidas put the decision to the vote of the Spartan assembly, as was his right as an ephor. Once the shouting was over, he said that he could not tell whether it was louder for war or for peace, but it probably wasn't as close as he claimed – he wanted to make the Spartans declare their opinions openly, and to increase the enthusiasm for war. So he pointed to a spot, and said, 'All the Spartans who are of the opinion that

Athens has broken the peace, get up and go there.' All the Spartans who were of 'the opposite opinion' were directed to go to another spot. In the end, the Spartans who wanted war were in the clear majority. They summoned their allies and told them about their decision: Athens had broken the peace. Although the allies would still have to put it to a vote, once the Spartans had decided they were prepared to fight, war with Athens was inevitable.[67]

7

The Archidamian War: Humiliating Failure?

431–421 BCE

Spartan shield taken from the hoplites who surrendered at Pylos in 425 BCE. Badly damaged, the shield was deposited in a cistern, apparently as a lid, before 300 BCE.

The cause of the first phase of the Peloponnesian War, known to the ancient Greeks as the 'Archidamian War' – ironic, given the Eurypontid king's vocal opposition – is much debated. At the time, both sides accused the other of starting it. But Thucydides claims the 'truest but least publicised' cause was that Sparta feared Athens' growing power.[1] Modern scholars have never been able to reach consensus. Some have argued that Athens had stopped growing by the 430s BCE, and that the war was caused by mistakes and confusion. According to this line of thought, neither Sparta nor Athens really wanted the war but were drawn into it by the actions of others. Other interpretations make Sparta the aggressor.

In recent years, the political scientist Graham T. Allison has used Thucydides' assertion that Sparta feared the growth of Athenian power as the basis for a theory called 'the Thucydides trap'.[2] Allison presents sixteen case studies – from the sixteenth century CE to the present day – when war broke out after an emerging power threatened to displace a great power, which he claims not only bear out Thucydides' claims about the inevitability of the war between Sparta and Athens, but also 'prove' that war between the US and China is inevitable. In many ways, however, the underlying premise is flawed – we have already seen that Athens, and not Sparta, was the dominant force in the middle of the fifth century BCE; Sparta was weakened, flailing, and had never *yet* ruled the Greeks. It was only by defeating the Athenians that they could become the dominant power in Greece and beyond. Sparta seems to have been motivated more by fear of the break-up of the Peloponnesian League than by fear of Athens. Conquest by diplomacy had got them to a position where they led the Greeks against the Persians, but they had effectively lost their network of allied city-states for much of the fifty years that followed. Having only now clawed it back, they couldn't afford to lose it again. This was probably what really drove the Spartans to war against Athens. But it would be a stretch to suggest that we can detect any form of strategic foreign policy from the Spartans at this time. The security of Sparta was probably still the driving force in Spartan decision-making.

∗   ∗   ∗

The Spartans had decided on war and their allies were in total agreement, but they still felt the need to seek divine approval. On asking Apollo 'whether it would be well with them if they went to war', the response was more than they could have hoped for. Apollo told them that victory would be theirs 'if they put their whole strength into the war', and promised that he would be with them whether they invoked him or not.[3] Quietly confident, the Spartans delivered the Athenians a series of blunt ultimatums that they knew would be rejected, demanding that they 'leave the Greeks independent', 'expel the accursed' – that is, Pericles, the scion of the Alcmaeonids – and revoke the Megarian decree.[4]

The Athenians responded with their own unrealistic ultimatums. They demanded that the Spartans atone for the sacrilegious killing of the helots at Cape Taenarum, and insisted that they suspend their 'alien acts' and allow the Athenians and their allies into the marketplaces in Lakonike, even in Sparta itself. Naturally, the Spartans refused. But even after all this posturing, the war only started when Sparta's ally Thebes attacked Athens' ally Plataea – after which the Spartans launched a massive invasion of Attica.

* * *

The two sides had very different strategies. Sparta's – naturally – was land-based. The Spartans were painfully aware that the Athenians ruled the waves, but they knew well that they themselves were the dominant force on land. The Spartans were the best hoplites in Greece, and they – finally – had the support of the Peloponnesians (except Argos), the Boeotians (except Plataea), the Locrians and the Phocians. Even Pericles conceded that the Spartans and their allies would be able to defeat 'all Greece' in a single land battle.[5] All the Spartans would have to do was invade Athens just before the harvest, live off the land for a few weeks and destroy Athens' food supply. This would compel the Athenians to fight a pitched battle and defeat them. It would require at most a couple of years.

There was only one problem: the plan didn't work.

Every summer for six years, the Peloponnesians occupied the Athenian countryside for weeks on end, hoping to provoke the Athenians to march out and fight them. And year after year, the Athenians simply refused to rise to the bait. Knowing that the Peloponnesians, who brought only the necessary supplies, and lived off the land, could only occupy their territory for a few weeks, Pericles ordered the Athenians to evacuate the countryside and move all their possessions within the fortifications of Athens. Rather than go out to battle, he insisted the Athenians should trust in their fleet, 'in which their real strength lay.'[6] The Athenians had long ceased pretending that they could be self-sufficient in terms of food; their massive fleet of more than 300 triremes was able to protect the merchant ships supplying the city. Unlike the cash-poor Spartans, the Athenians' massive wealth allowed them to effectively buy their way out of trouble.

Evacuating the countryside meant that all the Athenians

– men, women, children and slaves – were crammed into a small area between the city and the bay of Phaleron, and protected by the so-called 'Long Walls'. Their sheep and cattle were evacuated to nearby islands.[7]

With thousands of Athenians crammed into a hastily built shanty town in increasingly squalid conditions, disease inevitably struck. Scholars have spent much time trying to determine exactly what the illness was, based on Thucydides' vivid eyewitness account of fever, sneezing, violent coughing, red eyes, blisters, diarrhoea and even post-recovery amnesia. The fevers were so terrible that many victims plunged into the cisterns containing Athens' drinking water, polluting the water supply and spreading the disease further; Thucydides recognised that the impact of the plague was exacerbated by the cramped conditions and the baking summer heat. Typhoid, cholera, smallpox, bubonic plague, influenza, viral haemorrhagic fever and even Ebola have been suggested for this mystery plague, which is said to have originated on a cargo ship from Ethiopia. Thousands of Athenians died – perhaps a third of the adult men of fighting age, and as much as a quarter of the population. Modern excavations in Athens have revealed mass graves of bodies clearly disposed of in panic. Pericles lost his son in the early phases of the plague, and in 429 BCE he succumbed himself. Things looked grim for the Athenians.

The fact that the plague left the Peloponnese largely unaffected naturally led some Athenians to believe that it had been punishment meted out by Apollo. Zeus' son was not just a god of prophecy; he was also responsible for disease. Some recalled that he had promised to assist the Spartans, and drew the conclusion that the plague was the god's way of giving them a helping hand. Others recalled an old oracle that had proclaimed darkly, 'A Dorian war will come, and with it plague.' If any further signs of Apollo's displeasure were needed, the island of Delos – his place of birth – was struck by an earthquake for the first time in living memory.

* * *

Pericles' death could have spelled the end for Athens. But as his strategy had clearly kept the city safe from outside invasion, the leaders who came after him followed the same general principle while turning defence into attack – they invaded Spartan and allied territories by sea, and built fortresses there. The strategy worked spectacularly when the Athenian general Demosthenes managed to occupy a part of Messenia near Pylos. The presence of an Athenian fort immediately attracted runaway helots, which caused the Spartans to panic and hurry back home from their annual invasion of Attica.[8] They would not return for more than a decade.

The Spartans and the nearest of the *perioikoi* marched straight to Pylos to deal with the Athenian threat, while also sending the bulk of their small fleet to blockade the Athenian fort. Thucydides writes that the Spartans initially intended to assault the fortress by land, which makes sense given their expertise in land warfare and the small number in the Athenian garrison. But the Spartan military leaders then came up with an alternative plan that proved disastrous.

It is difficult to explain just how extraordinarily bad their decision-making was, especially to anyone who has not seen the region first-hand. They aimed to block the entrances to Navarino Bay with their ships, in order to deny the Athenians access to the harbour and long stretches of sandy beach there. The Spartans rightly believed that they could block the northern entrance, which today can be easily swum, with just two triremes, presumably moored with their prows pointing out to sea. But their belief that they could block the southern entrance, which is more than a kilometre across, with just nine triremes, is so wrong-headed that some modern scholars have argued that they must have been trying to block a now silted-up entrance to the Osmanaga lagoon, and that this is the 'harbour' to which Thucydides refers, rather than Navarino Bay.

Their attempt to block the entrance to either bay against the vastly superior Athenian navy now seems doomed to failure, which makes the third part of the Spartans' plan – ferrying hundreds of hoplites across to occupy the uninhabited 'desert' island of Sphacteria, nearly five kilometres long – seem positively foolhardy. To make matters worse, Sphacteria was covered in dense woodland, and had no water or food supply, requiring the Spartans to regularly rotate the contingents of men occupying it. When the Athenian fleet arrived they caught the Spartan fleet entirely unprepared and swept into Navarino Bay, routing the Spartan ships, disabling some and capturing five. This left 420 Lacedaemonians – Spartiates and *perioikoi* – marooned on Sphacteria. It was a complete disaster for the Spartan leaders, who immediately concluded a truce with the Athenians that required them to surrender their entire fleet. In return, the Athenians promised to supply the marooned men with rations.

The peace negotiations broke down quickly, with the Athenians accusing the Spartans of violating the terms of the agreement, and refusing to hand back the Spartans' ships. This meant that the Athenians stopped sending provisions to the marooned Lacedaemonians. They thought that the Spartiates and *perioikoi* would surrender quickly, but they were able to hold out because volunteers – often helots – smuggled food supplies to them. Some swam, diving out of view of the Athenians, carrying skins filled with poppy seeds mixed with honey. Local helots smuggled wheat, wine and cheese across in boats. Back home, many Athenians started to grow restless that the blockade was taking too long.[9]

The orator Cleon seized on the discontent, boasting that he would have captured the Spartans on Sphacteria by now, were he in charge. Thucydides was particularly hostile to Cleon, the son of a wealthy tanner, but not part of Athens' social elite. Based partly on Thucydides' complaints about him, Plutarch claims that Cleon debased the speaker's rostrum by yelling, throwing back his robe to slap his thigh, and running about while speaking.[10] The conservative and wealthy Athenian politician Nicias called Cleon's bluff, offering to resign his commission as general and hand it to him. Thucydides and Plutarch both say that Cleon was afraid and tried to back out, but the masses clamoured for him to go. Caught out by his own bravado, Cleon accepted the generalship – and even found the nerve to double down on his boast, promising to deliver the Spartans from Pylos – dead or alive – in just twenty days.[11]

Cleon was extremely fortunate. Just as he arrived on the scene, a fire lit by Spartan sailors smuggling supplies to Sphacteria denuded the island of vegetation, allowing the Athenians to see exactly where the Spartans were, scattered across the island. Cleon's first act was to send 800 Athenian hoplites across at dawn, which caught the Spartans unaware. After the hoplites had landed, the Athenians sent across around 800 archers, 2,000 light-armed troops, 8,000 rowers armed with whatever weapons they had, and some free Messenians from Naupactus.[12] One can only imagine just how keen the liberated helots were to besiege their former masters.

Despite being vastly outnumbered, the Spartan hoplites wanted to attack the Athenian hoplites and seem to have thought that being outnumbered two to one was not a problem. Yet Thucydides reports the Spartans were not able to show their 'experience' or 'skill',[13] because the Athenian light-armed troops were effectively able to act as a screen, rushing up to prevent the Spartan hoplites from engaging their own hoplites, before turning tail and outrunning their heavily armed Spartan opponents. The Spartans were unable to advance around the light-armed troops as they were hemmed in by the archers and slingers and increasingly disoriented by the dust and ash from the fires. Things were made worse by the fact that at some point the Spartans had stopped using the face-covering Corinthian-style helmets and switched to conical *pilos* helmets that sat on top of their head; these provided little protection from the showers of arrows, stones and other missiles.

During the fighting, the senior Spartan officer Epitadas was killed, and his deputy Hippagretas was mortally wounded. Now led by the third-in-command, Styphon, the Spartans formed up in close order and withdrew to a fort on the north of the island, leaving the body of Epitadas and the dying Hippagretas behind. They made a catastrophic and seemingly elementary mistake in assuming that the cliff behind them was too steep to be climbed. The Messenian commander led a force of archers and light troops on a wild scramble up the steep cliff-face, and attacked the Spartans from the rear.[14]

With the Spartans 'caught between two fires', as Thucydides puts it, Demosthenes and Cleon realised that they would soon all be killed, as Spartans would fight on regardless of the circumstances, as they had done at Thermopylae. 'Indeed,' he writes, describing the scene, 'to compare small things with great, they were in the same situation as Thermopylae, where the Spartan army was destroyed by the Persians getting around behind them by the path.'[15] There was one crucial difference, however: unlike Xerxes at Thermopylae, Demosthenes and Cleon gave the Spartans a chance to surrender – and to everyone's surprise, they took it with both hands.

The fact that the Spartan senior officer Epitadas had been killed and his next-in-command Hippagretas left for dead might have been a significant factor in their decision to throw in the towel. Styphon asked the Athenians for permission to send a herald to the Spartans on the mainland to ask for instructions. Demosthenes and Cleon allowed it, and in response to the question of what he should do, Styphon received the blunt reply: 'Decide for yourselves; but do nothing shameful.' Reading between the lines, their message was clear – he should fight to the death – but Styphon and his men either could not or would not read between the lines. A total of 292 Lacedaemonian hoplites – including 120 Spartiates – surrendered and left the island as prisoners-of-war. One hundred and twenty-eight Spartiates and *perioikoi* had fallen, while Athenian losses were negligible as the fighting had not been at close quarters.

In a famous line from his work, Thucydides claims:

> Nothing that happened in the war surprised the Greeks so much as this. It was the opinion that no force or famine could make the Spartans give up their arms, but that they would fight on as they could, and die with them in their hands: indeed, people could scarcely believe that those who had surrendered were of the same stuff as the fallen.[16]

One of the Athenians' allies insulted the prisoners, musing, 'I suppose it was the "gentlemen" who fell.' He received the scathing reply that 'the arrow would be worth a great deal if it could tell men of honour from the rest', but the sharp rejoinder cannot hide the shame and embarrassment of the speaker, who in surrendering had broken a seemingly iron Spartan law.

The shame of the Spartans was more than matched by the immense pride the Athenians felt at having forced the Spartans to surrender. To commemorate their achievement, they displayed the shields of the Spartans who surrendered at Sphacteria, smeared with pitch to protect them from corrosion, in the

'Painted Stoa', alongside paintings of Theseus fighting against the Amazons, and Miltiades defeating the Persians at Marathon.[17] Today, visitors to the Athenian Agora Museum can still see one of those shields on display. On it were inscribed the words 'The Athenians, from the Lacedaemonians at Pylos'.

*   *   *

Success at Pylos put Athens on the front foot. With 120 precious Spartiate hostages, the annual Spartan invasions of Attica were ended – for fear that the Athenians would execute them. Modern scholars often suggest that the Spartans' panic at the possibility of losing just 120 citizens shows that their citizen population was in serious decline. We do know that Spartan citizen numbers fell significantly in the late fifth and fourth centuries BCE – but another way of thinking about the Spartans' fears is to consider how strong an in-group they had forged. It might be that their fear was as much about losing valued members of the collective as it was about losing bodies in their hoplite phalanx.

Things were now going so badly for the Spartans that they even started to think that the gods were no longer on their side – perhaps because they had refused to accept the Athenian offer of arbitration.[18] But in a moment of despair, the Spartans stumbled upon the idea of sending a force to target the Athenian colony of Amphipolis, founded in 437 BCE near the Chalcidice peninsula in the north of Greece. Amphipolis protected the Athenians' access to gold and silver mines in the Pangaion hills, timber for shipbuilding and grain supplies in Thrace. If the Spartans could destabilise Athenian interests there, it might give them the breathing space they needed to get the war back under control.

The task was delegated to Brasidas, a prominent Spartan

who had served as ephor in 431 BCE. Brasidas was a rare beast in Sparta at the time: a fighter who had distinguished himself during the Archidamian War. In the first year of the war, his swift actions had rescued the perioikic town of Methone in Messenia from a seaborne attack by the Athenians.[19] When he spotted what was happening, he gathered together a hundred hoplites and broke through the ranks of enemy marines besieging Methone and burst into the town, causing the Athenians to give up in the face of this show of 'boldness'. In 428 BCE, Brasidas' reputation was sufficiently high that he was sent out as one of three advisors to the Spartan admiral Cnemus, who had been defeated by an Athenian flotilla in the Corinthian gulf. During this campaign, the Spartans were so arrogant that they were unable to understand why they had been defeated by such a small number of ships.[20] They assumed that it must have been caused by 'softness'; in fact, the Athenians were simply more experienced at sea warfare.

Brasidas had even fought bravely at Pylos, where he served as a ship captain. In a failed effort to capture the Athenian fort at Pylos, he gave orders to his steersman to drive his ship directly onto the rocks, so that he and his marines could launch themselves at the enemy. Brasidas was first onto the gangway to hurl himself at the Athenians, but he was struck down by so many Athenian blows that he fell into the bow of his ship. As he slipped into unconsciousness, his shield slid from his left arm and into the sea. The Athenians later displayed that shield as a trophy, too.[21]

Now, Brasidas was given the command of the army that would head to the north of Greece. Given the successes that followed, it would be easy to paint his expedition as a stroke of genius by the Spartan authorities. Thucydides, however, claims that Brasidas was given the task largely at his own initiative, so his success may well have been just dumb luck for the Spartan high command. Brasidas was given the most meagre resources – just 1,700 hoplites (comprising 700 freed helots and 1,000 Peloponnesian mercenaries), in addition to a handful of Spartiate advisors. Brasidas' strategy was designed to compensate for the fact that the Spartans lacked the citizen numbers to project their power beyond the Peloponnese. Brasidas' force was so small that it has been described as a 'virtual Spartan army',[22] a means for the Spartans to project their power without risking too many actual lives, or placing them in the position where they might surrender, as so many had done at Sphacteria. If the leader was a man like Brasidas – brave, bold, charismatic and a good speaker ('not incapable, for a Spartan', as Thucydides would put it) – this virtual army could generate significant goodwill. Indeed, Thucydides states that Brasidas was 'the first who went out and showed himself so good a man at all points as to leave behind him the conviction that the rest were like him.'[23] We will see further evidence of the 'Brasidas effect' later.

Brasidas' status as a man of action was further cemented before he marched north. While he was gathering forces near Corinth, he was able to frustrate an Athenian attack on the city of Megara.[24] Arriving in the north, Brasidas rallied the locals to the Spartan cause by announcing that he had come to 'liberate' them from Athens and promising that they would remain 'autonomous': that is, free from Spartan rule.[25] Brasidas swiftly captured the cities of Acanthus, Stageira and Torone from the Athenians, but his greatest success was taking advantage of factional disputes at Amphipolis to prise the city from Athenian control. The Athenian general in the region, Thucydides – *the* Thucydides – was blamed for the disaster and went into exile. It is surprising how infrequently modern scholars link his glowing portrayal of Brasidas' tactical skills to his own failure against the Spartan. It seems only natural that Thucydides might have over-egged his depiction of Brasidas to explain away his own failings.

This run of successes for Brasidas led the Athenians to agree to a one-year truce with the Spartans in 423 BCE.[26] During the truce Brasidas – ever the action man – campaigned with the Macedonian king Perdiccas against the Illyrians. Brasidas is said to have bitterly opposed any cessation in the hostilities, but the Spartan authorities felt that if they gave the Athenians a taste of peace, they might agree to a longer peace that would allow them to get the hostages back. The Athenians, though, had other ideas; they felt that they could use the time the truce bought them to prepare for Brasidas' next onslaught on their possessions in the north.

Once the truce had expired, the general Cleon swiftly sailed north and recaptured Torone, before setting his sights on the big prize – Amphipolis – where Brasidas was based. With Cleon's forces lined up outside the main gate to the city, Brasidas gave a rousing speech in which he reminded the Peloponnesians that they were Dorians, and that they were well used to beating Ionians.[27] Thucydides is not kind to Cleon, whom he clearly loathed. The way he paints it, Brasidas quickly realised how disordered the Athenians were under Cleon's leadership and ordered his men to attack when the opportunity presented itself. Brasidas split his forces in two; he would lead the main force out through the main gate himself, while his deputy Clearidas would lead a smaller force through the Thracian gate to the east of the city to attack the flank of the Athenian forces. Brasidas told his deputy to 'show yourself a brave man, as a Spartiate should', before telling the allies, 'Follow him like men, and remember that zeal, honour and obedience mark the good soldier – and that this day will make you either free men and allies of Lacedaemon, or slaves of Athens.' Later tradition had it that Brasidas wrote home to the ephors, 'I'll achieve my wishes in this war, or I'll die.'[28]

The opportunity Brasidas was awaiting came when Cleon decided not to attack the city but instead to wait for reinforcements to arrive. When Cleon gave the order to withdraw, Brasidas spotted that his opponent's troops were disorganised and unprepared for an attack from within the city. Brasidas reportedly announced, 'Those men will not stand against us. It is clear from the movement of their spears and heads. Anyone who does this will not stand firm.' He led his men out through the gate in a full-on assault on the retreating Athenians, who were panicked by their own disorder and astounded by Brasidas' daring.

The sudden arrival of Clearidas and his men caused Cleon to panic and run. He was one of no fewer than 600 Athenians who were killed as they fled back to the main base at Eion. Only seven members of Brasidas' forces were killed, but the daring general was one of them, leading from the front. Thucydides stresses that Brasidas 'lived to hear of the victory of his troops' but died soon afterwards from his wounds. At the orders of Clearidas, his men stripped the Athenian dead and set up a trophy to commemorate Brasidas' victory.[29]

After the battle, Brasidas was formally recognised as a founder demigod by the Amphipolitans. His body was paraded through the streets of Amphipolis and given a public burial in the marketplace. The Amphipolitans are said to have torn down the building honouring their actual founder, Hagnon the Athenian, and instead began to honour Brasidas, making annual blood sacrifice and holding games in his honour. Excavations have unearthed a small stone tomb, known as a cist grave, inside a small building in the Amphipolitan marketplace. This is thought to be the site of Brasidas' hero-sanctuary; a silver ossuary with a golden wreath in the grave is thought to have contained his remains.

In Plato's *Symposium*, Brasidas is likened to the great hero

Achilles.[30] Today, Brasidas is a heroic character in the action role-playing video game *Assassin's Creed Odyssey*, a powerful warrior and close friend of the protagonist Kassandra. As in reality, the game has Brasidas killed at Amphipolis in the mission 'We will rise'. By all accounts, Brasidas' own mother Argileonis might not have understood the veneration of her son. When some Amphipolitans travelled to Sparta and told her about her son's great achievements, calling him 'the best of all the Lacedaemonians', Argileonis replied bluntly: 'Foreigners, my son was good and brave, but Sparta has many better men than him.'[31]

*　*　*

The deaths of Cleon and Brasidas in 422 BCE removed the major stumbling blocks to peace between Athens and Sparta. Cleon's greatest rival Nicias was able to convince the Athenians that they wanted peace – partly because they had recently suffered a serious defeat against the Boeotians at the Battle of Delium, where the Thebans had made up for their lack of numerical strength by drawing themselves up to a depth of twenty-five ranks, rather than the standard eight.[32] The Spartans did not require much convincing, provided they got the Pylos captives back – in part because they were aware of the fact that their thirty-year peace with Argos was about to expire. An initial one-year truce between Sparta and Athens was agreed, with a view to exploring a longer-term deal.[33]

Much of the winter and spring was spent in fruitless negotiations, until the Spartans made it clear that they were intending to invade – and occupy – part of Attica, which spooked the Athenians into agreeing a fifty-year peace. The terms of the treaty required the Spartans to restore Amphipolis, the other northern Greek *poleis* and the border fortress between Boeotia and Attica at Panactum to the Athenians, while the Athenians agreed to restore Pylos, Cythera and any captives to the Spartans. The terms were sworn to by seventeen representatives from each city – including Brasidas' father Tellis on the Spartan side and Nicias on that of the Athenians.[34]

The Spartans and the Athenians seemed to be on the road to a long-term peace deal. However, some of Sparta's key allies – the Boeotians, Corinthians, Eleans and Megarians – were still so aggrieved by Athenian imperialism that they refused to swear to the treaty, which became known as the Peace of Nicias. The fact that the Spartans were prepared to risk the ire of their Peloponnesian allies by forcing through the deal shows just how far many Spartans were prepared to go to ensure Spartan security.

The following year, the Spartans and Athenians tried to shore things up by upgrading the peace treaty to a fifty-year alliance requiring both parties to defend each other in the event of an attack by a third party. Another key term of the alliance stipulated that the Athenians would assist the Spartans in the event of the 'slave population' (*douleia*) rising up against them. The exceptional danger the helots posed to Sparta can be seen in the fact that there is no corresponding clause requiring the Spartans to help the Athenians in the event of their own slaves rebelling.

After the swearing of oaths, the Athenians finally returned the captives from Sphacteria. Sparta now had peace with Athens, security in the event of a helot rebellion, and her precious hoplites at home. Everything seemed on course for the Spartans to slowly regroup and recover their strength and regional influence.

The agreement with Athens would not last long, though. Some of Sparta's allies would display their dissatisfaction with the peace with Athens by, somewhat bizarrely, making a separate alliance with the Athenians and going to war against Sparta themselves, fighting alongside the Athenians. Greek interstate politics were always unpredictable, but the Spartans' allies taking out their frustrations on the Spartans for ending the war with Athens by allying themselves *with* the Athenians *against* the Spartans – that really does take some explaining.

8

The Athenian War:
Sparta Betrays Greece?

421–404 BCE

Roman-period mosaic showing the Athenian statesman
Alcibiades (first to fourth century CE).

Over the next fifteen years, the Spartans would claw their way to power – in Greece and beyond. They would stand at the head of a secure alliance system, and their Athenian rivals would be smashed. But few would have predicted this when the Peace of Nicias was signed – and certainly not once Sparta's allies started falling away in droves. In many ways, the Spartans brought their isolation on themselves. They were so desperate for the captives from Sphacteria to be returned to them that they ignored the wishes of their allies.

As soon as the fifty-year alliance with Athens was agreed, the Corinthians went straight to Argos, complaining that the alliance with the 'most hateful' Athenians proved that the Spartans must be contemplating the complete subjugation of the whole Peloponnese.[1] Clearly the Corinthians were afraid that the Spartans would betray their fellow Dorians and use their alliance with the Athenians as a means to properly conquer the Peloponnese. The fact that the Spartans had previously conquered the Messenians and tried to conquer the Tegeans (both Dorians) lent some credibility to these fears. The Corinthians told the Argives it was their duty to try to stop the Spartans, and offered them a mutual-defence treaty, which would oblige them to defend each other in the event of attack by a third party, including Sparta, but not require the Corinthians to get involved if the Argives attacked Sparta. The Corinthians also promised the Argives that many of Sparta's other allies also hated them. One can also imagine that after the fiasco at Sphacteria, many of the allies were now starting to doubt Sparta's strength.

The Argives didn't need a second invitation to encourage

them to make a play to increase their regional influence at the expense of the Spartans. They immediately agreed to the mutual-defence agreement with Corinth, before going on to make full alliances with Sparta's renegade allies, Mantinea and Elis. Both states had recently extended their territories and influence, carving out mini-empires of their own, and feared that the peace would leave the Spartans free to undo all their hard work.

Things got messier for Sparta when the Thebans tore down the fortifications at Panactum before handing the territory back to Athens, in accordance with the treaty. The Athenians naturally saw the destruction of the fort as bad faith on the Spartans' part, as they really ought to have handed it back intact. In the midst of this febrile atmosphere, a new player emerged: the Athenian statesman Alcibiades, whom Thucydides calls 'young in age and distinguished in ancestry'.[2] The great-grandson of Cleisthenes, nephew and ward of Pericles, and a student of Socrates, Alcibiades was extremely ambitious. He was also keenly aware that his grandfather had been the Athenian *proxenos* for the Spartans. In Greek city-states *proxenoi* looked after the interests of visitors from the foreign state they represented, and were expected to use their influence to promote policies of friendship or alliance between their homeland and the city-state they represented. Alcibiades was irked that the Spartans had negotiated the peace treaty with Nicias rather than him, even though his grandfather had long ago renounced the family's relationship with Sparta.

When Spartan ambassadors travelled to Athens to try to calm the Athenians down about the destruction of Panactum, Alcibiades saw an opportunity. He reached out to the Spartan ambassadors, reminding them of his family's long-standing connection with the Spartans and giving the impression that he wanted to help. He bamboozled them into thinking that they would get a better reception from the Athenian assembly if they told the citizens that they had not been sent with full powers to negotiate – directly contradicting what they had told the Athenian council the previous day. Alcibiades promised that he would fix things to their advantage – but he had cleverly deceived them. When they told the assembled Athenians that they had not come with full powers, Alcibiades railed against them as men who gave different answers when asked the same question on successive days. The Athenians were so angered at what they saw as Spartan bad faith that Alcibiades was able to convince them to make a one-hundred-year alliance with Argos, Mantinea and Elis.[3]

Sparta was soon so diplomatically isolated that the Eleans, who managed the Olympic Games, fined them 200,000 drachmas (£20 million or $30 million in today's money) for violating the truce, and banned them from participating at the games in 420 BCE. The Spartans were unable to pay, and not being able to compete at the Olympics would have stung. Indeed, one of them, Lichas, was so desperate for the glory of competing that he entered his horses in the four-horse chariot race as part of the Boeotian team. When his horses won, Lichas could not stand missing out on the glory, and tried to crown his charioteer. This was too much for the referees, who gave Lichas a very public – and very humiliating – flogging. Although all the Greeks feared that the whole thing might take a nasty turn, the Spartans kept quiet, and the rest of the games passed uneventfully.[4]

* * *

For some time, the Spartans tried to avoid provoking the Athenians and the Argives into a conflict. But things came to a head in 418 BCE when the Spartans placed a garrison in the city of Epidaurus, which was around forty kilometres from Argos, to protect it against the Argives. The Spartans took care to travel by sea to avoid facing an Argive army, which was a good tactical decision, only for the Argives to complain to the Athenians that they should have stopped the Spartan fleet from landing. They told the Athenians that if they did not immediately send a force to attack Pylos, they would have to reconsider their options. The Argives clearly hoped that the Athenians would be able to distract the Spartans by attacking Pylos, just as they had seven years before, in 425 BCE.

The intervention was just what Alcibiades needed to stir the Athenians up against the Spartans. At his urging, the Athenians inscribed the words 'The Spartans did not keep their oaths' on the stone stele recording the peace treaty.[5] The chorus in Aristophanes' comedy *Peace*, which said the Spartans were 'children of foxes, their heads are treacherous, their minds are treacherous'[6] when it was staged for the first time at the Dionysia festival just a few days before the Peace of Nicias was formally ratified in 421 BCE, would not have been surprised that the peace broke down. Having made it clear who was in the wrong, the Athenians sent a force of Messenians to raid Pylos.

Just as during the Archidamian War, the attack on Pylos prompted the Spartans to react. Rather than defend Pylos as they had earlier, however, this time the Spartans put together a massive allied army, to strike against Argos. The Eurypontid king Agis led out these troops, which Thucydides deems the finest Greek army ever assembled. It was made up of the Spartans 'in all their strength', plus their allies from Tegea, Arcadia (except Mantinea), Boeotia, Corinth, Phlius, and 3,000 horsemen from Sicyon, Pellene and Megara.[7] The Argives marched out to meet them near Mantinea, accompanied by the Mantineans and Eleans. But on the cusp of what would have been a truly major confrontation – Plutarch says that if they had been defeated 'the very existence of Sparta would have been at stake'[8] – two Argives, the general Thrasylus and Alciphron, the *proxenos* for Sparta, offered to negotiate terms. Neither of them had the authority to do so, but strange things can happen in war. Agis stepped forward to meet them alone and came back announcing that he had agreed to a four-month truce with Argos.

To say that it did not go down well – with either side – is an understatement. Thrasylus' own men tried to stone him to death, and he was only able to survive by seeking sanctuary in a nearby temple. The Spartans were just as furious, but grudgingly obeyed their orders to return home. When they got back, their resentment at having to abide by Agis' unauthorised deal overwhelmed them. Although Thucydides claims the Spartans' fury was 'out of character',[9] we have already seen their simmering resentment explode on numerous occasions. Agis fared a little better than Thrasylus the Argive, but the furious Spartans threatened to raze his house to the ground and to fine him 100,000 drachmas (roughly £10 million or $15 million today). To mollify the Spartans, he promised that he would redeem himself with a 'great deed' when he next led them to the field of battle. This promise saved Agis' house and finances, but the Spartans insisted on clipping his wings; from now on he would be accompanied by ten 'advisors', without whose approval he would not be authorised to withdraw an army from enemy territory. Cleomenes had been allowed to call up an allied army and lead it all the way to Athens without telling anyone his intentions; the rules for Agis were very different.

One can only imagine how tense things must have been in Sparta and Argos for the next few months, while both citizen bodies waited for the short truce to expire. Almost as soon as it had lapsed in 418 BCE, the Spartans were given word that the Tegeans were thinking about leaving their alliance and joining the Argives. Exactly why is not clear, but this threat to their authority prompted the Spartans to act swiftly. Agis was sent out to attack Argos with an army made up of the Spartans 'in full force', accompanied by thousands of freed helots, including the so-called 'Brasideioi' – those who had served with Brasidas at Amphipolis. Agis led his army straight at the Argive forces that marched out to meet him, even though they held the higher ground. This was clearly a dangerous idea; so dangerous that when they were within a javelin-throw of the enemy, one of the older Spartans – perhaps one of the advisors – shouted out that Agis was intent on 'curing one ill with another'.[10]

Agis suddenly led his army away to Tegea at great speed, before the Argive forces could engage. Was this a response to the criticism of the older man, or a planned feint? We shall never know. Whatever the reason, the Argive hoplites were baffled by how quickly the Spartans disappeared and started to criticise their own leaders for letting the opportunity slip. They were even more alarmed when they learned that Agis had set about diverting the course of a stream to flow into Mantinean territory. It has since been argued that Agis was hoping to draw the enemy into attacking him in a favourable position, but Thucydides says he was caught by surprise when the Argives and their allies arrived suddenly. If it was a plan, Agis was bizarrely unprepared for it to work.

The battle that followed – the so-called Battle of Mantinea – was one of the most important in Classical Greek history. As Thucydides describes it, on the Spartan left were 600 *perioikoi* known as Skiritiai, who 'always have this post'. To their right were the Brasideioi and the freed helots known as *neodamodeis*; then the Spartans themselves (with the *perioikoi*); then their allies, the Heraeans and Maenalians. On the Spartan right wing were the Tegeans with 'a few' Spartiates on the very end. Agis deployed his cavalry on each wing to screen his movements. Opposite the Spartan army, the Mantineans lined up on the right. The other Arcadians allied to them were on their left, followed by 1,000 elite 'picked' Argives, who had been given military training at the city's expense, then the other Argives; the men from Cleonae and Ornae; and finally the Athenians and their cavalry. Thucydides says that Agis' forces 'seemed' larger, but he was unable to be sure because of the Spartans' characteristic secrecy in their dealings with foreigners.[11]

The mindsets of the two armies were very different. The Argives rushed forward boldly, while the Spartans marched slowly and evenly to a rhythm set by flute players. Nonetheless both sides started shifting to the right, as the men on the extreme end, who were not protected by a comrade's shield, instinctively edged in that direction to keep their unarmed side away from the enemy. Thucydides stresses how each man's 'fear spreads to the others who follow his example'. The consequence was that both armies edged so far to the right that Agis realised that the Mantineans would end up outflanking the Skiritai on his left.

To solve the problem, he came up with a bold solution, ordering the Skiritai and the Brasideioi to move left, away from the main body of the army, to cover the Mantineans. This left a gap, which he ordered two of his senior officers, the polemarchs Aristocles and Hipponoïdas, to plug, by crossing over from the right (of the Spartan forces in the centre) with two *lochoi* of the Spartan hoplites. If it had worked, it would have been genius – but Aristocles and Hipponoïdas refused to obey their orders, leaving a huge gap in the Spartan line. When he realised what had happened, Agis tried to move the Skiritai back, but it was too late. The Mantineans routed the isolated Skiritai and Brasideioi, and then joined the picked Argives in rushing into the space Agis' failed manoeuvre had left in the line. The leftmost Spartans were driven all the way back to their waggon train by the advance of the Argives.

The rest of the army, however – especially those in the centre, where Agis himself was stationed with his bodyguard of 300 elite knights – fared far better. These Spartans fell upon the Argives, Cleonaeans, Orneates and Athenians, and routed them. Thucydides writes that many of the enemy did not even wait for the Spartans to attack. Rather, they panicked and ran away, with some even trampled by their own men as they fled.[12]

Agis then ordered the men in the victorious right and centre to wheel to the left to tackle the Mantineans and the elite Argives. But as the Spartans bore down on them, they too panicked and fled. The Athenians – and it must have pained Thucydides to say it – effectively watched the Spartans sweep by them before skulking away. Thucydides claims that the Spartans did not pursue the fleeing enemy very far, as was their customary practice. Pursuing a routed enemy was inherently dangerous, as it risked being surprised by an enemy who suddenly turned back to defend itself. This Spartan practice may even have been designed to encourage the enemy to run away, rather than risk fighting to protect themselves. The same might apply to the Spartan practice of advancing slowly towards the enemy: marching slowly gave the enemy a chance to panic and run, which would have been an even more appealing option if they knew the Spartans wouldn't pursue them very far. On the other hand, Diodorus claims that Agis only let the Argives go after he was urged to do so by one of his advisors.[13] As Diodorus tells it, Agis was so anxious to achieve a great deed that he almost risked undoing his great victory.

So ended the biggest pitched battle in Greece since Pausanias' victory over the Persians at Plataea in 479 BCE. Thucydides reports that 700 Argives, Orneates and Cleonaeans were killed, along with 200 Mantineans and 200 Athenians (including both generals). He also estimates that around 300 Spartans were killed, but Spartan secrecy once again prevented him from knowing the true number.

The outcome of the battle resonated throughout the Greek world. Thucydides claims that this single action wiped out the shame of the Spartans' surrender at Sphacteria, and the charges of 'softness, slowness and inaction' that had followed that embarrassing defeat. The Spartans were now thought to have been the victims of bad luck on that occasion, and were 'the same men in spirit that they had always been'.[14] In other words, the Spartans were back.

*   *   *

Although hundreds of Spartans and Athenians had died in a pitched battle, the Battle of Mantinea did not spell the end of the Peace of Nicias. One of the major reasons why was the fact that the Spartans managed to tempt the Argives into agreeing to a fifty-year peace treaty. One of the key brokers of the deal was the recently flogged Olympic 'victor' Lichas.[15] It has been argued that his Olympic success was one reason why the Spartans chose him as their envoy to Argos, but the fact that he was the *proxenos* for Argos at Sparta was surely a more significant factor: as a quasi-official representative of Argive interests at Sparta, Lichas must have had influential friends at Argos, and been a figure to whom the Argives would listen. With a peace treaty in place between Sparta and Argos, the Athenians would have understood only too well that they were on their own against the Spartans when fighting on land, while the cautious Spartans would not have wanted to risk jeopardising their regained air of invincibility by tangling further with Athens. With both parties eager to avoid crossing each other, the Athenians turned their attention to the small Aegean island of Melos, the one island in the Aegean that was not part of the Athenian empire. Feeling confident that the Spartans would not risk facing them at sea, the Athenians gave the Melians a blunt ultimatum: surrender and pay tribute to Athens, or face destruction.

The Melians asked to remain neutral. They pointed out that they were Dorians, and even claimed to be a Spartan colony. This meant, they argued, that becoming a tribute-paying subject of Athens would offend their Spartan forefathers – but they added that their neutrality could cause no harm to the Athenians. Irrespective of whether Melos *was* a Spartan colony or not, the Athenians rejected the Melians' offer, taking the line that if you're not with us, you're against us. They also argued that 'the strong do what they have the power to do, while the weak accept what they must'.[16] One of the reasons for this stance was their confidence that the Spartans would not help the Melians. They bluntly – and rightly, as it turned out – told the Melians that they were wasting their time hoping for Spartan assistance. The Melians made one last play, arguing that 'one falling in danger should be treated with fairness and justice'. They warned the Athenians that 'this is a principle that touches you as much as anyone, since your fall would result in the most terrible vengeance on you and would serve as an example to others'.

The Athenians would have done well to heed this warning, but they did not listen. They easily defeated the Melians and, in a brutal act that is often cast as genocide, killed the entire adult male population and sold the women and children into slavery, before repopulating the island with Athenian settlers. The last island state that was not subject to Athenian control had been wiped out. The Spartans may have returned to dominance on land, but the Athenians were Greece's maritime superpower.

Yet just as they were making the Aegean their own, the Athenians made their biggest miscalculation of the war – providing the Spartans with the opportunity they had been seeking for half a century.

*   *   *

After receiving an appeal for help from the city of Segesta against Selinus, a nearby city on Sicily, the Athenians set their sights on conquering the whole island. However you look at it, the Athenian campaign in Sicily did not start off on firm foundations. Alcibiades championed the cause – but his aim was not to better Athens, nor to help Segesta against Selinus. Rather, he wanted large-scale war against Selinus' ally Syracuse, the largest and most powerful Dorian Greek *polis* on Sicily. Alcibiades was motivated by a toxic mix of ambition and spite: his rival Nicias was opposed to helping the Segestans, so Alcibiades opposed *him* for the sake of it. He also reportedly believed that commanding the Athenians in Sicily would bring him wealth and fame.[17]

Thucydides stresses that most Athenians had no idea how large Sicily was, how many people lived there, or that they were taking on a war of a similar magnitude as that they had waged against the Peloponnesians.[18] Thus, many Athenians probably thought they were tackling another small island like Melos, and Alcibiades made easy headway in stirring up support for his plan. Nicias tried to explain just how dangerous it would be, and how unsuitable Alcibiades was as a leader. Alcibiades responded by listing his own virtues – he was so rich that he had once entered seven teams of horses at the Olympic Games (his teams coming first, second and fourth) – and stressing how much support the Athenians would get from the other Sicilians. He then flattered the Athenians, reminding them that their boldness had given them an empire, and being bold would help them prevail in Sicily. When Nicias changed tack, arguing that the 60 triremes they were sending would not be enough to get the job done, his dire warnings backfired: the Athenians resolved to send 40 more warships as well as 5,000 hoplites. This desire to devote so many resources to the Sicilian expedition would turn out to be an even bigger long-term disaster than Nicias could have imagined.[19]

Even before the Athenian fleet left there were problems. One night, someone mutilated the Hermae – stone sculptures with Hermes' head above a plain, square column, on which male genitals were carved, usually placed at street corners – and Alcibiades was blamed for the sacrilegious vandalism. Although modern scholars often fixate on the idea that the genitals on the Hermae were mutilated, Thucydides only mentions damage to their faces. Despite the accusation hanging over his head, Alcibiades was allowed to lead the fleet to Sicily. But before anything could be achieved, he was recalled to Athens to face trial, leaving the Sicilian expedition in the hands of Nicias, the man who had led the opposition to the campaign in the first place. Even worse for Athens, rather than face trial in Athens, Alcibiades defected to Sparta.[20]

Despite Alcibiades' absence – or perhaps because of it, Nicias might have thought – the fighting in Sicily began comparatively well for the Athenians. After an opening indecisive land battle against the Syracusans, the Athenians managed to occupy Epipolae, the plateau above the city of Syracuse. Once they were there, they set about building walls to cut off the Syracusans from their Sicilian allies by land and blockading them by sea with their superior fleet.[21]

Circumstances changed when Alcibiades started advising the Spartans. He was well received there – the Spartans were amazed by the ease with which he abandoned his hitherto luxurious lifestyle and took to wearing his hair long, taking cold baths and eating the 'black broth and barley cakes'. Plutarch compares Alcibiades to a chameleon for the ease with which he changed his appearance, noting that in Sparta he had been all for 'gymnastics, simplicity and sternness of face'.[22] A Roman-era mosaic displayed in the archaeology museum in Sparti, showing a handsome but sly-looking Alcibiades sporting longish hair, is perhaps meant to represent his brief flirtation with the Spartan way of life. Alcibiades encouraged the Spartans to attack Athens and set up a permanent base in Attica rather than rely on annual invasions there. The Spartans did just that, occupying and fortifying the rural township (deme) of Decelea; thus many scholars refer to this phase of the Peloponnesian War as the 'Decelean War'. With a Spartan force based in Attica, the Athenians were forced to abandon the countryside once more. In the confusion, thousands of slaves fled from the silver mines at Laureion, damaging the Athenian economy.[23]

Alcibiades also encouraged the Spartans to send a general to Syracuse to help the Sicilians against the Athenians, and they duly sent Gylippus to advise the Syracusans. Gylippus' role in Sicily was similar to that of Brasidas in the north of Greece in 424 BCE; his presence symbolised Spartan involvement, without any commitment of significant manpower or naval resources. Put simply, the Spartans would be committing only a handful of men and getting the Syracusans to do the hard work for them.

Gylippus annoyed the Athenians straight away, sending a herald to offer them safe passage from Sicily provided they left immediately. Nicias refused to respond, but one of the rank-and-file Athenians asked the herald if the presence of 'a single Spartan cloak and staff' had made the prospects of the Syracusans so secure that they could risk mocking the Athenians, who had captured 300 Spartans 'far sturdier and longer haired' than Gylippus. The Syracusans were initially unimpressed by Gylippus too, mocking his shabby cloak and long hair. However, he swiftly proved himself to be what Plutarch calls an 'owl', overseeing operations that led to the completion of a counter-wall, which rendered the Athenian siege useless. He was also able to rally the Syracusan fleet, which trapped the Athenian fleet in their own harbour and left the invaders hemmed in on land and sea.[24]

The Athenian general Demosthenes was sent out with a relief force to help, but by the time he arrived he found the situation so desperate that he advised Nicias to return home. Not only does this show how desperate things were in Sicily, it is also a clear indication that the Spartan occupation of Decelea was working. Yet Nicias would not give up on the campaign – perhaps afraid that his initial lack of enthusiasm would lead him to be blamed for the failure. By the time he tried to break out several months later it was far too late; the verb 'to Niciasise' would become an Athenian euphemism for shilly-shallying. More than 7,000 Athenians were captured, including Nicias himself and Demosthenes. The generals were executed by the Syracusans – against Gylippus' wishes – and the rank-and-file Athenians were sold into slavery.[25] The few surviving Melians would have appreciated the irony.

* * *

Despite the limited Spartan involvement in the fighting, it is hard to overstate just how important the failure of the Sicilian expedition was in Sparta's rise to dominance in Greece. For the Athenians, the loss of resources was as damaging as the military defeat. Not only did they lose two generals (or three, including Alcibiades), but they also lost some 7,000 hoplites and skilled rowers, and more than 100 triremes. These were resources that the Athenians desperately needed in the campaigns that were to follow.

The Sicilian expedition also energised Sparta's Peloponnesian allies,[26] especially because they realised that the Syracusans would now be able to help them offset the numerical superiority of the Athenian navy by supplying them with a large naval force. It also seems to have spurred the Spartans into action. Agis sailed north to Thessaly almost immediately, where he took hostages to ensure that the Thessalian cities would join the Spartan alliance against Athens.[27] The Spartans resolved to build 25 warships, and asked their allies to start building 75 more. The Boeotians were to contribute 25, the Phocians and Locrians 15 between them, the Corinthians 15, the Arcadians, Pellenians and Sicyonians a further 10 between them, and 10 more from the Megarians, Troezenians, Epidaurians and Hermionians. Prior to the Sicilian disaster, there would have been little point in the Spartans and their allies trying to build enough ships to challenge the Athenians – and even if they did, the Athenians could always muster better rowers. But Sicily had cost Athens dearly in terms of both ships and rowers, and Athens was also short of cash now that the Spartan base was at Decelea. The Athenians could build more ships, but rowers weren't easy to come by, and they needed to be paid. If Sparta could find the cash to build enough ships and pay the best rowers, Athens would be in serious trouble.

Trouble duly arrived in 412 BCE, when Sparta did the unthinkable and asked Persia for help, in the form of ships, manpower and money. Given that the Spartans had gone into the Peloponnesian War with the stated aim of ending Athenian 'tyranny', the price they paid for Persian support was heavy; they had no choice but to agree that 'All the territory and the cities held now by the King or held in the past by the King's ancestors shall be the King's.'[28] This meant that the Spartans would be handing over the Greeks of Asia Minor – whom they had previously effectively liberated by defeating Xerxes and

Mardonius – to the Persians. In fact, if one took the wording literally, they were effectively handing over most of mainland Greece outside the Peloponnese to the Persians too – for Thessaly, Locris, Phocis, Boeotia and even Athens had at one time been possessed by Darius' father Xerxes. This terrible bargain shows how desperate the Spartans were to defeat the Athenians, and how low they were prepared to go to claw their way to the top of the heap.

There were, however, two subsequent updates to the agreement between the Spartans and the Persians that were fractionally less terrible for Sparta's reputation as a liberator. The first was a comparatively standard mutual-defence pact, which nonetheless included the wording that 'Neither the Lacedaemonians nor the allies of the Lacedaemonians shall make war against or otherwise injure any country or cities that belong to King Darius or did belong to his father or to his ancestors.'[29] After this deal was made, the Spartan Lichas insisted that it was monstrous that the Spartans had promised the Greeks they would give them freedom, but were instead giving them a Median master. So a second update clarified that only the Asian Greeks would return to being subjects of the Persian king. In all three treaties, the key detail for the Spartans was the promise that the Persian king – via his satrap Tissaphernes – would provide significant funds to finance their ongoing war with the Athenians.[30]

The Persian intervention had an almost immediate impact. Some of the Athenians' allies started to rebel because of increased Spartan naval activity in the Aegean. Things very quickly got so bad for Athens that the rich oligarchs bullied the assembly into handing them the government of the city-state. As odd as it sounds, the Athenian democracy held a vote, and voted itself out of existence. The new powerholders in Athens flirted with making peace with the Spartans, but ultimately decided to keep on with the war, and – most significantly – to bring Alcibiades back into the fold.

Alcibiades was at that point in Asia, having weaselled his way into the entourage of Tissaphernes, the Persian satrap of Lydia and Ionia. He had been forced to flee Sparta after he was accused of seducing Timaea, the wife of the Spartan king Agis. Timaea was reportedly so thoroughly corrupted by Alcibiades that she made no denial of their affair, even calling her newborn son Leotychides 'Alcibiades' in front of her friends and helot attendants.[31] After revoking Alcibiades' exile, the new Athenian oligarchic regime appointed him as a general in the fleet – a move that would prove almost an immediate success.

While all this was going on, the Spartans were getting ready to try out their new Persian-built navy against the Athenians. But the first major naval battle in 410 BCE was an utter fiasco. The Spartan admiral Mindarus led between 60 and 85 triremes against an Athenian fleet of a similar number, led by Alcibiades – and the experienced generals Thrasybulus and Theramenes – near Cyzicus in northern Asia Minor. Alcibiades lured the overconfident Mindarus out with a small decoy force, after which Theramenes and Thrasybulus swept in behind the Spartan admiral and encircled his fleet. Mindarus spotted the trap before everything was lost and fled for land, beaching his ships south of Cyzicus, but he was killed in the fighting, and the whole Spartan fleet was captured by the Athenians, except for those of the more experienced Syracusans who burned theirs.

The triumphant Athenians intercepted the desperate laconic message sent home by Mindarus' deputy: 'Ships lost, Mindarus dead, men starving, we don't know what to do.'[32] The fact that they could read it suggests either that the more junior officer did not have the coded *skytalē* that Spartan commanders were given, or that Spartan codes were not that difficult to crack.

*   *   *

Mindarus' failure showed that the Spartan alliance with the Persians was not a magic fix, and the Spartans showed how low in confidence they were by responding to this single failure by suing for peace immediately. The war was now seeming to go so well for the Athenians, however, that they refused the offer and returned to democracy. In the next few years, they restored their finances and grew their fleet. But just as things seemed to be slipping away from the Spartans, everything changed.

In 408 BCE, the Persian king Darius sent his younger son Cyrus to serve as governor of Lydia, Phrygia and Cappadocia, and as his general commander of the Persian forces against the Athenians. His appointment as Tissaphernes' superior was a game-changer. Tissaphernes had been lukewarm in his support for the Spartans, but Cyrus was all for it – not least because his appointment coincided with the arrival of Lysander as admiral in 407 BCE. The son of an aristocratic but impoverished Spartan who had risen by way of talent, Lysander was the other missing piece of the puzzle for the Spartans, a man with the flexibility of thought to work effectively with the Persians and with the nous to command a fleet.

Lysander set about cultivating Cyrus' friendship and was soon able to squeeze a lot of money from the Persian prince's sizeable coffers: Cyrus told Lysander that he had brought 500 talents (roughly £300 million or $450 million) and was pre-pared to spend more of his own money if necessary. One story goes that when Cyrus offered Lysander a gift that would 'please him', the Spartan asked Cyrus to increase his sailors' pay, as well as giving them backpay that had been withheld by his predeces-sor.[33] When Lysander managed this sudden change in finances, which increased his rowers' morale and encouraged more of Athens' allies to switch sides, Lysander must have looked as self-satisfied as he does on a plate painted by the eighteenth-century Italian potter Francesco Antonio Xaverio Grue, now held by the Pottery Museum in Abruzzo, on which a clean-shaven, long-haired Lysander meets a goateed Cyrus wearing a traditional Arabian turban.

Lysander was also a very canny admiral. Finding himself blockaded by Alcibiades' fleet at Ephesus, he refused to engage due to the Athenians' superior numbers and experience. All he was prepared to risk doing was to send three ships out as a patrol. When the Athenians sent ships out from their base in Notium in response, Lysander's three ships would return to base. The impression created was that Lysander was afraid to fight, which likely prompted Alcibiades to make a crucial error. Confident that Lysander was no threat, he sailed out to Phocaea where his co-general Thrasybulus was based, leaving his helmsman Antiochus in charge of the Athenian fleet.

It was obviously a huge mistake, as Antiochus was far too junior for this responsibility. It was rather like an admiral leaving a naval rating or an enlisted sailor in charge of a fleet today. Although Alcibiades had given Antiochus strict orders not to act in his absence, the helmsman couldn't help himself: he sent a small squadron of ten ships sailing past Lysander's position. Antiochus was probably hoping to lure the three ships that Lysander regularly sent out into an ambush, but the whole operation went awry.

Lysander had heard from deserters that Alcibiades was gone, and saw an opportunity 'to strike a blow worthy of Sparta';[34] rather than sending out just three ships, he sent out his whole fleet. Antiochus' flagship was sunk straight away, and the remaining nine ships raced back to the safety of the main Athenian force at Notium. The speed of Lysander's attack took the whole Athenian fleet by surprise (the lack of a senior officer must have been telling here); fifteen Athenian triremes were captured in the fighting and seven were sunk. Lysander set up a trophy near Notium to commemorate the first ever Spartan victory over the Athenians at sea and sailed back to Ephesus.

Learning of the disaster, Alcibiades sailed back and tried to lure Lysander out to fight again, but the wily Spartan refused to budge. Soon after this fiasco, Alcibiades was deposed as general; he would remain in exile for the rest of his life. A few years later, Lysander brought about his execution on the orders of the Spartan authorities – either they too were scared by the threat Alcibiades represented, or they were trying to gratify the cuckolded Agis.[35]

*　*　*

The war seemed to be swinging in Sparta's favour. But just as they had found an admiral with the skills to take on the Athenians, their progress was stalled by one of the key rules of Spartan government: annual rotation of office. As no Spartan could serve as admiral for more than one year, Lysander was replaced by Callicratidas, whom Diodorus calls 'young, guileless and straightforward' because he had not yet experienced foreign ways,[36] very much the yin to Lysander's yang. Plutarch contrasts Callicratidas' scrupulous honesty with Lysander's propensity for deceit, arguing that his predecessor was prepared to overlook justice and honour if it was profitable to do so. One of Lysander's most famous aphorisms was 'Sometimes the lion's skin must be patched out with that of the fox'.[37]

When Callicratidas arrived to replace him, Lysander boasted that he was handing him complete mastery of the sea. At this, Callicratidas told him that if this was true, he should sail from Ephesus to Miletus, passing the Athenian base at Samos on the way: 'If you do this, I shall be quite prepared to recognise that you are the master of the sea.'[38] Lysander did not risk taking up

Callicratidas' challenge, and in a fit of pique returned the money Cyrus had given him.

When Callicratidas went to beg for it back, the meeting didn't go well. In one particularly cringeworthy incident, the gauche Callicratidas tried to meet with Cyrus but was told that the Persian prince was unavailable because he was 'drinking'. 'No matter,' Callicratidas naively replied, not realising that Cyrus was drinking at a banquet, rather than just having a drink; 'I will stand here and wait until he has finished.' The Persian guards laughed at him, considering him a 'country bumpkin'. After Callicratidas had waited a while – presumably long enough in his mind for Cyrus to have finished his drink – he was refused entry for a second time. Callicratidas was now so indignant that he swore in front of bystanders that he would do everything he could when he got back to Sparta to reconcile the Greeks and strike fear into these 'barbarians'.[39]

Even more embarrassingly for Callicratidas, Lysander's friends set about undermining him, following his orders only slowly and spreading a message around the fleet that the Spartans were making a huge mistake in replacing a skilled admiral with a clueless landlubber who did not know what he was doing. This placed Callicratidas in an awkward position, but given the formidable emphasis Spartans placed on obedience, his response was particularly astute. He summoned all the senior officials – Spartan and non-Spartan alike – to a meeting where he announced that he would have preferred to have stayed at home in Sparta and was by no means an expert in naval warfare, but had no choice but to carry out his orders to the best of his abilities. Callicratidas then asked for their advice: 'Do I stay here, or do I go home and report back what I find here?'[40] The threat worked; after that, none of the other Spartans were prepared to do anything other than promptly follow his orders.

Having failed to persuade Cyrus to return the money,

Callicratidas sailed to Miletus and got the locals to stump up the money to pay his rowers. He then attacked the Athenian general Conon at Samos, whose troops were so demoralised that he could only man 70 of their 100 triremes. Rather than flight, Conon fled north to the island of Lesbos – the gateway to the Hellespont and thus to the Black Sea region, a vital source of grain for Athens. Callicratidas pursued Conon with 170 triremes, defeating him in battle and blockading him in the harbour of the city of Mytilene. In a few short months, Callicratidas had carried out what he had challenged Lysander to do – and more besides. Callicratidas may have been gauche, but he was also very effective.

* * *

Thus far, Callicratidas had proven a surprisingly successful replacement for Lysander. If he was able to overcome Conon's forces, he would control the grain routes to Athens, and might even strangle the city into submission. But the game changed when the Athenians sent 110 triremes to the northern Aegean to relieve the pressure on Conon – hastily constructed ships manned by crews cobbled together from citizens, resident aliens and even slaves. Callicratidas responded by leaving 50 of his ships to bottle up Conon at Mytilene and taking the remaining 120 – all manned by well-paid and experienced crews – to oppose the Athenians at the nearby Arginsuae islands. There Callicratidas prepared for battle against 155 Athenian triremes commanded by no fewer than eight experienced generals. The Spartan admiral's rowers had the skills, but he lacked leadership experience – and it showed. The Athenian generals came up with a plan to nullify the disadvantage of their crews' limited skill: to draw up their ships in two lines, which meant that if the Spartans tried the usual Greek tactic of racing through the gaps between the ships, wheeling around and striking them in the side, they would be leaving themselves vulnerable to attack from the second line of ships. The fact that Callicratidas was significantly outnumbered (so much so that his helmsman, a Megarian named Hermon, advised him not to force the battle) made traditional tactics even more dangerous – and to make matters worse for Callicratidas, the seers had foretold that he would die in the fighting.

Like Leonidas at Thermopylae, Callicratidas was not daunted; according to Xenophon, he replied, 'If I die, Sparta will go on just the same; what is disgraceful is to run away.' And die he did, disappearing into the sea after his ship struck one of the opposing ships. Whereas Xenophon says Callicratidas' ship was struck in the first moments of the battle, Diodorus reports that he rammed the Athenian general Lysias' ship, sinking it and disabling many others. Finally, he rammed the ship commanded by Pericles the Younger, but while the two ships were locked together, Pericles used a grappling iron to fasten them so that his marines could board Callicratidas' ship. Pericles' men swarmed onto the Spartan flagship, and the admiral was surrounded and struck down.[41]

After Callicratidas perished, the Battle of Arginusae went badly wrong for the Peloponnesians. The Spartans lost nine of their ten ships, and sixty more of the allied triremes were sunk. The Athenians, meanwhile, lost only twenty-five ships. Their victorious generals set up a trophy to commemorate their achievement, delegating the task of collecting the remains of the Athenian dead to the experienced ship captains Thrasybulus and Theramenes, both former generals. Everything should have gone smoothly. But a late-afternoon summer thunderstorm ultimately prevented them from doing so,[42] setting off a sequence of events that would lead to the Spartans winning both the war and the hegemony that they had sought for so long.

* * *

Victory at Arginusae should have turned the war firmly in Athens' favour, but things soured when the relatives of those who died railed against the generals for failing to arrange proper burials. Xenophon suggests that Theramenes was particularly vociferous in attacking the generals, clearly hoping to protect himself. The Athenian people turned on the generals, deposing all eight who had fought in the battle, and summoning them back to Athens to face trial. Sensing which way the wind was blowing, two of them went into exile, but the other six returned home to face trial. The precise details are messy, but the key fact is that the Athenians tried the six generals en masse before the assembly rather than giving them separate trials in the law courts, and the citizens voted to condemn them all to death.[43] During the Enlightenment, political commentators often highlighted this episode as evidence that Athenian-style democracy was too dangerous to be inflicted on the modern world. Rather oddly, some commentators at the time felt that Sparta was a better model for a modern democracy.

The spectacularly self-destructive decision to execute the victorious generals meant that the Athenians were not able to capitalise on their victory. Moreover, their disastrous defeat at Arginusae made the Spartans realise that they needed Lysander in charge. As the rules prevented him from being reappointed, the Spartans sent out Aracus as admiral in 405 BCE, with Lysander as his notional deputy. Aracus' orders were implicit: do whatever Lysander says.[44]

Lysander was summoned by Cyrus, who advised him to not repeat Callicratidas' error; he should fight the Athenians only when he had numerical superiority. Cyrus also gave Lysander all the tribute he'd levied from the cities he controlled in Asia, and even promised to melt down his golden throne into coins if it would help recruit the rowers Lysander needed. Lysander seems to have taken Cyrus' warning onboard. Plutarch claims that he sailed to Attica and displayed his fleet to Agis, only to flee when he learned that the Athenians were sending ships to confront him.[45] Lysander ended up at the Hellespont, where he captured the city of Lampsacus. The Athenians responded by sending an enormous fleet of 180 triremes to face him. They landed on a long stretch of beach at Aegospotami, opposite Lampsacus. There the Hellespont is only three kilometres in width, so they were able to track Lysander's movements closely.

The next day, the Athenians rowed across to the harbour at Lampsacus to challenge the Spartans to battle. Lysander prepared his fleet as if he were going to row out but did not give the orders to attack. Each day for almost a week he did the same thing, drawing his fleet up in the mouth of the harbour at Lampsacus to face the Athenians as they rowed out to challenge him to fight, and sending a small squadron to follow them back to the beach where they landed their ships and observe their movements. Anyone who had witnessed Lysander's tactics at Notium might have suspected something was coming. Indeed, Alcibiades, who was holed up in the nearby city of Pactya, could see what was happening from his tower home and advised the Athenian generals to shift their anchorage to Sestos, where they would have a harbour and a city at their backs and ready access to supplies. But the Athenian generals at Aegospotami rebuffed his advice, telling him, 'We are in command now, not you.' Their overconfidence would cost Athens the war.

On the fifth day, Lysander again drew his fleet up in the harbour, once more refusing to respond to the Athenian challenge. But this time, the ships he sent to follow the Athenians had special orders: when it was clear that the Athenians had scattered to search for provisions, they were to sail back, signalling with a shield when they were halfway across the straits.

When Lysander saw the signal he launched a rapid attack with his whole fleet, catching the Athenians entirely unprepared. Lysander thus captured almost their entire fleet without a fight. Only the Athenian general Conon responded to the danger, rallying just seven ships. Having seen what happened to the generals who were victorious at Arginusae, Conon sailed off to foreign service with the Cypriot king Euagoras of Salamis, rather than return home to face the music. Lysander sent a Milesian pirate named Theopompus back to Sparta to announce the good news. When they learned just three days later that the Athenian fleet had been captured, the Spartans would have known that the end was nigh.[46]

Lysander commemorated the victory by dedicating bronze tripods in the sanctuary of the Graces at Amyclae, and two golden statues of Nike, the goddess of victory, on the Spartan acropolis, with each holding a golden eagle to signify his victories at Notium and Aegospotami.[47] Lysander also erected an extraordinary colonnade just inside the entrance to the sacred way at Delphi. Here he added bronze statues of himself and his steersman, and in the treasury of Brasidas and the Acanthians was placed a magnificent gold and ivory model of a trireme two cubits (90 centimetres) long, which Cyrus had sent as a prize for the victory at Aegospotami.[48] Lysander also set up a particularly bold and self-aggrandising dedication, composed for him by Ion of Samos: 'He set up a statue on this monument, when he won with swift ships and sacked the power of Cecrops – Lysander, having crowned unravaged Lacedaemon, the acropolis of Greece, country of fine dances.'

* * *

After capturing the Athenian fleet, Lysander really did control the seas, as he had once boasted to Callicratidas. To make this clear to the defeated Athenians, he sailed there and anchored off Piraeus with 150 of his 200 warships and closed the harbour to merchant ships. He then gathered together the survivors of the Athenian atrocity on Melos and restored them to their home. While Lysander was blockading Athens by sea, and King Agis was blockading them by land, the other Spartan king, Pausanias, gathered together an army of 'all the Peloponnesians' except Argos and marched on the city. In what must have been a mocking reference to the pleasure the Athenians had taken in intercepting the desperate letter home by Mindarus' deputy after the Battle of Cyzicus, Xenophon wrote that 'they had no ships, no men, no food; and they did not know what to do'.[49]

The desperate Athenians sent envoys to Agis, telling him that they would be willing to join the Spartan alliance if they were allowed to keep their walls and Piraeus. Agis told them he did not have the authority to negotiate – clearly learning from the mistake he had made fifteen years earlier when hammering out the truce with the Argives – and sent them on to Sparta. The ambassadors made it as far as the perioikic town of Sellasia in northern Laconia, only to be rebuffed by a delegation of Spartan ephors. They told the Athenians bluntly that if they really wanted peace they would have to come back with better proposals.

After several months of blockade, the Athenians were ready to accept whatever terms they could get. They sent Theramenes and nine other envoys to Sparta. The ephors once again made a show of meeting them at Sellasia; this time the Athenians were sufficiently submissive that they admitted them to Sparta. The Corinthians and Thebans wanted Athens to be wiped off the face of the earth, but the Spartans said that they would not enslave a Greek city that had previously done such good things when Greece was faced with supreme danger. The argument that they had fought alongside the Spartans against Xerxes had not helped the Athenians avoid the war in 431 BCE, but it did help them survive the defeat twenty-five years later.

Nonetheless, the price the Spartans exacted for peace was heavy. The 'Long Walls' (the fortifications protecting Piraeus and the ship-sheds that housed Athens' vast fleet) were to be destroyed, and the Athenian navy would be reduced to just twelve warships. Oligarchic exiles were to be recalled, and Athenian affairs overseen by an oligarchic puppet government of the thirty Athenians, known in later sources as the 'Thirty Tyrants'.[50] Of these, Theramenes nominated ten, the ephors chose ten more, and the Athenian assembly chose the final third. They were tasked with drawing up new laws under which Athens was to be governed. The most prominent of the new ministers was the well-known Spartophile Critias, a former student of Socrates, who once observed that 'the best constitution is that of Sparta',[51] which gives a good idea of the flavour of government the Thirty might have in mind. The peace deal also required Athens to become an ally of the Spartans, bound to swear an oath of loyalty and 'to follow them whithersoever they might lead'.[52]

Once the Athenians had accepted these terms, Lysander sailed into Piraeus and his men set about destroying the walls and ship-sheds. He was said to have gathered all the flute-girls from the city of Athens and arranged for them to play as an accompaniment to the destruction. An inventory from the treasuries of Athena indicates that Lysander dedicated a golden crown weighing almost 300 grams to the goddess.[53] Sadly, we must discount Plutarch's wonderful story that Lysander sent a three-word message to the ephors – 'Athens is taken' – only for the ephors to write back that the single word 'Taken' would have sufficed:[54] with both Spartan kings present, sending such a message back to Athens would not have been Lysander's call to make.

The Spartans' allies reportedly wore garlands to celebrate the freedom of Greece from Athenian tyranny. According to Xenophon, 'It was thought this day was the beginning of freedom for all Greece.'[55] Others record that the Spartans' victory meant that they now had 'hegemony on land and sea by common agreement',[56] making them the only Greeks ever to do so.[57]

With an undisputed empire, and the wealth that came with it, the Spartans had every intention of enjoying it. Yet they should have realised that their supremacy had been achieved through effective expenditure of Persian cash rather than their own strength of arms. 'Virtual' Spartan armies and navies might have won them the war against Athens, but the Spartans would require further and actual manpower resources if they were to maintain and extend their hegemony. Otherwise, their super-power status would disappear as quickly as it came.

9

'Glad to Eat Them, Even Raw': Inequality and the Downfall of Sparta

Hoard of Athenian silver tetradrachms (fifth century BCE). Stamped on one side with the head of Athena, and with her owl on the other (the iconographic symbol of the Athenian *polis*), it was such currency that Gylippus allegedly stole from the booty he was escorting back to Sparta.

Almost as soon as the Spartans defeated the Athenians, an event took place that highlighted the weak foundation for empire provided by the very structure of Spartan society. In 397 BCE, when the Eurypontid king was making a sacrifice on behalf of the state, the official seer announced: 'The signs that I read are just as would be given if we were surrounded by enemies.' Just five days after this malign portent, an informant reported to the ephors that a young Spartan called Cinadon was conspiring against the state. Despite being 'strong in body and heart', he was not a Spartiate but rather one of the so-called 'inferiors' – those former Spartan citizens who had had their status as one of the *homoioi* taken away from them. Cinadon had told the informant that, whenever Spartiates were mentioned, he knew well that all the underclasses – 'inferiors' like him, helots, freed helots and even the *perioikoi* – 'could hardly conceal the fact that they would be glad to eat them, even raw'.[1]

Cinadon had then taken the informant – who must himself have been from one of these underclasses – to the Spartan marketplace to show him that together they vastly outnumbered their Spartiate superiors, where he was invited to count the number of Spartiates present. Having tallied up the kings, ephors and about forty other Spartiates, Cinadon explained to him that these people were the 'enemies', and that everyone else there – more than 4,000 – were 'allies'. Cinadon had then led him through the streets of Sparta, labelling the one or two Spartiates there enemies, and everyone else allies. Then they wandered through some of the nearby estates owned by Spartiates; almost everyone they saw was an ally. The informant added that Cinadon had told him that those conspirators who served in the army had weapons; the rest of the 'allies' in town would get knives, swords, skewers, axes, hatchets and sickles from the iron market, while those who worked in the countryside would use the tools they used when working the land, timber and stone (presumably hoes, adzes and chisels).

The ephors wanted to act swiftly, but they were afraid to arrest Cinadon in the city of Sparta, because they did not know how many people were involved in the plot. They also wanted to get the names of Cinadon's accomplices out of him before they could realise that they had been fingered. So they resolved instead to send him as far away from the city as they could, while keeping him within the bounds of Lakonike, and have him arrested there. They chose Aulon, a perioikic town in western Messenia, near the border with Elis, and gave Cinadon orders to bring back a number of Aulonians and helots whose names were written in a coded *skytalē*. They also asked that he bring back a woman who was said to be the most beautiful in Aulon: she was accused of corrupting the Spartans who had travelled there.

The ephors were so well organised that some modern scholars see the episode as proof that the Spartans were able to control their underclasses through state terror. The ephors told Cinadon to ask the senior officer of the elite military unit called 'the knights' to provide him with six or seven men, but they had already arranged that the officer should send trustworthy men who had been told that their actual task was to arrest Cinadon. The ephors even told Cinadon that they would arrange three waggons, so that he wouldn't have to bring the prisoners back on foot. A regiment of horsemen were dispatched, ostensibly to help him round up the men on the list; the authorities didn't want to give Cinadon any clue that the only man who was going to be arrested was him.

The arresting officers had their own orders: to write down any names Cinadon divulged, and send them on to the ephors. When they arrested him, he quickly gave up some names. Although Xenophon doesn't disclose how he was encouraged to do so, Polyaenus – writing later – is open about the fact that Cinadon was tortured.[2] When the 'hit list' arrived in Sparta, the ephors immediately arrested the most influential conspirators, including the seer Tisamenus, which nipped the plot in the bud. When Cinadon was brought back to Sparta, the ephors extracted even more names from him. Before binding Cinadon's hands, fixing his neck in a collar and dragging him through the city under lashes and goads, the ephors demanded to know what he hoped to achieve. Cinadon replied simply, 'To be inferior to no one in Lacedaemon.'[3]

Not only does this episode show us how well organised the Spartan state was when it came to dealing with potential insurrections, the very existence of these social 'inferiors', and Cinadon's conspiracy itself, further points to an inherent flaw in Spartan society: the supposed 'equals' were not as equal as they were meant to be. However, explaining the nature of Cinadon's inferiority has proved challenging, as this is the only reference to 'inferiors' in all the ancient literature about Sparta. We know that Cinadon was not deemed physically inferior – Xenophon calls him 'young in body and stout in spirit', and Aristotle calls him 'manly'.[4] Nor does the fact that the ephors made extensive use of Cinadon's skills in a military context suggest that he had been degraded due to cowardice or intellectual deficiency, and there is no hint that his inferiority relates to birth. Furthermore, he clearly distinguished himself from the other classes who hated the Spartiates: the *perioikoi*, freedmen and helots. The only logical explanation, then, for Cinadon's inferiority is poverty. Most modern scholars assume that the inferiors were Spartiates who had been deprived of full citizen status because they were unable to make the food contributions required to maintain their membership in a common mess.

Losing his place as one of the *homoioi* must have been a bitter blow for a man like Cinadon. Indeed, Aristotle says that plots of this kind were an inevitable consequence of depriving otherwise excellent men of a share in the 'honours'.[5] Despite his manly nature, and excellence in war, after years of learning to be part of the in-group, Cinadon was suddenly one of the out-groups. His former peers would surely have treated him differently once he was no longer an 'us' but a 'them'. One can imagine them suddenly shunning him, or perhaps even bullying him – just as Spartiates reportedly mistreated cowards. From Cinadon's own words, we can see that finding himself 'inferior' cut him deeply.

* * *

How was it possible for Spartiates who were supposedly equal to become impoverished? The simple answer is that the *homoioi* were not really equals, but 'similars'. There is clear evidence of wealth inequality throughout Spartan history; their habit of calling themselves equals and dressing like high-status gentlemen represented part of a compromise between richer and poorer Spartiates. Thucydides claims that 'the Spartans were the first to adopt a more modest style of dress', such that 'the rich adopted a lifestyle more on equal footing with the poor'.[6] As noted earlier, coloured dyes were banned for non-military clothing, and no Spartan citizen was allowed to go outside better dressed than another. Aristotle criticised the excessive simplicity of Spartiate clothing, deeming it a form of 'boastfulness',[7] or what we might today call 'humblebragging'. Yet by focusing on how the rich had to dress more modestly within the confines of Spartan society, our sources are missing the fact that poorer Spartans were expected to 'style up', with elaborately braided hair and expensively dyed – albeit shabby – military cloaks.

Some Spartiates clearly owned vastly more land than others, as 'rich' Spartiates were able to bring extras like wheaten bread to the common messes.[8] As Spartan citizenship was dependent on producing large fixed amounts of barley, only those Spartans who had considerable land to spare would have been able to grow wheat, which was itself a prestige crop in Greece, with a failure rate five times that of barley. Other wealthy men might offer generous extras from their large flocks of sheep and goats for the 'afters' course.[9]

Wealth inequality in Sparta is also revealed by hunting practices. Xenophon notes that Spartans were legally permitted to borrow hunting hounds from other Spartiates – as long as they invited the dogs' owner to hunt with them.[10] This surely implies that the Spartiates who owned hounds were wealthier than those who didn't. In a rare moment of praise for Sparta, Aristotle argued that in 'well-run states', each person has his own possessions but also makes some available for 'communal use'; in Sparta, he noted, they use each other's slaves, horses and hunting dogs 'practically as their own'.[11]

The clearest indicator of wealth inequality is the fact that Spartans were conspicuously engaged in horse-breeding for sport, which in ancient Greece – as it remains – was the province of the wealthy. The Spartans appear to have been highly successful at the four-horse chariot race, which was the blue-ribbon event at the Olympic Games from the time of the conquest of Messenia through to Sparta's period of hegemony. The Spartan Euagoras won three consecutive races in 548, 544 and 540 BCE,[12] the Spartan king Demaratus won in 504 BCE,[13] Polypeithes won in 484 BCE, Arcesilaus won back-to-back in 448 and 444 BCE, and a Spartan team of horses won at every

Olympics between 432 and 420 BCE, and again between 396 and 388 BCE. The winner in 424 BCE, Polycles, was nicknamed Polychalcus ('abounding in bronze'), because his team of horses also won at the other great Panhellenic games – the Pythian, Isthmian and Nemean events – earning him four commemorative bronze statues.[14]

Spartans also competed successfully at the Panathenaic Games in Athens, with numerous fragments of Panathenaic amphoras unearthed at both the temple of Athena Chalkioikos and the Menelaion; these depict chariot scenes showing the winners dedicating their prizes to the gods. Spartans also competed in events within Lakonike. The so-called 'Damonon stele', a marble dedication to Athena Chalkioikos dating from around 400 BCE, commemorates the remarkable sporting achievements of Damonon and his son Enymakratidas at games throughout Lakonike, including more than forty four-horse chariot victories by Damonon and more than twenty horse-race wins by father and son. Topped by a relief depicting a four-horse chariot and driver, the dedication stresses that 'Damonon won with his own four-horse chariot, himself holding the reins'.

The known Spartan victories in Olympic chariot racing include two by the Spartan princess Cynisca,[15] sister of the Eurypontid kings Agis and Agesilaus, in 396 and 392 BCE. Her fame and prowess earned her a posthumous hero-shrine near the exercise grounds for Spartan male youths. She could probably have driven her team herself had she been allowed to compete, as rich Spartan girls drove racing chariots – the ancient Greek equivalent of a flashy sportscar – when the population of Sparta processed to Amyclae during the religious festival of the Hyacinthia.[16] But not all girls had such luxuries; Xenophon praises the Spartan king Agesilaus for insisting that his daughter took the 'public cart'.[17] Agesilaus' daughter did not take the public cart because of poverty – after all, she could surely have borrowed a racing chariot from her aunt; Agesilaus was trying to make a point about the insignificance of wealth with a performative act of austerity. Tradition had it that he encouraged Cynisca to enter her horses at the Olympics not for personal glory, but to show the men of Sparta that winning at chariot racing was a sign not of excellence but rather of 'having some money and spending it'.[18]

The property controlled by Spartan women indicates another sign of wealth inequality: some Spartan brides came with larger dowries than others. The wealthier the family, the bigger the dowry, which explains why when a poorer Spartan girl was asked what dowry she would bring to her husband, she replied, 'The family virtue.'[19] Aristotle complained about Spartan dowries, arguing that they ought to have been prohibited or at least limited in size.[20]

The Spartans may have felt the need to put special measures in place, in order to help poorer girls find a husband. A later source describes a bizarre ritual version of Spartan marriage by capture; unmarried maidens were locked in a dark room with eligible young men, and each Spartan married whichever girl he 'grabbed'. The notoriously poor Lysander acquired his wife this way, although he is reported to have tried to swap the girl with a prettier one when he saw what she looked like.[21]

*   *   *

The story of Lysander acquiring his wife thanks to a marriage lottery for the poor points to another sign of wealth inequality in Sparta: the existence of yet another social class of lesser Spartans, the so-called *mothakes*. Lysander was said to have started life as a *mothax*, as did Gylippus and Callicratidas. Although there is some confusion in our sources, it is generally agreed that *mothakes* were the sons of inferiors, free boys who would participate in the public upbringing alongside the sons of wealthy Spartiates as 'brothers by adoption' (*syntrophoi*). Spartan fathers would adopt one, two or more *syntrophoi* depending on their means,[22] to enhance their reputation and status – and that of their sons. As sons of Spartiates who had completed the public upbringing, the *mothakes* were eligible for Spartan citizenship – as long as they could pay for the necessary mess contributions. Thus it seems that if a wealthy Spartan wanted to, he could effectively reward a *mothax* with full citizenship by continuing to sponsor him into adulthood.

The Spartiate 'foster-brother' of the *mothax* would probably have been crucial in this decision. Having spent the best part of fifteen years with his foster-brother, it would surely have been hard for some not to have that relationship continue. Although Plutarch implies that Lysander was rewarded by the state with citizenship for showing 'manly excellence' during his upbringing,[23] it was more likely that a rich sponsor supplied him with the funds to join a mess. Sponsorship from a richer Spartan would probably explain how Gylippus, whose father Cleandridas had skipped town in 445 BCE to avoid paying a massive fine for allegedly taking a bribe from Pericles, acquired full citizen status.

Gylippus' impoverished background might also explain why, when Lysander entrusted him with the task of bringing 1,500 talents of silver plundered from Athens – the equivalent of £900 million or $1,350 million today – he couldn't resist the temptation to line his pockets. Thinking he was being immensely cunning, he opened the sacks at the bottom and took a large sum of money from each, before sewing them back up again. Gylippus then stashed his embezzled cash – some 300 talents (£180 million or $270 million today) – under his roof tiles. Had his crimes remained undetected, he and his family would have become filthy rich, even by Spartan standards.

Unfortunately for Gylippus, he was not nearly as sneaky as Lysander, who had left a note at the top of each sack indicating the precise amount that was inside. When the bags were collected and the money was counted, the ephors were confused as to why the amounts didn't tally. Then one of Gylippus' helots informed on him, telling the ephors that there were many owls sleeping under the roof tiles at Gylippus' house. The ephors realised that this was a reference to the fact that Athenian silver coins bore an image of an owl; they searched Gylippus' house and found the cash. By this one 'disgraceful and ignoble act', Gylippus undid his previous achievements in the Peloponnesian War, and was driven into exile.[24]

Gylippus was by no means the only Spartan to succumb to greed. Indeed, later sources cite an oracle from Apollo that prophesied that 'greed alone will destroy Sparta'.[25] We have already seen King Leotychidas being caught sitting on a sleeve full of silver,[26] Cleomenes being told by his daughter Gorgo to leave the room to avoid the temptation of bribes,[27] Eurybiades taking cash from Themistocles before agreeing to fight at Artemisium,[28] and Pleistoanax and Gylippus' father Cleandridas taking a bribe from Pericles.[29] Aristotle also found fault with the entire Spartan system of government, which allowed citizens he regarded as 'quite poor' to be elected as ephors. As far as he was concerned, the poor lacked the integrity to hold elected office, and could be easily bribed because of their poverty. Yet he provides only one example – some ephors who took bribes in 'the affair at Andros'.[30] Unfortunately we have no other evidence about this incident. Aristotle also suggests that Elders were easily bribed – though he makes no allegations regarding their comparative poverty. The problem Aristotle saw there was that the Elders were not required to submit accounts relating to their period in office. Had their activities been more closely scrutinised, they could have avoided the temptation to take bribes.[31]

*　*　*

It was not so much that Spartans didn't possess wealth, rather that they weren't meant to desire it or flaunt it – and Sparta's unwieldy iron currency made it awkward for Spartans to make flashy purchases. It may be that apart from the money they spent breeding horses, Spartans were effectively hoarding their wealth at home. Socrates claimed that more gold and silver was held privately in Sparta than elsewhere in Greece, but while there were 'tracks' showing the wealth going into their homes, there were none heading back out.[32]

It is probable that Sparta had a 'don't ask, don't tell' culture when it came to wealth. Dionysius of Halicarnassus claims that the Spartans paid no attention to what took place in each other's homes, 'holding that each man's front door marked the boundary within which he was free to live as he pleased'.[33] This rather undermines Xenophon's extravagant praise of the fact that the doors on Agesilaus' house were so old and unadorned they might have been the one set up for his mythical ancestor Aristodemus, the father of Procles and Eurysthenes, the first kings of Sparta.[34] Agesilaus was known to be very rich, and he helped make his friends rich, too;[35] but his wealth was safely hidden behind plain old doors.

Wealth inequality was closely connected to another key problem for the Spartans: the small size of their citizen population, often inadequate for Sparta's ambitions – and particularly so at the time Sparta achieved hegemony. Indeed, Aristotle considered *oliganthrōpia* – literally 'the scantiness of men' – the main cause of Sparta's eventual collapse.[36] The problem was partly a result of the fact that the Spartans set such a high bar for citizenship, requiring citizens to own at least fifteen hectares of land to maintain that status. This bar was so high that the largest Spartan army we ever hear about – the 5,000 Spartiates and 5,000 *perioikoi* at Plataea in 479 BCE – was barely one-third of the 30,000 hoplites and 1,500 cavalry that Aristotle thought Lakonike should be able to support. Modern estimates suggest there were between 115,000 and 145,000 hectares of land in Lakonike available for the Spartiates, enough for between 7,500 and 9,500 Spartiate families. Had the financial threshold for citizenship been lower, the Spartans could have had far more citizen hoplites available for their wars of conquest. If they had been able to put together armies of 30,000 hoplites, literally no Greek state – or even coalition of Greek states – could have stopped them.

Yet that was only part of the problem. Aristotle also noted that in the second half of the fourth century BCE there were not even 1,000 Spartiates. Indeed, studies have shown that during the years that followed Xerxes' invasion, there was a severe decline in Spartiate numbers, borne out by examination of the size of Spartan armies. Close reading of the sources suggests the following numbers for Spartiate males aged between twenty and forty-nine: 5,000 Spartiates at Plataea in 479 BCE, fewer than 3,000 Spartiates at Pylos in 425 BCE, little more than 2,000 at Mantinea in 418 BCE, fewer than 2,000 at the Battle of Nemea River in 394 BCE, and fewer than 1,000 at the Battle of Leuctra in 371 BCE. Put in simple terms, in around a century, the number of adult Spartiates available to fight in the phalanx decreased by more than 80 per cent.

To plug the gap, the Spartans seem to have relied increasingly on non-Spartiates: *perioikoi*, freed helots and allies. After sending the same number of *perioikoi* as Spartiates to Plataea, the proportion of *perioikoi* in the 'Spartan' army rose steeply; by the time of the fiasco at Pylos in 425 BCE and the great victory at Mantinea in 418 BCE, the proportion had risen to 60 per cent. This disparity worsens in the fourth century BCE, with the *perioikoi* contributing 66 per cent of the Spartan army at the Battle of Nemea River in 394 BCE, and as much as 75 per cent at the Battle of Leuctra in 371 BCE.

The decline in Spartan numbers means that after 479 BCE the Spartans were essentially reliant on the *perioikoi*, freed helots and their allies to project Spartan power and influence abroad. The disparity grew so great that the allies went so far as to tell Agesilaus that they were sick of being led 'hither and thither' each year to their destruction, when it meant so 'many' of them following so 'few' Spartan soldiers. Agesilaus had to resort to a trick to prove that the Spartans really did have sufficient soldiers to earn the right to lead the allies wherever they liked. He ordered the Spartans to sit in one place and the allies to sit elsewhere at random. Then he asked the potters to stand up, followed by the smiths, the carpenters, the builders and every other type of craftsman. In the end, only a few allies remained seated, and *all* the Spartans were still sitting, vastly outnumbering those of the allies who did not have to work for a living. Agesilaus then retorted, 'See, men, how many more *soldiers* we send out than you.'[37] (In the graphic novel and film *300*, this one-liner is given to Leonidas, to counteract criticism for sending only three hundred hoplites to Thermopylae. In Miller's version, the thwarted Arcadian ally mutters under his breath, 'Damn Spartans! They always know what to say.'). But witty one-liners were never going to fix the problem of *oliganthrōpia*, which has been likened to a spreading cancer that was poisoning Sparta from within.

* * *

How can we account for this dramatic fall in the number of Spartan citizens? An obvious answer that has been discussed, accepted, rejected and increasingly accepted again, is fatalities in combat. Research into combat casualties in the ancient world suggests that 5 per cent of fighters were killed in victories, and 14 per cent in defeats. Given the sheer amount of battles, skirmishes and sieges the Spartans were involved in between 480 and 371 BCE, this would account for a considerable amount of the decline in Spartiate numbers.

We know that at least 391 Spartiates died fighting against the Persians in 480 and 479 BCE – some 7.5 per cent of the Spartiates aged between twenty and forty-nine. To put that into perspective, 6 per cent of the adult male population of the UK died in combat during the First World War. We know of other significant combat losses in the decades that followed, including the 300 Spartiates who died with Arimnestos while fighting against the Messenian rebels on the Stenyclarus plain, and around 300 who fell at Mantinea in 418 BCE. Large numbers of Spartiates must have fallen in other battles – for example, at Dipaea against the Tegeans and Argives, when, as we saw earlier, the Spartans were reportedly so outnumbered they were stretched out in a single line, and the 'heavy' casualties the Spartans suffered in 457 BCE at the Battle of Tangara. There were other significant Spartiate losses in the fourth century BCE, such as the 250 Spartiates from Amyclae who fell at Lecheum in 390 BCE, and the 400 who fell at Leuctra in 371 BCE. There will have been other combat deaths in various other skirmishes and confrontations for which we have no real data. Together, these numbers would account for a significant amount of the decline in citizen numbers – but there were nonetheless other factors at play.

The earthquake in the 460s BCE also had a significant impact on the number of Spartan citizens. Diodorus' claim that 20,000 Lacedaemonians were killed suggests that a significant number of Spartiates would have been killed along with the families. Plutarch even claims that all the 'ephebes' (presumably the *paidiskoi* aged between fourteen and twenty) were killed when their gymnasium collapsed on them. They were apparently exercising with the 'neaniskoi' (presumably the young adults aged between twenty and thirty) in the interior of the colonnade. Just before the earthquake was felt, a hare appeared, and the oiled-up neaniskoi dashed out to chase it 'like boys'. But the 'ephebes' remained behind, and they perished together when the gymnasium fell on them.[38] The loss of a significant number of teenagers will have not only cost the Spartans future hoplites at a crucial time; it will have had an impact on future fertility rates.

Spartan sexual practices after marriage might have also been part of the problem. Spartan husbands were actively discouraged from having sex with their wives too frequently, to ensure that they would be 'full of longing' for each other when they copulated. It was thought that this would ensure that their offspring would be healthier and stronger than if the lovers were 'glutted with one another'. The comparative infrequency of intercourse would have obviously reduced the chance that Spartan women were ovulating when they did copulate. Spartan women also married later in life than women elsewhere in Greece. Unlike Athenian girls, who would marry soon after puberty, Spartan girls married 'in the prime of their bodies', probably in their late teens. The Spartan rationale was that their offspring would be bigger and stronger, but a later marriage age would have reduced the number of years in which married Spartan women were fertile, compromising their childbearing potential. However, deaths in combat and natural disasters, and unusual sexual practices, were not the only cause of *oliganthrōpia* at Sparta; landownership rules were also to blame.

*   *   *

The problem was in some ways simple: the Spartiates could not all be both wealthy and equal at the same time. The notion that the Spartans were genuine equals comes from the unreliable story that Lycurgus redistributed Laconia into 9,000 equal, indivisible and legally inalienable plots called *klaroi*.[39] As we have seen, it was the conquest of Messenia that enabled the Spartans to reimagine themselves as the 'equals', wealthy gentleman of leisure. The unequal distribution of the conquered lands meant that the problem of wealth inequality was temporarily masked – but over the following centuries, Spartan wealth inequality grew increasingly worse, pushing more Spartans to the brink of poverty.

In other Greek city-states, a citizen could be dirt poor but still produce children who were citizens and might eventually become wealthy enough to be a hoplite. But in Sparta, a citizen needed at least fifteen hectares of land to maintain his citizen status, making *all* the Spartiates wealthy by ancient Greek standards. Indeed, Socrates claimed that the Spartans were far wealthier than Athenians in terms of the size of their estates, the number of slaves they owned, their livestock – especially horses – and even cash.[40] Provided every family had the 'correct' number of sons and daughters, this could have produced a stable pool of very wealthy Spartan citizen hoplites. Put simply, if a Spartiate had one son to inherit his property, that son's financial future would be secure. But if a Spartiate had two or even three sons, their inheritance would be divided and perhaps spread too thin to meet the output required for their mess contributions, leaving the next generation in danger of sliding into 'inferior' status. This is why Aristotle argued that the Spartans ought to have paid for the messes from public funds or ensured that contributions were means tested,[41] rather than requiring a flat fee. The wealthier Spartans could thus have subsidised the less well off. This was the case on Crete, where the messes were supplied from a public pool of produce and livestock that was stockpiled from citizen contributions, which in turn were based on a tithe rather than a flat fee.[42]

What would happen if our hypothetical Spartiate produced a son and a daughter? As Spartan women were able to inherit property in their own right, the inheritance would be split. If a Spartiate had *only* a daughter, the pressure on land available for citizens would have been even greater; unlike in Athens, where sole heiresses were immediately married off to their nearest male relative on their father's side, in order to keep the wealth in the family, there was no obligation in Sparta for heiresses to marry. If an heiress kept hold of her own landed wealth, it would potentially be lost forever from the pool of land available to support Spartiate hoplites. This was why Aristotle argued that the fact that two-fifths of the land in Lakonike was owned by women was a sign that Sparta was badly regulated.[43]

If a Spartan heiress did marry a citizen from another family, she would provide him with a more secure financial footing – but that would have led to further inequality due to what anthropologists call 'assortative mating patterns'. In other words, the Spartan men and women who inherited the most property would likely have married each other, rather than poorer Spartans. If this pattern continued generation after generation, more and more land in Lakonike would have been concentrated in fewer and fewer hands. The rich would get richer, the poor would get poorer, and the pool of inferiors and *mothakes* would have grown ever bigger.

What could the Spartans have done to address this problem? If a citizen was in danger of defaulting on his mess contributions, the options open to him might have included bachelorhood (to avoid the cost of raising children and to minimise the risk of dividing his estate between too many heirs), wife-sharing (in effect, leaving someone else to pay for 'his' child), borrowing from richer Spartans (perhaps using land as security for the loan), or selling off some land to release funds to buy the necessary foodstuffs. Both of the latter options would have been dangerous in the long term. So too would chasing one of the incentives the Spartans did put in place to encourage child-rearing, such as exempting fathers of three from garrison duty, fathers of four from all forms of taxation, presumably including mess contributions, and allowing fathers of five to marry off their daughters without a dowry.[44] As tempting as these might have been for poorer Spartans, aiming for these incentives would have been risky; falling short would have stretched the family resources to no benefit.

Wife-sharing (polyandry) would not have helped raise the Spartan birth rate either, even if it might have been intended to. If a Spartan did not wish to be married, it was legal for him to have children by 'any fertile and well-bred woman', provided he had her husband's consent. If an older man had a young, fertile wife, he could choose to 'introduce' her to any young man whose physical or moral qualities he admired – for the purpose of begetting children.[45] Later sources suggest that it was 'common custom' for three or four poorer Spartans to share a wife.[46] This would have allowed a family's limited land resources to stay intact, but it would have reduced the potential growth of the Spartan citizen population. Although Spartan women are often seen as sexually liberated, there is no hint in our sources that they had any choice in how their husbands farmed them out.

The Spartans clearly did try to increase the birth rate, imposing penalties on long-term bachelors. In winter, the magistrates would order them to parade naked in a circle round the marketplace; as they did so, they had to sing a song stressing that their punishment was fair because they were flouting the laws.[47] This 'festival' sounds like an inversion of the choruses at the Gymnopaidiai festival, when choruses of men and boys would parade while singing during the searing summer heat. The reverse-Gymnopaidiai might be the same festival at which unmarried Spartan girls dragged bachelors around an altar while beating them with sticks, supposedly in order to 'make them fall in love'.[48] Mature bachelors were also deprived of the honour and attention which the young normally bestowed on elders. No one criticised a young Spartan who refused to give up his seat to the fifth-century BCE general Dercylidas, a long-term bachelor. The young Spartan bluntly told Dercylidas, 'No, for you are not the father of any son who will rise and offer his seat to me.'[49]

The Spartans could have increased citizen numbers by making Spartiate status accessible to non-Spartans, as indeed Aristotle suggested,[50] but it was not until the third century BCE, when the reforming kings Agis IV and Cleomenes III tried to revive Spartan power, that the Spartans tried opening up citizenship to the *perioikoi* and even foreigners. At the time they achieved their hegemony and were seeking to extend their power and influence into Asia, there just weren't enough Spartiates on the ground to secure their position, let alone permit expansion. Sparta was like a dying tree, hollowed out and ready to be cut down by enemies both at home and abroad.

10

Spartan Hegemony:
Empire at Last?

404–386 BCE

Modern impression made from a grey banded chalcedony cylinder seal (sixth to fourth century BCE), depicting a Persian warrior striking at a Greek hoplite, beneath a winged solar disc.

When Gylippus attempted to steal 300 of the 1,500 talents of silver Lysander had entrusted him with bringing back from Athens (the equivalent of £180 million or $270 million today), it was hardly a good omen for how Sparta would handle being the dominant Greek power. After all the noises they had made about liberating Greece from Athenian tyranny, they simply replaced it with their own. One ancient Greek historian compared them to dishonest barmaids who add bitter and sour wine to the best and sweetest; having enticed the Greeks to war by promising them freedom, they imposed tyrants, puppet regimes and 'harmosts' – a Spartan term for a military governor.[1] Even the normally partisan Xenophon describes himself as observing that the Spartans – both collectively and individually – could do 'whatever they want' in any Greek city.[2]

Xenophon (c. 430-354 BCE) is our main narrative source for the period of Spartan hegemony. A one-time student of Socrates, and later a mercenary commander, he was a very different writer from both Herodotus and Thucydides. He wrote two historical works: the *Anabasis*, an account of the expedition of the 'Ten Thousand', an army of Greek mercenaries hired by Cyrus the Younger to help him seize the throne of Persia from his brother, Artaxerxes II, in 401 BCE; and a narrative history covering the period from 411 to 362 BCE. Xenophon also wrote an encomium of the Spartan king Agesilaus, an account of the *Constitution of the Lacedaemonians*, as well as various works of philosophy, including *Apology of Socrates to the Jury* (a defence of his former teacher) and a work on the *Art of Horsemanship*. Xenophon was friends with Agesilaus, and often writes more glowingly of the Eurypontid king than an impartial observer might. He also frequently highlights Sparta's uniqueness to demonstrate what he perceives as the superiority of Spartan society over other Greek states. Despite his wealth of insider knowledge, Xenophon's partiality towards the Spartans, and especially Agesilaus, makes him a challenging source to use effectively when exploring the period of Spartan hegemony.

As Xenophon noted, this period opened up a new world of opportunities to the Spartans. This was especially true for Lysander. Statues of him were erected in cities throughout Greece, and governing councils of ten individuals called 'dekarchies', which he imposed on Athens' former subjects, were prepared to toady to him throughout Asia. The Samians literally worshipped Lysander as a demigod, building an altar to him, offering sacrifices to him and singing hymns, as if he were a god.[3] One of them began: 'We sing a hymn to the general of blessed Greece from spacious Sparta, O, Io, Paean!' The Samians even renamed their major religious festival, held in honour of the goddess Hera, the 'Heraea Lysandreia'. As odd as this may sound, a damaged inscription found at Hera's sanctuary on Samos, honouring an athlete who was 'victor in the *pankration* for the fourth time at the Lysandreia', confirms that it really did happen.

Despite this ascendancy, however, Lysander and the Spartan hegemony would soon be tested, when civil war broke out in Athens.

*   *   *

The Thirty, who ruled Athens with Spartan backing, had set about reorganising Athenian government to suit themselves. They established a new council of 500, and appointed ten officials to manage the Athenian port of Piraeus. They put the Athenian politicians who had opposed the peace deal with Sparta on trial in the new council, and having found them guilty, put them to death. They also tried and executed a range of Athenians they deemed 'undesirable'. The Thirty limited citizenship – and (as they put it) the right to share in the government – to 3,000 selected Athenians, but they never quite got round to finalising their list, allowing them to act as they pleased.

Two of their number – Aeschines and Aristoteles – were closely linked with Lysander, whom they convinced to install a Spartan garrison in Piraeus. The garrison, which was most likely manned by freed helots, was ostensibly put in place to help the Thirty deal with the 'criminals' in Athens. In reality, though, they used it to help them rule Athens with an iron fist. Protected by their Spartan garrison, the Thirty – Critias in particular – embarked on what can be best described as a bloodbath. They hired 300 'whip bearers' to police the city, and executed, murdered or exiled hundreds of wealthy political opponents and resident aliens. They often targeted the wealthy, in order to confiscate their assets. Among the prominent victims were two wealthy resident aliens: Lysias, a prominent speech writer, and his brother Polemarchus, who ran a shield-making workshop in Piraeus. In his prosecution speech *Against Eratosthenes*, Lysias provides a vivid account of their arrest on trumped-up charges by Eratosthenes – one of the Thirty – so that the Thirty would have cause to confiscate their substantial wealth and property. Lysias managed to escape through the back door of the house in which he was imprisoned, but Polemarchus was executed, forced to drink poisonous hemlock. The Thirty even targeted one of their own; Critias accused Theramenes of treason and put him on trial in the council. When forced to drink hemlock, Theramenes went out with some style; as he drained his cup, he flung the dregs on the floor, and made a toast to Critias' good health as if he were drinking wine at a banquet.

While the Thirty were embarking on their reign of terror, the Spartan garrison commander Callibius scarcely covered himself with glory either. Plutarch reports an incident when he tried to strike the champion Athenian athlete Autolycus with his staff – only for the pentathlete, an accomplished wrestler, to seize Callibius' legs and throw him to the ground. When Callibius complained to Lysander, he rebuked him for not understanding how to govern free men. Callibius was by no means the first Spartan to fail to cope with foreigners not showing him what he deemed to be due respect, and nor would he be the last, but the Thirty had Autolycus put to death.[4]

Soon after Theramenes was executed, the former Athenian general Thrasybulus seized the Athenian border fort of Phyle with a ragtag bunch of democrats, resident aliens and slaves, before marching down to Piraeus, well known as a hothouse of democracy, and rallying the so-called 'men of Piraeus' to his cause. Thrasybulus led the rebels to victory over the forces of the Thirty in a pitched battle near the port. Critias was killed in the fighting, and the survivors of the Thirty fled to the Athenian deme of Eleusis on the western fringes of Athenian territory, where they set up a new mini *polis*. The 'Ten', previously in control of Piraeus, took control of the city of Athens itself, and then both oligarchic groups begged the Spartans for help. They responded by lending them 100 talents (equivalent to £60 million or $90 million today), with which the oligarchs could hire mercenaries. They also sent Lysander to take control of the city, and his brother Libys led a naval force to blockade Piraeus.

The Spartans might have regained control of Athens, but the Eurypontid king Pausanias, who was said to be jealous of Lysander, intervened to stymie his plans. Xenophon claims that he brought an army to Attica, nominally to support the Thirty Tyrants against the democratic rebels, but in reality to undermine Lysander. Before he set off, Pausanias was wise enough to convince the ephors that his plan was the right course of action. He camped near Piraeus, where the democrats were based, and ordered them to disperse. When they refused, Pausanias took a detachment of two *morai* – one-third of the whole Spartan army – and three units of Athenian cavalry, to see whether he could shut off Piraeus with a wall. However, while they were away from the main army, Pausanias and his men were attacked by a contingent of Athenian democratic rebels who were fighting as light-armed soldiers rather than hoplites. Angered by this, he ordered the Athenian horsemen, and those Spartans aged between twenty and thirty, to chase the Athenian troops, while he followed with the rest of his detachment. The young Spartan hoplites and the Athenian cavalrymen killed nearly thirty light-armed Athenians and chased the rest to the theatre in Piraeus.[5]

Once the Spartan hoplites entered the theatre, they found themselves facing the rest of the light-armed troops, the democratic Athenian hoplites and the general Thrasybulus. The light-armed troops threw javelins, stones and sling-bullets, and launched arrows, causing the Spartans to fall back. Xenophon is at pains to stress that they did not turn their backs on the enemy – the Spartans definitely didn't retreat. Thrasybulus drew up his hoplites in a phalanx eight ranks deep and pressed Pausanias' men back by four or five stadia (between 750 and 900 metres), to a hill where they regrouped and linked up with the rest of his army. Pausanias then formed what Xenophon calls 'an extremely deep phalanx' and pushed downhill, driving the democratic Athenians back to the marshes near the Athenian deme of Halae, several kilometres away. Nearly 150 Athenians were killed in the fighting, and Pausanias set up a trophy on the spot where the Athenians had retreated to indicate his victory.[6]

The Spartan polemarchs Chaeron and Thibraechus were killed in the fighting, as well as the Olympic victor Lacrites.

Xenophon says that they and the rest of the Spartans were buried in front of the gates of Athens in the region called the Kerameikos, where the Athenians buried their dead, and archaeologists have even identified their tomb: an inscription (in Doric script) bears the names and titles of Chaeron and Thibraechus, and the first two letters of the word 'Lacedaemonians'. The tomb, which is around twenty-four metres long, four metres wide and nearly three metres high, lies roughly parallel to the ancient road that leads to Plato's Academy. All of the twenty-three interred individuals are male, with their bodies placed parallel to each other in an extended supine position, and their heads facing roughly east. All the bodies seem to have been wrapped in cloth before they were buried, and the only surviving grave offering is a small flask (*alabastron*) found alongside one of the skeletons – which seems to corroborate Plutarch's claim that Spartiate soldiers who died in combat were buried with just their red cloak and olive leaves. Two skeletons were separated from the others by large stone blocks. Given the age at which they died – approximately thirty-three and fifty years old – the excavators have suggested that these might be the bodies of the polemarchs. Another skeleton, approximately twenty years old at the time of his death, has been tentatively identified as the Olympic victor Lacrates.

Pausanias was not angry with the democrats despite their attack, and set about orchestrating a deal between them and the oligarchs. This saw the return of democracy to Athens, and the exile of the remaining members of the Thirty. The Athenians proclaimed a general amnesty – perhaps the first in history – swearing oaths that they would 'forget' everything that had happened in the past. Xenophon stresses that at the time he was writing, some fifty years later, the Athenians were still abiding by their oaths.[7]

When Pausanias returned to Sparta he was put on trial for

his leniency towards the Athenians; the court that tried him consisted of the Elders, the ephors and his co-king. Fourteen of the elders voted to convict Pausanias, but the ephors – who had pre-approved his plans for Athens – swung the vote in his favour. His co-king Agis, however, voted to condemn him,[8] which must have made life at the kings' mess table interesting.

*   *   *

Around this time, the Spartans proclaimed that all the Greek cities were free to be governed according to their 'ancestral constitutions', thus ending the rule of Lysander's dekarchies. Giving the Greeks their freedom after decades of Athenian rule might sound altruistic, but 'freedom' was, after all, the official reason why the Spartans had gone to war against Athens in the first place. However, the proclamation was probably a move by Lysander's opponents to rein in his influence in Asia.

It also gave the Spartans a pretext to revenge themselves on the Eleans, with whom, Xenophon says, they 'had been angry for a long time' because of the alliance they made with Athens, Argos and Mantinea in 421 BCE, and for banning them from the Olympics. When the Eleans refused to accept that the small neighbouring *polis* of Lepreum should be independent, the Spartans decided to 'bring them to their senses' and sent an invasion force to plunder Elean territory and set up a garrison. The Spartan intervention prompted a revolt by the Lepreans and other small *poleis* subjugated by the Eleans. The show of force from Sparta was enough to prompt the Eleans to submit. Spartan control of the Peloponnese now seemed very secure indeed.

*   *   *

After dealing with their allies close to home, the Spartans became embroiled in war with ones further afield when they supported Cyrus the Younger in a rebellion against his elder brother Artaxerxes II. When Cyrus asked for their help, thirty-five Peloponnesian warships were dispatched eastwards under the command of the Spartan admiral Samius, accompanied by 700 hoplites (probably mercenaries), commanded by the Spartiate Cheirisophus.[9] These forces linked up with more than 10,000 Greek mercenaries who were under the command of another Spartan, Clearchus; although he was formally exiled from Sparta, the Spartans sent a *skytalē* to him ordering him to give Cyrus every assistance.[10] Xenophon describes Clearchus as 'level-headed in the most dangerous conditions', a harsh disciplinarian, and 'good at impressing upon his companions that he was to be obeyed'. Clearchus could have enjoyed a quiet and peaceful life in Sparta after the Peloponnesian War, but he effectively engineered his own exile – as Xenophon puts it, he was 'not just good at warfare, but absolutely devoted to it'.[11] A man who was too warlike for the Spartans must have been warlike indeed.

At the decisive Battle of Cunaxa, Cyrus' troops won the day, though he himself fell in the fighting as he tried to reach his brother, desperate to fight him in single combat. Clearchus' troops reportedly didn't suffer a single casualty. Cyrus' death meant that Artaxerxes' throne was secure, but Clearchus' mercenaries had proved such formidable fighters that the Persians were afraid of the havoc they could cause. So Artaxerxes' general Tissaphernes came up with a means of removing them, luring Clearchus into a meeting under the pretence of arranging a safe withdrawal from Persian territory for Clearchus and his 10,000 Greek troops. When Clearchus arrived for the meeting, Tissaphernes had him arrested and thrown into prison. The shocked mercenaries elected new leaders, including Xenophon, and eventually fought their way back to the Black Sea region, where Xenophon ended up joining up with the Spartans, and ultimately with the Eurypontid king Agesilaus.

Clearchus never left Asia. When Ctesias, a Greek doctor at Artaxerxes' court, visited him in prison, he found the Spartan gaunt and dishevelled. When he asked Clearchus if he could do anything to help him, the Spartan asked only for a comb so that he could prepare for death by tending to his long, bedraggled hair. When his wish was fulfilled, Clearchus was so grateful that he gave Ctesias his signet ring as a token of friendship, which he might show to his kindred and friends in Sparta if he ever travelled there. When Ctesias arranged for extra meat portions to be sent to the half-starved Clearchus, the Spartan asked for a knife to be secreted into them so he could end his life on his own terms. Sadly, Ctesias was unable to help, and Artaxerxes had Clearchus executed.[12]

Once Cyrus was dead, the Spartans seem to have considered their alliance with the Persians void. Their next step was to launch an invasion of Asia Minor to liberate the Greek cities there from Persian rule – a huge challenge, and one that Sparta didn't have the manpower to take on. The campaign was almost certainly the brainchild of Lysander, who saw the war as an opportunity to grow his power and influence. So, too, did his protégé, the new Eurypontid king Agesilaus.

*   *   *

Lysander had become Agesilaus' mentor during the Spartan upbringing, after the younger man had caught his eye with his 'disciplined nature'.[13] But for the ambitious Lysander, the fact that Agesilaus was the then king Agis's younger brother might also have been part of the appeal.

In Classical Greece, a mentorship like Lysander's of Agesilaus entailed a homoerotic relationship. The ancient Greek term for this was 'pederasty', derived from *pais* ('boy') and *erasthai* ('to love'). In Athens, the term *erastēs* ('the one who loves') was generally used to describe the elder partner in such a relationship and *erōmenos* ('the one who is loved') to describe the boy. This has often been interpreted by modern scholars as implying that the older male played the active sexual role in anal intercourse, and the younger boy the passive, but this is by no means clear, and many Greek vase paintings depict lovers engaging while facing each other, implying they engaged in intercrural or 'thigh sex'.

What practices Spartan lovers engaged in is not clear. Xenophon is at pains to point out that pederastic unions at Sparta were not sexual, and that 'lovers [*erastai*] should refrain from molesting boys just as much as parents avoid intercourse with their children, or brothers with their sisters'. He describes the Spartans as taking the middle ground between Greek *poleis* such as Thebes or Elis, where sexual union between men and boys was promoted, and others where would-be lovers were debarred from even talking to boys. At Sparta, men were permitted to 'love' boys provided the man was of the 'right character', and his interest was 'innocent' and related to 'admiration for a boy's personality'.[14] Plutarch takes a similar line, claiming that 'affectionate regard for boys of good character was permissible, but embracing them was held to be disgraceful'. He goes so far as to claim that a complaint of 'disgraceful embracing' would lead to the older Spartiate being deprived of civic rights.[15]

Nonetheless, it seems that Xenophon and Plutarch might be protesting too much. The term *kusolakōn* – 'Laconian buttocks' – became a popular euphemism for anal intercourse outside of Sparta, particularly in Athens, and Plato overtly rejected Sparta as a model for his ideal state where pederasty was forbidden.[16] We even have a painted Laconian cup from around

550 BCE, found at the sanctuary of Orthia, which appears to depict Spartan males engaging in anal intercourse. It is difficult to tell, because only poor-quality photographs have been published and a line drawing from the 1930s has been described as 'inaccurate', but one figure, who is bent forward while being anally penetrated, is almost certainly male. He even appears to have stripes on his back, perhaps suggesting that he is being whipped. Another male figure being pursued by a satyr-like figure appears to have drops of blood flowing from his backside.

A fragmentary Athenian vase painting from the early fifth century BCE depicts the naked god Zephyros thrusting his erect penis between the legs of the Amyclaean prince Hyacinthus, who is fully clothed. This image has been linked to a fragmentary text of Cicero, which claims that in 'amatory relations with young men' the Spartans 'permit intercourse with cloaks between'.[17] This Clintonesque get-out as to what constituted 'sexual relations' would allow us to see that Xenophon and Plato were both telling the truth about Spartan pederasty.

*   *   *

When Agis died in 400 BCE, his son Leotychides should have succeeded him. But Lysander and Agesilaus took advantage of the old story that Alcibiades had seduced Leotychides' mother Timaea and used it against him. But Leotychides received support from Diopithes, a man with great knowledge of oracles, who reminded the Spartans of Apollo's warning that they should 'beware the lame kingship'. This, he argued, should debar Agesilaus, who was lame in one leg.

Modern scholars have contorted themselves trying to explain how Agesilaus survived infancy. Plutarch claims that newborn Spartan babies were inspected by the eldest men in the tribe, who would immerse them in unmixed wine to test their reactions. Those who were weak or disabled were apparently cast into a 'precipitous spot' near Mount Taygetus, known as Apothetae (from the Greek *apotithēmi*, 'to put away').[18] However, given that Plutarch is the only source to mention this practice, and doesn't mention it in his biography of Agesilaus, it may just be a myth. Modern admirers of Sparta might be appalled to know that Adolf Hitler praised the Spartans' exposure of 'sick, frail, deformed children' as evidence of their 'racial superiority' in his 'unpublished' sequel to *Mein Kampf*, the so-called *Zweites Buch*.[19]

Lysander successfully argued that the oracle did not mean that the Spartans should beware of a king of theirs who might 'pull a muscle and become lame'; it rather meant that they should not allow someone who was not of royal blood to accede to the throne.[20] Clearly fearing that Leotychides may not have been a true descendant of Heracles, the Spartans made Agesilaus king in his place. Lysander presumably assumed that he would be able to take on the role of puppet master when Agesilaus became king, but it didn't quite turn out that way.

By all accounts, Agesilaus was an unusual Spartan king. This was partly due to the fact that he had been required to undergo the tough upbringing from which heirs-apparent were usually exempt. As Plutarch puts it, 'Agesilaus was singular in ... that he had been educated to obey before he came to command', and because he had endured the communal upbringing, 'he was much more in harmony with his subjects than any of the kings'.[21]

Nonetheless, Agesilaus was by no means the typical Spartan. Not only was he lame, he was so short that the ephors were said to have fined his father Archidamus for marrying his mother Timarete, who was so tiny that she would produce 'kinglets' rather than kings.[22] Whatever disability caused his lameness was significant enough to be noticed, but not so serious that it held him back. Plutarch does not shed much light on how tough it must have been for Agesilaus undergoing such a physical upbringing with a disability. Despite the fact that he uses the word *pērōsis*, which can mean 'maiming' or 'mutilation', Plutarch claims that Agesilaus made jokes about himself, and writes that 'the beauty of his physique' during his youth effectively 'hid' the disability. But elsewhere Plutarch provides evidence of how callous the Spartans could be when it came to physical disability; when a Spartan who could only crawl around on all fours, having been wounded in combat, complained to his mother that he was mocked by his peers, her terse reply was: 'How much better, child, to be joyful over your *andreia* [courage], than to be ashamed of ignorant laughter.'[23] This might sound uplifting but fails to mask the fact that Spartans were laughing at a veteran, who had been disabled fighting in the phalanx alongside them. Later in life, a chorus master relegated Agesilaus to the back of a choir – presumably so that he could not be easily seen. Agesilaus laughed it off, claiming that his presence would bring the back row 'distinction', but being hidden from view clearly stung.

*   *   *

Not long after Agesilaus became king, the ephors discovered – and dealt with – the plot by the inferior Cinadon to overthrow the Spartans.[24] Soon after that, news spread that the Persian king was building 300 triremes, with a view towards 'driving the Spartans from the sea'. Agesilaus went before the assembly and offered to undertake the war if they would give him thirty Spartiates as 'advisors' and 8,000 hoplites (2,000 of the best *neodamodeis* and 6,000 allies).[25] Lysander travelled with Agesilaus as one of these 'advisors'. Xenophon suggests that the campaign was Lysander's idea;[26] it may be that he envisaged his role as similar to his full command of the fleet while nominally only vice-admiral at the Battle of Aegospotami in 404 BCE.

Agesilaus, however, was far too power-hungry to allow that. We can see Agesilaus' ambition in his sacrifice of a hind to Artemis at Aulis in Boeotia before crossing to Asia. With this act, Agesilaus was casting himself in the role of the great Achaean king Agamemnon, who sacrificed his daughter Iphigenia at Aulis – also at the command of the goddess Artemis – to ensure he received the right winds for the expedition to Troy. The night before, Agesilaus had had a dream in which a voice told him that no one except Agamemnon had ever been appointed general of all Greece; since they waged wars on the same foes, it was right that he should sacrifice to the goddess as Agamemnon had done. But the Thebans were angry that a Spartan was making a sacrifice in their territory, contrary to their laws and customs; they interrupted Agesilaus' sacrifice, literally flinging remains of the sacrificial victim from the altar. By all accounts Agesilaus was furious at being thwarted, and Xenophon says he called on all the gods to witness his being wronged.[27]

Nor did things get off to an auspicious start in Asia. When they arrived in Ephesus, Agesilaus soon spotted that the local statesmen were addressing their petitions to Lysander rather than him and was 'maddened' by the attention the other man received.[28] The other Spartan advisors were equally peeved, rounding on Agesilaus to complain about Lysander's behaviour.

Rather than showing his anger to Lysander, Agesilaus set about subtly humiliating him by sending his wealthy and powerful foreign contacts away empty-handed. When Lysander realised what was happening, he advised them to go straight to the king, rather than risk being ignored, but that didn't stop crowds of ordinary people thronging around Lysander – who had after all been recognised as a demigod in the region – when he walked about town or exercised in the gymnasium. Agesilaus, who frankly seems rather petty, now found the ultimate way of putting Lysander in his place, appointing him not as a general or a governor, but as his 'carver of meats'. Humiliated, Lysander told Agesilaus, 'You know well how to cut down your friends,' to which Agesilaus retorted, 'Yes, if they would try to be mightier than me.'

Soon afterwards, Agesilaus sent Lysander away. The older man was so angry that he resolved to change the whole constitution of Sparta and make the kingship open to all Spartiates. Long afterwards, when Lysander was dead, Agesilaus found a speech that he had commissioned – and reportedly memorised – from the philosopher Cleon of Halicarnassus, arguing that Spartan kings should be chosen on merit rather than birth. Agesilaus was so enraged that he wanted to show it to the Spartans, as proof of what Lysander was really like. But the ephor of the day – Lacratidas – wisely advised Agesilaus not to 'dig Lysander up again'.

Freed from Lysander's interference, Agesilaus set about trying to deal with the Persians, who had given him a blunt ultimatum that he should get out of Asia or face the consequences. Agesilaus had no intention to leave and set about trying to stir up trouble for the Persian satraps Tissaphernes and Pharnabazus. When the Spartan king learned of a falling-out between Pharnabazus and yet another satrap – Spithridates – he made an alliance with the latter.

The connection with Spithridates allows Xenophon to tell a story about Agesilaus' habitual self-control. Apparently, Agesilaus 'ardently loved' Megabates, the handsome young son of Spithridates, but refused to even receive kisses from him. But when his self-restraint led the slighted Megabates to stop trying to kiss him, Agesilaus asked one of his companions to persuade Megabates to honour him with kisses again. When the Persian asked the short and lame Agesilaus if he would ever kiss Megabates, the Spartan king said, 'No, by the Twin Gods, not if I were to become straight away the fairest, strongest and fleetest man on earth!' Agesilaus then added an oath: 'I swear that I would rather fight that same battle over again than that everything I see should turn into gold.'[29] The way Xenophon tells it, it was not enough for Agesilaus to merely follow the rules: he actively enjoyed having his resolve tested, and proving himself to have real self-control.

Love affairs aside, Agesilaus achieved several minor victories over the Persians and performed well enough against Tissaphernes that Artaxerxes had his satrap executed and replaced. But Agesilaus' ambitions in Asia were undermined by a lack of manpower and cavalry – a virtual army was never going to cut it when faced with the might of the Persians. When Alexander the Great invaded Asia in 334 BCE, he took 30,000 infantry and 5,000 horse, followed up by tens of thousands of reinforcements over the years that followed. Agesilaus had nothing even close to that.

In the winter of 396 BCE, Agesilaus tried to increase his forces; he called up the Greeks of Asia for service as hoplites and light-armed troops (known as 'peltasts'), and levied the best possible cavalry by offering the richest Greeks exemption from military service if they provided a horse and a fit cavalryman. Xenophon describes Agesilaus' army training; the hoplites exercised in the gymnasium while the horsemen practised in the hippodrome, and the peltasts and archers undertook continual target practice.[30] This passage is the closest we get to primary source evidence of what training a Spartan army might undertake. Agesilaus also made the Greeks of Asia build 120 triremes; he gave command of the fleet to his brother-in-law Peisander, reportedly to please his wife.[31]

According to Xenophon and Plutarch, Agesilaus had grandiose hopes of invading the Persian heartland.[32] But even if he really did hope to take his tiny army all the way to Persia, he never got the chance – for at that point, Artaxerxes sent substantial sums of money to Athens, Thebes, Argos and Corinth and encouraged them to make war on the Spartans. All four states agreed to an alliance, and although Xenophon says the Athenians refused the Persian money, Diodorus says they were happy to take the cash. All of this seems to have come as a surprise to the Spartans, who had been so convinced that they did not need help from the Persians anymore that it never seems to have entered their heads that the Persians might turn on them. The Spartans also seem to have been caught out by the fact that less than a decade of Spartan rule had led the Corinthians and Thebans, who had previously wanted to wipe Athens from the face of the earth, to seek an alliance with the Athenians against them.

*　*　*

The Corinthian War, which began in 396 BCE, was a serious threat to Sparta's hegemony in Greece. In fact, the historian Polybius treats the beginning of the war as the end point of Spartan hegemony, observing that 'the Spartans after disputing for the hegemony of the Greeks for many years, eventually attained it, but held it only for twelve years.'[33]

As with the Archidamian War, when actions far from Sparta led them into the conflict, the dispute that started the Corinthian War took place on the fringes of the Spartan sphere of influence. When the Thebans interfered in fighting between the Phocians and the Locrians, the Phocians appealed to Sparta for help – at which Lysander persuaded the Spartans to intervene and install a garrison in Thebes to ensure their obedience to Sparta. Lysander also persuaded the ephors to place him in command, even though land warfare was not obviously part of his skill set, given that he had only previously held commands at sea. The plan the Spartans hatched was for Lysander to descend on Thebes from the north, while Pausanias would lead a larger force from the Peloponnese; the two would rendezvous at the Boeotian city of Haliartus, a key ally of Thebes.

Unfortunately, the timing went wrong. Lysander arrived first and sent a rider with a message to Pausanias, telling him that he was at Haliartus and ready to attack. But the rider was caught by the Thebans, who then sent hoplites to Haliartus to help – and somehow Lysander failed to notice the Theban troops entering the city. The next day, Lysander was either too bold or too foolish and brought his troops too close to the walls of the city. The Thebans sensed an opportunity and sallied out; Lysander was killed. Pausanias then arrived with his army, but it was too late. He made a truce with the Thebans to collect the dead, and Lysander was given a proper burial, but many of the Spartan hoplites were angry about this and told Pausanias that he ought to have fought to recover Lysander's body. It would have been better to die with the general, they said, than to get his body back in such a shameful manner. Pausanias countered by arguing that it was not worth the risk, as Lysander's body was too close to the city walls, some of his men had run away, and the allies weren't really prepared for a fight.[34]

When he returned home, Pausanias was put on trial, charged with incompetence. His lenience towards the Athenians ten years earlier, when he allowed Athens to recover its democracy from the Thirty, was dredged up against him as well. Seeing the writing on the wall, Pausanias absconded to Tegea and was condemned to death *in absentia*. While living in exile he reportedly produced a pamphlet called '*kata* Lycurgus', which due to some ambiguity in the word *kata* meant either 'On Lycurgus' or 'Against Lycurgus'. Pausanias' son Agesipolis succeeded him.[35]

In desperate need of Agesilaus' troops, the Spartans recalled him from Asia, effectively ending the ambitions of both Sparta and Agesilaus for conquest there. Agesilaus was angry, but Xenophon stresses that he rushed home – he had 'no intention of arriving too late to aid his fatherland'. Agesilaus reportedly grumbled that the Persian king was driving him out of Asia with ten thousand 'archers', a reference to the Persian gold coins known as 'darics' (each worth 25 drachmas) that bore the image of an archer. If Agesilaus' one-liner is true, Artaxerxes had bribed the Greeks to go to war with Sparta with a mere 250,000 drachmas, the equivalent of just £25 million or $37.5 million today. If we trust Xenophon, the Thebans, Corinthians, Athenians and Argives didn't need that much convincing to shake off the Spartan shackles – but one of our less partial sources, the so-called 'Oxyrhynchus Historian', claims that Artaxerxes' bribes were not a decisive factor in beginning the war.[36]

* * *

By the time he reached Amphipolis in 394 BCE, Agesilaus learned that the Spartans had won a great victory at the Battle of Nemea River. According to Xenophon, the Spartans' opponents initially considered attacking the Spartans nearer to home, but thought better of it after the Corinthian Timolaus observed that when people try to get rid of a wasp nest, they succeed if they set fire to the nest while the wasps are inside, but tend to get stung if they try to catch the wasps on their way out of the nest.[37] It seems unlikely, however, that anyone would have dared suggest attacking the Spartans so close to their own territory at this stage, as they were still seen as the best fighters in Greece. The battle, which ended up taking place in Corinthian territory, near the Nemea river, underlined that superiority.

As at the Battle of Mantinea in 418 BCE, both armies edged to the right. This time the Spartan general Aristodemus – acting as regent for Agesipolis, the son of the exiled Pausanias

– did not try any complicated manoeuvres. But the allies on the left, who had been outflanked, were pushed back by the advancing Argives and some of the Athenians. In fact, many of the Spartans' enemies pursued their opponents far from the field of battle, but the Spartans on the right were able to out-flank the Athenians facing them, wheeling behind them as they advanced and killing large numbers, all while maintaining good order. This was a prime example of what Xenophon described as Sparta's greatest strength: 'fighting well in disorder'.[38]

As the Spartan hoplites continued to advance across the enemy lines, they encountered the Argives returning from routing their opponents. Xenophon writes that just as the polemarch was going to order the Spartans to meet the Argives head-on, someone shouted out from the Spartan ranks, 'Let their first ranks go past.' After they let the leading Argives pass by, the Spartans then struck down hordes of Argives as they came running past, their right sides being unprotected. Once the Argives were gone, they used the same tactic against the returning Corinthians, and then the Thebans. According to Diodorus, there were 1,100 casualties on the Spartan side, and 2,800 of the enemy died. But Xenophon adds the stunning detail that only *eight* Spartiates fell. When Agesilaus heard the good news, he is said to have exclaimed, 'Alas for Greece! Those who now lie dead were enough to defeat all the barbarians in battle had they lived!'[39]

*   *   *

On his way back home, Agesilaus was attacked by a large force of Thessalian cavalry – for the Thessalians were at this time allied to the Thebans. Although the Thessalians were famous for the quality of their horsemen, Agesilaus ordered his cavalry, which he himself had trained in Ephesus, 'to charge at full speed ... and not to give the enemy a chance of rallying'. This unexpected boldness worked, and Agesilaus was victorious. He proudly set up a trophy to commemorate his victory, mightily pleased to have defeated an enemy inordinately proud of their own horsemanship with his own horsemen.[40]

It was not all good news for the Spartans, though, who suffered a severe blow when the Persian fleet commanded by the Athenian general Conon crushed their fleet at Cnidus. The defeat was avoidable, but Agesilaus' brother-in-law Peisander chose to take Conon on even though he was heavily outnumbered – just as Callicratidas had done at Arginusae fourteen years earlier. Xenophon says that Peisander's trireme was rammed and forced out of the water. The other Spartans abandoned their ships, but Peisander died fighting onboard – yet another commander who perished in a defeat. The loss was so heavy that Agesilaus chose to lie about it to his troops, telling them that the Spartan fleet had been victorious, rather than risk demoralising them by revealing the truth. Meanwhile, Conon returned to Athens with a bag of Persian money and helped rebuild Athens' walls and navy.

Not long after he learned of his brother-in-law's death, Agesilaus entered Boeotia, where he found himself facing the Thebans, Athenians, Argives, Corinthians, Aenianians, Euboeans and both the Locrian tribes near the city of Coronea. Two Spartan ephors arrived in time to deliver Agesilaus reinforcements and orders to fight the enemy. Xenophon, who was himself present at the battle, describes it as the most remarkable of his lifetime. Both armies advanced towards each other in complete silence; when they were less than 200 metres from each other, the Thebans gave a loud war cry and rushed towards the Spartan line. Then, when they were only around 100 metres apart, Agesilaus and the Spartans came running out, and when they were within a spear thrust, most of the Thebans' allies

– particularly the Argives – bolted, without even daring to fight the Spartans. Xenophon says Agesilaus' mercenaries were about to present him with garlands to celebrate his victory, when he suddenly noticed that the Thebans had routed the Orchomenians on his left and were heading back in his direction.

According to Xenophon, there was no question that what Agesilaus did next was brave, but it was by no means the safest course of action. He might have done exactly what Aristodemus did at the Nemea river: allow the Thebans to pass by, follow them, and annihilate those in the rear. But instead, Agesilaus made a furious frontal attack: 'So with shield pressed against shield they struggled, killed and were killed.' By the end of the day's fighting, many were dead on both sides; Agesilaus himself was severely wounded, and it was by no means clear who had won the encounter. The next morning Agesilaus ordered the polemarch Gylis to draw up the Spartan survivors in battle order to show that they were ready to fight the Thebans, but insisted that they wear garlands to show that they were celebrating the fact that they had won the previous day's encounter. When the Thebans sent heralds to ask for a truce to collect their dead – the standard Greek way of accepting that you had lost a battle – Gylis set up a trophy to celebrate Agesilaus' 'victory'.

The battle had been very close, and one could say that Agesilaus had allowed his hatred of the Thebans to get the better of him. Indeed, many Spartans criticised him at the time; when Antalcidas saw that Agesilaus was wounded, he said, 'What a splendid tuition fee you are receiving from the Thebans for having taught them to fight when they had neither the wish nor the knowledge to do so.'[41] In future battles, the Thebans would remember how close they came to victory; the Spartans' standing was starting to diminish.

*　　*　　*

After this battle at Coronea, Sparta's enemies confined their military activities around Corinth, which is why the Corinthian War was so named. With the Spartans constantly campaigning near Corinth, the Corinthians' allies began to fear they would take the easy route and return to the Spartan fold. They consequently encouraged a massacre of pro-Spartans in Corinth, and engineered the political union of Argos and Corinth in 392 BCE. The unification of the Spartans' nemesis and long-time supporter into one mega-*polis* could have been an enormous blow for them, but in 391 BCE the Spartans were able to capture the Corinthian port of Lechaeum, and later destroy the Corinthian 'long walls'. The following year Cnidus and Samos rejoined the Spartan alliance, a sure sign that Sparta was consolidating its naval power.

Yet just as the Spartans seemed to be gaining the upper hand, there was an unmitigated fiasco. In 390 BCE, a whole regiment (*mora*) of Spartan hoplites was annihilated by Athenian light-armed troops at Lechaeum. The Spartan operations there coincided with the annual Hyacinthia festival, when the Spartiates from Amyclae always went home to celebrate, even when they were fighting abroad. Agesilaus ordered one of the polemarchs to escort the Amyclaeans safely past Corinth; he achieved the first part of his task, only for the Athenians there to spot that he had made the mistake of marching out without any support from cavalry or the light-armed troops known as peltasts. The Athenian general Callias marched his hoplites out of the city to meet the Spartans on their way back to Lechaeum, drawing his men up in battle formation, while his colleague Iphicrates attacked the Spartan hoplites with his peltasts.

When their first volley of javelins struck down a fair number of Spartans, the so-called shield-bearers (*hypaspistai*) were ordered to carry their bodies back to Lechaeum, and the polemarch sent his youngest hoplites, the men aged between twenty and thirty, to rush at the Athenian peltasts. But the light-armed Athenians ran, and before the Spartans could catch them, they reached Callias' phalanx. Faced with well-organised hoplites, but in disorder themselves, the Spartan hoplites withdrew and were once again set upon by the peltasts, who took advantage of the fact that their right sides were unprotected. Many Spartans fell.

When the staggeringly obtuse Spartan polemarch now ordered all the surviving hoplites aged between twenty and thirty-five to try the same tactic, exactly the same thing happened; the Spartans were not fast enough to catch the peltasts before they reached the safety of Callias' hoplites, and even more Spartans were cut down as they withdrew in disorder. By now, Spartan cavalry had been dispatched from Lechaeum to help, and so the polemarch tried the same tactic a third time, this time with horsemen in support. But Xenophon – who knew a thing or two about the cavalry – says the polemarch bungled it yet again. Rather than using the cavalry to chase the peltasts from the field, the cavalry tried to stick close to the hoplites as they chased the peltasts for a third time. Once again they failed to catch them, and the disorganised cavalry and hoplites had to rush away when faced with the snarling ranks of Athenian hoplites, and many more Spartans fell. Eventually, the Spartan hoplites panicked and ran. Some of them managed to escape back to Lechaeum with the cavalry, but 250 Amyclaeans perished. Xenophon rightly calls the defeat at Lechaeum the type of disaster that the Spartans were unused to suffering.[42] The Spartans' opponents and allies alike will have taken note of their discomfort.

*   *   *

The Spartan campaign against the Persians had been halted by a lack of manpower and unity, and their effort in the Corinthian

War was hampered by a lack of manpower and sometimes idiotic leadership. But the forces ranged against them were equally fragmented, and by 387 BCE the Spartans had managed to recover sufficiently on land and sea that their admiral Antalcidas pulled off a masterstroke, convincing the Persians to support a peace treaty that included all the Greeks. The Spartans desperately needed peace. As Xenophon puts it, they were not enjoying having to keep an eye on their allies, to stop the ones they trusted from being destroyed by their enemies, and to stop the ones they didn't trust from revolting. Furthermore, there was constant fighting near Corinth.[43] After Agesilaus' half-brother Teleutias raided Piraeus, and Antalcidas himself defeated the Athenian fleet at the Hellespont, the Athenians also felt that peace was in their best interests.

A conference was held in Sparta to ratify the peace, but the Persian king Artaxerxes was the real power broker. His representative Tiribazus showed the assembled Greeks the king's seal before reading his message:

> King Artaxerxes thinks it just that the cities in Asia should belong to him, as well as Clazomenae and Cyprus among the islands, and that the other Greek cities, both small and great, should be left autonomous, except Lemnos, Imbros and Scyros; and these should belong, as of old, to the Athenians. But whichever of the two parties does not accept this peace, upon them I will make war, in company with those who desire this arrangement, both by land and by sea, with ships and with money.[44]

The Spartans called this treaty the 'Peace of Antalcidas', but the rest of the Greeks called it 'the King's Peace' – the Persian king would police it, with the Spartans acting as his right hand if anyone broke it. The price of Antalcidas' dodgy deal with the

Persians was the freedom of the Greeks of Asia and Cyprus. When someone accused the Spartans of 'Medising', Agesilaus retorted that the Persians were 'Lacedaemonising' – which might sound good but still rings hollow.

Agesilaus was able to delay the swearing of the peace until Corinth had been split from Argos and Thebes had been compelled to accept back pro-Spartan exiles. He was even able to get one over the Thebans when they swore their oaths. As Xenophon explains, all the Greeks swore to the treaty as autonomous states, but when it was the Thebans' turn, they argued that they should be able to swear on behalf of all the Boeotians and not just as Thebans. Agesilaus, however, refused to let them swear unless they swore exactly as the king's writing directed: every city, whether small or great, should be autonomous. That meant that the other Boeotian cities needed to be independent of Thebes.

The Thebans refused to do that, because that was not the instruction they had received from home. At this, Agesilaus told them they could go home and ask what the other Thebans thought they should do, but he warned them that if they did not swear now they would be 'shut out' of the treaty. Xenophon reports that Agesilaus hated the Thebans so much that he immediately convinced the ephors to allow him to launch a campaign against them. Having made the necessary sacrifices preparatory to a campaign, he marched out to Tegea, from where he sent horsemen to muster the *perioikoi* and the 'guides' (*xenagoi*) to summon the allies. But just before he left Tegea, the Theban ambassadors arrived and agreed that they would leave the cities autonomous after all. As Xenophon puts it, 'Things had gone just as the Spartans wanted.'[45] The Spartan hegemony was intact, though with the benefit of hindsight we can see that it rested on increasingly shaky ground.

11

Sparta's Decline and Fall

386–371 BCE

The restored victory monument (*tropaion*) set up by the Thebans to commemorate their victory over the Spartans at the Battle of Leuctra in 371 BCE.

The King's Peace restored Sparta to the top of the tree in Greece. Over the next sixteen years, they would try to use the treaty as a means of policing the activities of the other Greeks and bending them to Sparta's will. The leading player in this was almost always the Eurypontid king Agesilaus – in many ways the architect of both Sparta's hegemony and its collapse.

As soon as the King's Peace was agreed, the Spartans 'turned their attention' – as Xenophon puts it – to their allies who had either been against them in the war or were more inclined to side with their enemies. These, the Spartans decided, should be punished or reorganised in such a way that they could not be 'disloyal' in the future.[1] The Spartans' reasoning seems remarkably similar to that of the Corinthians during the Thirty Years' Peace, when they convinced the Spartans not to intervene when Athens was attacking its rebellious ally Samos, on the grounds that every hegemonic state had the right to 'punish' its own allies.[2] It is almost as if the Corinthians unintentionally gave the Spartans a blueprint for imperial rule. It was not a good one for either the Spartans or their allies.

First up were the Mantineans, whom the Spartans had never really forgiven for allying with Athens, Argos and Elis in 421 BCE. The timing was right, because the thirty-year truce made after the Battle of Mantinea in 418 BCE was about to lapse. But the Spartans had more recent grudges against them. They were angry that the Mantineans had sent grain to Argos when Sparta was at war with the Argives, fought badly or unwillingly during the Corinthian War, and – after Lechaeum – been openly derisive of Spartan misfortunes. The King's Peace gave the Spartans the opportunity to right these wrongs. They demanded that the Mantineans tear down their walls, and launched an invasion when they refused. Agesilaus declined the opportunity to lead the campaign on the grounds that the Mantineans had helped his father Archidamus at the time of the helot revolt. It might sound high-minded, but it is possible that he was trying to make life difficult for his co-king Agesipolis, whose own father, the exiled former king Pausanias, was on good terms with the democratic faction in Mantinea.[3]

Agesipolis led a large allied army to Mantinea and ravaged their lands. When the Mantineans appealed to Athens for help, it was declined on the grounds that they couldn't fight against the Spartans without breaking their oaths.[4] Agesipolis dammed the Ophis river, causing it to flood, thus destroying a large section of Mantinea's mudbrick walls. Knowing that they would not be able to survive a siege, the Mantineans agreed to tear down the rest of the fortifications. But then the Spartans upped the ante, and insisted that the Mantineans not only destroy their walls, but also split up the city into separate villages. Having no real choice, the Mantineans agreed.

At the insistence of his father Pausanias, Agesipolis allowed the pro-Argive and democratic Mantineans to leave the city – at which the Spartan troops, who hated those Mantineans, lined up along the road leading from the main city gates, their spears pointing at them, as they left their home forever. Xenophon insists that this incident was an excellent example of the 'obedience' of the Spartans, who were able to control their hatred better than the aristocratic Mantineans.[5] Nonetheless, one can only imagine how terrifying this must have been for the exiled Mantineans, watching a sea of angry Spartans as they left and expecting to be cut down at any moment.

*   *   *

Taking note of what had happened at Mantinea, pro-Spartan exiles from the city of Phlius sensed an opportunity. They went to Sparta and pointed out that when they had been in charge, Phlius had always welcomed the Spartans into the city and willingly joined in allied campaigns. Yet now that their opponents were in charge, Phlius would not follow the Spartans, or admit them into the city. The ephors could join the dots, and sent a message to Phlius, demanding that the Phliasians allow the exiles to return. Having seen what the Spartans had just done at Mantinea – a far larger and more powerful city – the Phliasians wisely voted to allow the pro-Spartan exiles to return.[6]

Modern scholars often criticise the Spartans for their actions against the Mantineans and Phliasians, painting them as a violation of the autonomy clause in the King's Peace, but the Spartans could at least claim that they were merely policing the behaviour of their own allies, who had sworn oaths of obedience to them before the peace treaty was formalised. That does not mean, however, that the other Greeks would have perceived the Spartans as doing the right thing. They would have seen the Spartans as behaving like the Athenians did in the fifth century BCE. Spartan hegemony was turning into Spartan tyranny.

Nonetheless, the next Spartan intervention could indeed be justified on the grounds of enforcing the autonomy clause. Ambassadors from the northern Greek cities of Acanthus and Apollonia came to Sparta, complaining that the city of Olynthus was threatening the autonomy of all the northern Greek cities, particularly those in Macedonia. It was Sparta's responsibility, they argued, to intervene.[7] The counter-argument was that Macedonia was not legally a party to the King's Peace, and Sparta should have kept out of the dispute.[8] Thebes and Athens both took the latter line, but there was nothing they could do to stop the Spartans because of the treaty.

Whatever the legalities, the Spartans resolved to send out a 10,000-strong army against Olynthus. The command was placed in the hands of Eudamidas, who gathered 2,000 men, mostly *neodamodeis*, *perioikoi* and Skiritai, and convinced the ephors to allow his brother Phoebidas to bring the remaining troops to him once they had been mustered. This was a problem for everyone, as Phoebidas was a hothead; when he was passing Thebes with his army, he took advantage of factional squabbles there to seize the Theban acropolis, the Cadmea. It was perfect timing; the Cadmea was closed to men because the women were there celebrating the female-only Thesmophoria festival. With the women taken as hostages, the Thebans were forced to surrender to Phoebidas.[9]

When news of this dodgy episode was brought to Sparta by the Spartophile Theban politician Leontiades – who had convinced Phoebidas to seize the Cadmea in the first place – the ephors and the other Spartiates were angry at Phoebidas' display of unauthorised initiative. Given that the King's Peace guaranteed the autonomy of all the states who swore to it, including the Thebans, the Spartans ought to have ordered Phoebidas to restore the Thebans' freedom. This is what Agesipolis thought they should do,[10] but Agesilaus – who held a grudge against the Thebans – had other ideas. He argued that rather than following the letter of the law, the Spartans should determine whether Phoebidas had 'damaged' Sparta. If it had, he should be punished; but if what he had done was 'good for Sparta', they should let him off. In the end, the Spartans chose to have their cake and eat it; they fined Phoebidas for his crime but kept the garrison in the Cadmea. The Spartan troops there supported Leontiades, who effectively became the figurehead of a Spartan puppet government. While Xenophon seems keen to absolve

Agesilaus, Diodorus censures him as a 'war lover' and says that his terrible decision brought 'disrepute' on the Spartans.[11]

* * *

The campaign against the Olynthians was a mixed blessing for Sparta. It increased Sparta's power, but it did little to help their reputation. This was partly down to the involvement of Agesilaus' half-brother Teleutias. Xenophon is unclear how it happened, but in all the confusion, Teleutias ended up in charge of the whole Spartan campaign against Olynthus. Although Xenophon was close to Agesilaus, he damns Teleutias with faint praise, claiming that everyone was eager to serve him – both because he was 'not ungracious' to his subordinates, and because he was Agesilaus' brother. Teleutias had some initial successes against the Olynthians but was killed after losing his temper when the Olynthian cavalry casually rode past while he was destroying their crops. Teleutias ordered his light-armed troops to harass them, but they pursued too fast and too far, only to be cut to ribbons when the Olynthians wheeled around and counter-attacked. Xenophon says Teleutias was 'enraged' at this turn of events and ordered his whole army to chase the Olynthian horsemen into the city. In his rage, though, he led his men too close to the city walls. As they were being pelted with missiles, the Olynthian cavalry swarmed out with their own light-armed troops in support. Teleutias was killed, and his men withdrew in chaos. Xenophon gives a useful summary at this point, claiming that 'disasters' like this teach men to control their anger. In his opinion, 'It is utterly wrong to launch an attack under the influence of anger.'[12]

Controlling anger had long been a problem in Sparta. We have already seen the Spartans vent their rage against Leotychidas, Aristodemus, Cleandridas, Pleistoanax, Agis and

Pausanias. We have also seen Agesilaus and Lysander losing their tempers with each other. Plutarch even claimed that the disastrous earthquake in the 460s was caused by the Spartans not being able to control their anger (*thymos*).[13] No wonder that the directive to 'control anger' (*thymou kratein*) was one of Chilon's most famous aphorisms.

After the failure of Agesilaus' half-brother, the Spartans sent his co-king Agesipolis to deal with the mess. Agesipolis took a staff of thirty Spartiates with him, as well as some 'gentlemen' of the *perioikoi*, certain 'bastards' (presumably the illegitimate sons of Spartiates and helot women), and some volunteers from all the allies – but he died from a fever while besieging Olynthus. Remarkably, the monument that Agesipolis' exiled father Pausanias set up to his memory at Delphi has survived. It reads: 'As a memorial for his beloved son Agesipolis, Pausanias dedicated me. Greece sings of his excellence in unison.'[14] Agesipolis' replacement as commander, Polybiades, continued the siege, and the starving Olynthians ultimately had no choice but to sue for peace. The Spartans required the Olynthians to have the same friends and enemies as them and to follow them wherever they might lead. The Olynthians were now bound to the Spartans, just like the other members of the Peloponnesian League were. 'It appeared now, at last,' Xenophon concludes, 'that the Spartans' empire had been well and truly established.'[15]

∗   ∗   ∗

However, appearances can be deceptive; almost immediately, the Thebans rebelled from the Spartans and recovered their liberty. Xenophon is often accused of pro-Spartan bias, but even he saw this as proof that 'the gods are not indifferent to irreligion or evil-doing'. Xenophon goes on to explain that the Spartans had sworn to leave the *poleis* autonomous, only to seize the Cadmea, and were then punished by these very same men, despite having never been conquered by any single one of all the peoples that ever existed. He adds that the Theban partisans who helped the Spartan sacrilege were also punished.[16]

Yet even then, Xenophon couldn't bring himself to tell the story properly, refusing to mention one of the leading Theban rebels – Pelopidas – by name. He and his fellow conspirators assassinated the leaders of the Spartan-backed puppet government that ruled Thebes, and called the hoplites and cavalrymen to oust the Spartan garrison and regain their freedom. At this, the families of the Theban pro-Spartan partisans fled to the Cadmea. When the Thebans began to besiege it, with help from Athenian troops (whom Xenophon fails to mention), the Spartan harmost (governor) panicked, telling the Thebans that they would withdraw as long as they were allowed to keep their arms. The Thebans permitted the Spartans to go as they had sworn, but they butchered the pro-Spartan Thebans – and even their children.[17]

When the Spartans heard what had happened, the harmost was put to death for abandoning his post instead of waiting for a relief force. They then mobilised an army to send against Thebes. Agesilaus – in many ways responsible for the mess – refused to lead the army as he was 'too old'. Xenophon suggests that his real reason was that he feared being thought of as someone who would come to the help of tyrants, but it's more likely that he just didn't think he would be able to recapture Thebes. Even if Agesilaus thought he could, he shouldn't have tried – it would have meant violating the Thebans' autonomy for a second time. Instead, Cleombrotus, who had just succeeded his brother as Agiad king, got the job. The fact that he had never commanded an army before was not exactly ideal – and Cleombrotus achieved little in Boeotia, apart from installing a senior Spartiate named Sphodrias as harmost in the Boeotian city of Thespiae. Cleombrotus left a third of his army and all his money with Sphodrias, along with orders to hire additional mercenaries. The presence of such a large Spartan-led army reportedly spooked the Athenians into backing off, leaving the Thebans to face the Spartans alone.[18]

*   *   *

The promotion of Sphodrias proved to be a disaster. Soon after Cleombrotus left, Sphodrias decided to try to capture the Athenian harbour of Piraeus – for reasons that remain unclear. Xenophon alleges that the Thebans bribed him to do so, in the hope that it would force the Athenians to go to war against the Spartans. Yet it may be that Sphodrias, who Plutarch says 'lacked neither boldness nor ambition, but always abounded in hopes rather than in good judgement',[19] came up with the daft idea himself. After all, when Phoebidas captured the Cadmea, the Spartans had effectively let him off. If Sphodrias could capture the Athenian harbour, thereby neutralising the Athenian navy, he might just receive a hero's welcome on his return to Sparta. After giving his troops an early dinner, he led them out of Thespiae, intending to be at Piraeus by dawn. But the timing was entirely wrong; by the time the sun rose, Sphodrias and his men were still in the middle of the Athenian countryside. With no way of hiding, or of pretending that it was not a hostile invasion, they seized some cattle, looted some houses and returned to Thespiae. In short, it was a fiasco.

The Athenians were outraged. They arrested three Spartan ambassadors who happened to be staying at the house of the Athenian *proxenos*, assuming that they were in Athens because they were in on Sphodrias' plan. In reality, the Spartan ambassadors were equally astounded by what had happened. They assured the Athenians that Sphodrias would be put to death, and the ephors indeed recalled him to face trial. Although Sphodrias was initially too frightened to come home, he needn't have worried; Cleombrotus and his friends were already inclined to acquit him. And it just so happened that Sphodrias' son Cleonymus – the most handsome youth in Sparta – was the *erōmenos* of Agesilaus' son Archidamus.

Sphodrias urged Cleonymus to beg Archidamus to make Agesilaus 'favourable' to him at his trial. Cleonymus eventually summoned up the courage to go to see Archidamus at his common mess, to beg him to help his father. The sight of his young lover in tears brought Archidamus to tears himself; he explained to Cleonymus that his father was so strict that he normally found it difficult to look him in the eye. If Archidamus wanted anything, he tended to ask anyone other than his father. But he promised, nonetheless, to do his best.

The next day, Archidamus rose at dawn, keen to find the best opportunity to speak with his father. Everyone in Sparta, including Agesilaus, could see that Archidamus wanted an audience with him, but Archidamus gave way to any citizen – or even servant – who wanted to see the king. The day passed without Archidamus speaking with Agesilaus, and the same thing happened the next day. As everyone could see that Archidamus was deliberately avoiding Cleonymus – despite 'longing' to see him – Sphodrias' cronies feared that Archidamus had been rebuked by his father. Archidamus finally emboldened himself, however, and told his father that he and Cleonymus would like him to save Sphodrias. In response, Agesilaus said that he could not see how he could avoid being blamed if he didn't condemn a man who had benefited personally while at the same time harming Sparta. Archidamus went away disappointed, but returned later to make a second appeal, this time asking Agesilaus to acquit Sphodrias for 'our sake'. Agesilaus replied that he would do so only if it was 'honourable', at which point Archidamus left despondent.

Sphodrias' friends were also downbeat. One of them said to Agesilaus' friend Etymocles that he supposed all of Agesilaus' friends wanted to condemn Sphodrias. Etymocles surprised him by replying that this was not the case; Agesilaus, he said, had reached the conclusion that it would be 'dishonourable' to put to death a man who – until now – had been innocent of wrongdoing as a child, youth and young man, and continually performed all the duties required of him. Sparta needed such men as Sphodrias, Agesilaus had concluded. That he found an underhand way of absolving Sphodrias should not have been a surprise to anyone at Sparta, given that he had previously found a way to keep the garrison Phoebidas had illegally installed at Thebes. But why on earth did Agesilaus think it was a good idea to sacrifice the goodwill of Athens and the rest of the Greek world for the sake of his son's boyfriend?

Cleonymus was obviously delighted, and promised Archidamus that he would never give the crown prince cause to be ashamed of his friendship, but the Athenians were outraged by Sphodrias' acquittal, and any credibility the Spartans had left after the capture of Thebes was gone. Although Xenophon is coy about the details, it seems plausible that it was their outrage at this incident that led the Athenians to form a new defensive alliance system in 377 BCE, which is usually referred to as the Second Athenian Sea League. The decree announcing the alliance noted that it was being founded 'in order that the Lacedaemonians may allow the Greeks to live in peace, free and autonomous.'[20] Spartan hegemony meant Spartan tyranny – and the Athenians were not prepared to stand for it. Soon many Greek states joined them in their show of defiance against the Spartans.

*   *   *

The next few years saw numerous failed Spartan attempts to quell the Thebans. They could still pretend that they were defending the autonomy of those Boeotians who remained hostile to Thebes, but the other Greeks knew this was a sham. In 378 BCE, the Spartans ordered Agesilaus to lead an attack on Thebes. Agesilaus, whose hatred of the Thebans was now undisguised, jauntily replied that he would never go against a decision by the state.[21] Despite his obvious enthusiasm for the task, Agesilaus achieved little apart from plundering the Theban countryside up to the city walls. The next year the ephors asked him to lead an army against Thebes again, and once again he succeeded only in destroying the Thebans' crops. Although Xenophon talks up the fact that the Thebans were suffering, having been unable to produce a proper harvest for two years,[22] it was probably around this time that Sparta's allies began to openly criticise Agesilaus for his 'obsessive urge' to destroy Thebes; they complained that they were fed up with being led 'hither and thither' each year to their destruction, when so 'many' of them were following so 'few' Spartans.[23]

On his way back to Sparta at the end of the second unsuccessful campaign, Agesilaus was struck down with what medical experts now recognise as thrombophlebitis in his leg, the one that wasn't already lame, causing excessive swelling and extreme pain. The affliction presented itself in the most mundane of circumstances, when he was walking from the sanctuary of Aphrodite to the town hall at Megara. A Syracusan surgeon opened a vein in Agesilaus' ankle to relieve the pressure, but he almost died when they were unable to stop the blood flowing.[24] Such experiences probably explain why there are numerous Spartan sayings mocking the skills and knowledge of doctors. When a doctor declared to the Agiad king Pausanias, 'You have lived to be an old man,' for example, he replied, 'That is because I never employed you as my physician.'[25]

With Agesilaus out of action, the task of dealing with the Thebans fell to Cleombrotus, but he fared worse than Agesilaus, withdrawing his army from Boeotian territory almost immediately after finding his way blocked by an army of Thebans and Athenians. After this latest failure to capture Thebes, the Spartans suspended their annual invasions of Boeotia. By now they were afraid of Athens' growing naval power; in 376 BCE the Athenian general Chabrias defeated them at sea off Naxos, the Athenians' first significant naval victory since the Peloponnesian War.[26]

By 375 BCE the Spartans were also clearly struggling for manpower; so much so that they refused to intervene in a power struggle in Thessaly, in central Greece, between Polydamas of Pharsalus and Jason of Pherae. Xenophon reports that Polydamas made a long, impassioned speech, begging the Spartans for help against Jason, who was aiming to unite all of Thessaly under his control, an act that would give him control of 8,000 cavalry and 20,000 hoplites. Polydamas warned the Spartans that Jason already had a powerful army, and they should think again if they intended to send a force of freed helots commanded by a man who was not a Spartan king. The Spartans spent the next day calculating how many men they had serving abroad, and how many they had close to home, ready to deploy against the Athenian fleet and for the wars on their own frontiers. After completing their calculations, they told Polydamas that he would have to deal with Jason alone; they lacked the manpower to provide him with the help he needed.[27]

The year 375 BCE saw another disaster for the Spartans; though Xenophon omits it from his narrative, Plutarch and Diodorus both claim that the Thebans inflicted a heavy defeat on the Spartans at Tegyra in Boeotia.[28] Plutarch provides the more detailed account, explaining that Pelopidas led just 300 hoplites to battle against two *morai* of the Spartan army (between 1,000 and 1,800 men) and defeated them. This was the first known encounter between the Spartans and the Theban 'Sacred Band' – 150 pairs of lovers who were trained, housed and fed at state expense in the Theban citadel. The overconfident Spartan polemarchs Gorgoleon and Theopompus expected to defeat the small number of Thebans easily, not realising that they were the equivalent of the Spartan's elite knights. The polemarchs were killed in the early stages of the fighting; with their senior officers dead, the remaining Spartans panicked and ran. Plutarch and Diodorus both stress that this was the first time they had been defeated by a numerically smaller force. Little more than a century earlier, just 300 Spartans had struck terror into Xerxes' vast host; now it was a force of 300 Thebans that was terrorising the Spartans.

*   *   *

Sparta suffered further blows in 373 BCE, when the Thebans captured the cities of Thespiae and Plataea. Both Boeotian cities had resisted the Thebans for much of the last century, providing the Spartans with an excuse for their frequent interventions in the region. When the Thebans razed Plataea to the ground, the refugees were granted asylum in Athens.[29] The Athenians, who also accepted refugees from Thespiae,[30] began to fear the Thebans just as much as they had previously feared the Spartans. So when the Spartans called for a renewal of the common peace in 371 BCE, the Athenians were receptive. Another conference was held in Sparta, and representatives were sent from all the Greek *poleis*.

As had been the case in 386 BCE, the requirement for individual *poleis* to swear as autonomous states was a sticking point for the Thebans. The Spartans swore on behalf of themselves and their allies, after which the Athenians and their allies swore separately – and then everyone else did the same. The Thebans seemed to be happy to swear as the 'Thebans', but the next day they demanded that Agesilaus change it to the 'Boeotians'. Agesilaus was having none of it and told the Thebans that if they didn't like it, he'd strike their names off the treaty altogether. This version of events makes the Thebans look like dunces, who failed to remember what had happened sixteen years earlier. It also presents them as isolated and vulnerable. Xenophon writes that the Athenians enjoyed their plight, thinking that there was a good chance that the Thebans would now be 'tithed' – by which he meant decimated – by the Spartans.[31]

However, this is not the only version of events. Later sources reveal a debate between Agesilaus and the Theban statesman Epaminondas, during which the latter argued that the peace would only work if all the Greeks were autonomous and equal. Seeking to discomfort Epaminondas, Agesilaus asked him whether he thought all the *poleis* of Boeotia should be equal; in other words, whether the other Boeotian cities should be independent from Thebes. But Epaminondas turned the question back on the Spartan, asking him whether he thought all the *poleis* of Laconia should be autonomous. At the mere suggestion that the *perioikoi* should be independent of Sparta, Agesilaus jumped up in anger (yet another Spartan temper tantrum) and demanded to know whether Epaminondas would let the Boeotians be free – at which Epaminondas asked Agesilaus again whether he wanted the Laconians to be free.[32] This version of events suggests that Epaminondas and the Thebans may well have known exactly what they were doing: provoking the Spartans into going to war, so that they could crush them.

*　　*　　*

Cleombrotus, who happened to be in Phocis at the time with a large allied army, was given orders to 'lead it at once against the Thebans if they did not leave the cities autonomous'. He had perhaps 10,000 hoplites, including four *morai* of Lacedaemonians, of whom only 700 were Spartiates, and 1,000 horsemen. His campaign started off well – he entered Boeotia from an unexpected route, and captured twelve Theban triremes at the port of Creusis. The army then moved to Leuctra, in the territory of Thespiae. The Thebans marched out to meet Cleombrotus and encamped on a nearby hill, having brought only other Boeotians with them as allies. The subsequent battle would prove the pivotal moment in Spartan history, if not the whole history of Classical Greece.

Cleombrotus had superior numbers, but the Theban general Epaminondas, whom Xenophon refuses even to name, had home advantage, the motivation and the experience. Epaminondas lined up the 4,000 Theban hoplites fifty-men deep, directly opposite the Spartans, in an attempt to nullify Cleombrotus' numerical advantage while taking advantage of Sparta's dwindling authority. The other Boeotians were lined up eight to twelve deep, covering the Spartans' allies. Epaminondas calculated that if he defeated the part of the Spartan army that was closest to the king, the rest of them would fall like a house of cards. A later story had it that to encourage the Thebans to make a vigorous attack on the Spartans, Epaminondas produced a large snake from somewhere and crushed its head in front of the army. 'If you crush the head,' he said, 'you see how impotent the rest of the body is.' He went on to explain that if they crushed the Spartans, their allies would be as impotent as the snake's body.[33] Later legend had it that Epaminondas also had a secret weapon: the shield of Aristomenes the Messenian, which the oracle of Trophonius in Lebedaea had told the Thebans to take with them. The Messenians themselves claimed that the ghost of Aristomenes had appeared on the battlefield and helped defeat the Spartans.[34]

Cleombrotus' circle of friends urged him to fight the Thebans, warning him that if he let them escape without a battle, his previous failures against the Thebans would be held against him. Given what happened to Pleistoanax and Pausanias after their failures against Athens, Cleombrotus would have had good reason to fear the wrath of his subjects if they failed to fight the Thebans. There was even a rumour from the king's enemies that Cleombrotus and his friends drank wine at lunchtime in order to fortify themselves for the fight ahead.[35] Cleombrotus had never yet shown any great talent at war, and his decision to place his cavalry in front of his phalanx, perhaps hoping that it would screen his movements, has been much criticised. Xenophon stresses that the Spartan cavalry was of very poor quality at the time; the richest men provided the horses, but only at the time of a call-up, which meant that the poorer Spartans who actually served as cavalrymen lacked the time to hone their horsemanship. Xenophon complains that the Spartan cavalrymen were also the least strong and least ambitious among the Spartiates. It's worth bearing in mind a reported saying of Agesilaus relating to the cavalry: seeing a lame Spartan on his way to war asking where he might get a horse, Agesilaus said, 'Don't you realise that war has need of those who stand their ground rather than run away?'[36]

Plutarch and Diodorus both say that Cleombrotus tried to outflank the Thebans. But the Boeotians on the right retreated, while the left – where Pelopidas was leading the Sacred Band – continued to advance, at double-quick time. While this was happening, the Theban cavalry routed the Spartan horsemen, forcing them back into the advancing hoplites and disrupting their line. Diodorus writes that the heavy column led by Epaminondas bore down on the Spartans as if they were running a race.[37] Archidamus' lover Cleonymus fell, struck down three times in front of the king. Cleombrotus himself fell too, the first Spartan king to die in combat since Leonidas at Thermopylae. The 300 Spartan knights fought bravely to retrieve his body, with Diodorus describing a great number of bodies piling up around the king.

When senior officers, including the polemarch Deinon and Sphodrias, had also fallen, the knights and the polemarch's aide-de-camp started to fall back. The Spartans were unable to withstand the Theban onslaught; some 400 of them fell, including all the knights. Diodorus claims that had Cleombrotus survived, he would have rallied the troops, but the picture was bleak; with the best of the Spartans dead, the rest of the army fled. Epaminondas' men pursued the fugitives, killing many of them, and winning for themselves 'a most glorious victory'. Such was the speed of the Thebans' diagonal charge, the allies on both sides had scarcely been able to exchange a blow before the battle was over.[38]

Pausanias describes the Theban victory at Leuctra as 'the most famous ever won by Greeks over Greeks'.[39] To celebrate, the Thebans set up a magnificent stone trophy: a circular formation of nine round shields that created a dome-like feature, topped by a bronze figure. The Thebans were criticised for setting up such a permanent trophy,[40] as normal Greek custom dictated that such displays should be temporary.[41] When charged by the Amphictyonic Council on the grounds that it was not right, their response was reportedly, 'It *is* right.' Under any other circumstances, that was the sort of retort that the Spartans would have admired.

* * *

The defeat at Leuctra shattered Sparta's hegemony. They had recovered from the shame of Sphacteria, Lechaeum and Tegyra, but there was no coming back from Leuctra. There were just too few Spartans left for them to ever challenge for supremacy in Greece again. As Diodorus puts it, 'Since the Lacedaemonians had cast away many of their young men in the disaster at Leuctra, and in their other defeats had lost not a few, and were, taking all together, restricted by the blows of fortune to but few citizen soldiers ... they sank into a state of great weakness.'[42] Leuctra was the end of an era, a complete changing of the guard. A gravestone commemorating three of the Thebans who fought at Leuctra says it all: 'When the Spartan spear held sway, then it fell to Xenocrates' lot to carry the trophy in honour of Zeus, fearing neither the army from Eurotas nor the Laconian shield. "The Thebans are superior in battle," announces the trophy won through victory by the spear at Leuctra.'[43]

News of the disaster reached Sparta while the men's chorus was performing at the Gymnopaidiai. Such was the importance of the festival that the ephors did not interrupt the ceremony – but when the men had finished singing, the ephors announced the defeat and listed the names of the dead. Such were the rules of cowardice in Sparta that Xenophon claims the relatives of the dead walked about with big smiles on their faces, while the relatives of the survivors looked downcast.

The big question was what to do with survivors. No shame was attached to those who had fallen at Leuctra, but the 300 or so who ran from the enemy should have been degraded as cowards.[44] However, Spartiate numbers had sunk so low – there were probably only around 1,100 left – that the Spartans could not afford to disenfranchise so many citizens. It is further arguable that Spartan society could not have functioned properly with so many *tresantes* ('cowards') to manage. As Plutarch says, keeping an eye on so many cowards with so few proper citizens would have been taxing. To resolve the crisis, Agesilaus was appointed as 'lawgiver', the same title Lycurgus had reportedly held when he came up with the Spartan constitution of government, the Great Rhetra. It may have been an acknowledgement of Agesilaus' seniority and status – after all, his co-king, Cleombrotus' young son Agesipolis, was a mere boy – but it was surely also because his moral flexibility suited the occasion. Indeed, the man who had found a way to rescue Phoebidas and Sphodrias did not disappoint; he determined that while the laws of Sparta must always be obeyed, they should 'sleep' until tomorrow.[45]

*   *   *

Agesilaus may have been able to paper over the cracks in Spartan society, but he was unable to do the same for Sparta's hegemony. The moment the news of the disaster at Leuctra reached her allies, the game was up. As happens when a school bully is defeated by the new kid on the block, the old social hierarchy unravelled; no one feared the Spartans' bullying any longer. Mantinea re-established itself as a *polis* and as a democracy. The pro-Spartan oligarchs in Tegea were ousted and the Arcadian *poleis* formed a federal state. When Agesilaus led an army against Tegea to try to restore the oligarchs, the Arcadians appealed to the Thebans, who did not need a second invitation. Epaminondas led a massive army – Plutarch counts 40,000 hoplites – and invaded Laconia.[46] It is hard to put into words the significance of this invasion. As far as the Spartans were concerned, it was the first time that Laconia had been invaded from the north since they had arrived there as part of the Dorian invasion, or as Plutarch puts it, no less than six hundred years earlier.[47] Little wonder then, that the appearance of invaders prompted several communities of *perioikoi* to rebel against their Spartan overlords.

Epaminondas entered the Eurotas valley, destroying fields and the houses of Spartiates, and then marched on Sparta itself. Exactly what happened is confused by the discrepancies in our sources. Plutarch reports that Agesilaus took the few hundred citizens he had available, lined them up in front of the acropolis to defend the city, and watched with relief as the fast-flowing waters of the Eurotas prevented the Thebans from gaining access to the city. Plutarch even has Agesilaus watch on as Epaminondas desperately tried to ford the river at the head of the phalanx, before remarking, 'O ambitious man!'[48]

Xenophon and Diodorus both claim, however, that Agesilaus marched out to face their enemies – Xenophon says this was at Mantinea, Diodorus on the Laconian border with Arcadia – leaving the women, old men and children to defend the city.[49] Xenophon states that the Spartan women panicked, as they 'could not endure even the sight of the smoke, since they had never set eyes upon an enemy',[50] while Aristotle complains that the commotion of the panicking women 'caused more confusion than the enemy'.[51] It is possible that Aristotle was mistaken, and that the Spartan women were raucous not because they were afraid, but because they were frustrated at being denied the opportunity to help.

During the chaos, Antalcidas was allegedly so afraid that he sent his children away to the island of Cythera to keep them safe.[52] After Epaminondas moved his forces away from Sparta, ravaging the nearby countryside as he went, around 200 disaffected Spartans seized a building known as the Issorium near the temple of Artemis Orthia by the banks of the Eurotas. Rather than tackle them by force, as others wanted, Agesilaus decided to give the rebels a chance to reconsider. Donning his red cloak and taking just a single servant with him, Agesilaus marched up to the Issorium and called out to the assembled men that they had misunderstood their orders, and that rather than be stationed at the Issorium, they were meant to be else-where in the city. Once they had left, Agesilaus occupied the Issorium with troops loyal to him, and arranged for fifteen of the rebels to be executed that very evening.

Soon after, Agesilaus got wind of another conspiracy. This time, a large group of Spartiates was said to be plotting to change the constitution. As there was neither the time nor resources to hold a proper trial, Agesilaus had these Spartiates put to death without process of law – the first time Spartans had ever met with such a death.[53] The Spartans were so desperate that they even offered freedom to any of the helots who would fight for Sparta. But when 6,000 helots – surely Laconian, rather than Messenian – answered the call, they panicked. It was only when allies from Phlius, Corinth, Epidaurus and Pellene arrived that the Spartans felt safe from their own freed slaves.[54]

Epaminondas was not able to capture the city of Sparta, though he did lay waste to the area around Amyclae and Sparta's port of Gytheum. Xenophon talks up the fact that Epaminondas never dared to cross the bridge over the Eurotas, but Epaminondas didn't need to capture Sparta; by sweeping Messenia and liberating the Messenian helots after centuries of Spartan rule, in one fell swoop he was able to unravel the entire fabric of Spartan life.

Unfortunately, our sources for what is arguably the most important moment in Spartan history are meagre, to say the least. Plutarch's biography of the Theban hero Epaminondas is lost, and in his *Pelopidas*, which does survive, all he says is that 'they [Pelopidas and Epaminondas] united all Arcadia into one power; rescued the country of Messenia from the hands of its Spartan masters and called back and restored the ancient Messenian inhabitants, with whom they settled Ith-ome'.[55] If that sounds laconic, Xenophon makes Plutarch seem positively prolix, refusing to even mention the liberation of

Messenia, presumably to avoid labouring the most humiliating moment in Spartan history. We have to make do with the brief summary that Diodorus provides, which allows us to at least begin to imagine what happened. According to his account, it was Epaminondas' nature to attempt great enterprises and crave eternal fame, so he encouraged the Thebans, the Arcadians and the other allies to help the Messenians found a new city near Mount Ithome, which would serve as an excellent base for future operations against Sparta. Epaminondas registered any Messenians who wanted to be involved as citizens of the new independent *polis* of Messene, dividing the lands taken from the Spartans among the new citizens, even starting to construct a new city for the Messenians, and gaining widespread acclaim amongst the Greeks. Diodorus even claims that the whole venture – Theban invasion, Messenian rebellion, and foundation of the new city – took just 85 days.[56] Clearly it would take a lot longer than that for the Messenians to build a proper new city, but Messenian exiles from throughout the Mediterranean were soon flooding back home to make it happen.

The loss of their prime Messenian estates and the workforce that toiled on the lands for them was a blow from which the Spartans never recovered. Sparta's rise to superpower status had been slow, but the fall took less than three months. Sparta would never again make a significant impact on the international stage. Only in modern popular culture would Sparta rise again.

Epilogue:
No More Heroes?

Fragment of a sixth-century BCE terracotta votive mask dedicated to the goddess
Artemis Orthia, depicting a Spartan warrior.

The opening sentence of Xenophon's description of the Spartan constitution says it all. When explaining that the Spartans' renown had been a result of the laws imposed by Lycurgus, Xenophon observes that Sparta was able to achieve all this despite being 'among the scantiest populated' *poleis* in Greece.[1] He was well aware that Sparta's greatest strength was having between 6,000 and 9,000 wealthy citizens, all of whom bought into the system. But he also knew that the small size of the Spartan in-group was Sparta's great weakness; such a small number of fighting men could only take them so far.

The Spartans did their best to compensate for their lack of numbers by making alliances with other Peloponnesian states, each of which was led by oligarchs who owed their position and security to Sparta. On their own, none of these could hope to defeat the Spartans. After they had suffered a crushing defeat at Sepeia in the early fifth century BCE, even the Argives had to accept that Sparta was *the* power in the Peloponnese. The backing of Peloponnesian allies allowed the Spartans to grow their power and gain influence over the other mainland Greeks, and eventually – albeit briefly – the Greeks of the Aegean islands and Asia Minor.

As we have seen, however, Spartan power turned out to be illusory. Their alliance system gave the impression – both to insiders and onlookers – that Sparta could dominate the Greek-speaking world for generations, and even allowed them to think that they might be capable of taking on and conquering the Persians. In fact, none of this was really possible, because there were simply too few Spartans. It wasn't only that the city-state had too few citizens to survive the single great blow suffered at Leuctra: according to Aristotle, they had too few citizens, period. Had they taken full advantage of the resources available to them in Lakonike, and deployed armies 30,000 strong, things could have been very different. Trying to conquer the whole of Greece, and afterwards to take on the Persian empire, with no more than 9,000 hoplites proved to be a textbook case of what political scientists call 'hegemonic overextension.'

The problem for the Spartans was that, unlike the Romans, they never adapted their system for true empire. In the mid-sixth century BCE, the city of Rome was in a similar position to Sparta before the Messenian conquest; it had close to 10,000 male citizens, of whom no more than 5,000 were wealthy enough to fight as heavy-armed infantry. Like the Spartans, the Romans conquered neighbouring territories – such as Veii in 396 BCE and the population of Latium during the Social War (340–338 BCE). Unlike the Spartans, however, the Romans integrated these conquered territories into their system. Some of them were absorbed, while others were forced to yield territories that were then settled by Roman and allied *coloniae*; they lost their independent foreign policy, and were required to provide contingents of soldiers for Rome's wars. But this did not make them like the Spartan *perioikoi*, who were dependent and required to serve in Sparta's wars but ultimately kept apart. For in the Roman world, the 'outsiders' shared in the booty and benefited from the peace Rome maintained more tangibly than the *perioikoi* ever did. Local Italian elites were even able to join the Roman aristocracy. Thus the Romans were able to expand their territory almost exponentially in the decades and centuries that followed. From a starting point that was far smaller than in Sparta, the Romans expanded their power to the point that they eventually ruled over as many as 70 million people, and 5 million square kilometres of territory.

Further, unlike the Romans, the Spartans jealously guarded both their conquests and their power, consistently maintaining a distance between themselves and their allies. Spartan hegemony in the Peloponnese was a delicate balancing act, and there were too many occasions when even Sparta's most loyal allies – the Corinthians or the Tegeans, say – felt that they were better off going it alone, or seeking an alternative hegemon who might treat them better. The Spartans' stubborn refusal to share their wealth and conquests with other Greeks limited their potential to grow; at the height of their power, they were indeed more a virtual superpower than an actual one.

It was probably best for the future of the world that the Spartans overreached themselves. Their admirers have long tended to overlook the negative aspects of Spartan society and their hegemony in Greece because – as William Golding put it – they had stood 'in the right line of history' at the Battle of Thermopylae, by giving up their lives for Greek freedom.[2] The uncritical veneration of the Spartans' last stand at Thermopylae allows poets like Byron to paint them as freedom fighters, writers like Golding to see them as safeguarding an intellectual freedom that they could never have imagined, or firearms enthusiasts and rebellious British politicians to see them as forerunners of their own resistance to progressive change. Yet history shows that the Spartans didn't sacrifice themselves so that future generations could enjoy great works of literature, use assault rifles whenever they wanted, or even use a blue passport instead of a red one. Nothing could be further from the truth. The only freedom the Spartans were interested in was their own – and particularly the freedom to treat anyone they thought beneath them as they pleased.

It is only natural for modern Spartophiles to admire the heroics of Spartans like Othryadas, Leonidas and his 300,

Brasidas, Lysander, and even Agesilaus, as they appear in the pages of Herodotus, Thucydides, Xenophon and Plutarch. Who could not be moved by the stories of Othryadas taking his life in shame that he was the sole survivor of the Battle of the Champions, Dienekes laughing in the face of overwhelming odds at Thermopylae, or Brasidas boldly writing to the ephors, 'I'll achieve my wishes in this war, or I'll die'? There is an emotional intensity to their stories and a vividness in their portrayal that truly brings these distant characters to life. At the same time, however, we should never overlook how often these very same Spartans were prepared to trample on the freedom of others to further their ambitions. The Spartans could be heroes, but sadly, our heroes sometimes fall short of our hopes and expectations.

Endnotes

Prologue: Honour and Duty

1 Herodotus 1.82.
2 Tyrtaeus, fragment 10 (Lycurgus 1.107).
3 Herodotus 7.104.
4 Herodotus 1.82.
5 Xenophon, *Lac. Pol.* 4.
6 Tyrtaeus, fragment 11 (Stobaeus 4.9).
7 Eupolis, fragment 394 (Photius Λ 1).
8 Plutarch, *Moralia* 234.
9 Plutarch, *Moralia* 216.
10 Xenophon, *Lac. Pol.* 11.
11 Scholiast (on Aristophanes, *Lysistrata* 453).
12 Xenophon, *Lac. Pol.* 11.
13 Pausanias 2.20, 2.38.
14 Herodotus 1.82.
15 Xenophon, *Lac. Pol.* 11.
16 Plutarch, *Lycurgus* 22.
17 Plutarch, *Agesilaus* 31.
18 Plutarch, *Lycurgus* 27.
19 Heracleides Pontikos, *Constitution of the Spartans* 2.8.
20 Plutarch, *Agesilaus* 30; Xenophon, *Lac. Pol.* 9.
21 Herodotus 7.201–39; Diodorus 11.4–11.11.
22 Herodotus 7.109.
23 Herodotus 7.226.
24 Plutarch, *Moralia* 866.
25 Plutarch, *Moralia* 1225.
26 Diodorus 11.8.
27 Aristophanes, *Lysistrata* 1255–7.
28 Herodotus 7.212.
29 Herodotus 7.225.
30 William Golding, *The Hot Gates and Other Occasional Places* (London: Faber, 1965; 1974), p. 20; Frank Miller and Lynn Varley, *300* (Milwaukee, OR: Dark Horse Books, 1998), n.p.
31 Lord Byron, *Don Juan*, Canto III, stanza 86.
32 Joe de Sena, *Spartan Up!: A Take-No-Prisoners Guide to Overcoming Obstacles and Achieving Peak Performance in Life* (New York: Mariner Books, 2016), pp. 23–4.
33 Herodotus 7.228.
34 Stefan Rebenich, 'Reception of Sparta in Germany and German-Speaking Europe', in *A Companion to Sparta*, ed. Anton Powell (Malden, MA: Wiley-Blackwell, 2018), pp. 685–703 (p. 685).
35 Ibid., citing M. Bormann, *Hitlers politisches Testament. Die Bormann Diktate vom Februar und April 1945* (1981), p. 51.
36 Simone de Beauvoir, *The Second Sex*, ed. and trans. H. M. Parshley (London: Jonathan Cape, 1953), p. 112.

37 Xenophon, *Lac. Pol.* 1.

1. The Origins of the Spartan State: *c.* 1000–600 BCE

1 Euripides, fragment 995 (Plutarch, *Solon* 22).
2 Thucydides 1.10.
3 Plutarch, *Moralia* 210.
4 Strabo 8.20.
5 Strabo 8.5.
6 Thucydides 1.128.
7 Xenophon, *Hellenica* 4.7.
8 Strabo 8.5.
9 Homer, *Iliad* 2.494–760.
10 Strabo 8.4.
11 Tyrtaeus, fragment 3 (Strabo 8.4).
12 Plato, *Menexenus* 245.
13 Herodotus 5.72.
14 Pliny, *Natural History* 7.195.
15 Homer, *Iliad* 10.260–5.
16 Polybius 5.18.
17 Herodotus 6.61; Pindar, *Nemean Odes* 10.56.
18 Xenophon, *Hellenica* 4.5.
19 Strabo 8.5.
20 Apollodorus, *Library* 1.3.
21 Strabo 8.5.
22 Aristotle, fragment 538 (Plutarch, *Lycurgus* 28).
23 Plato, *Laws* 776.
24 Aristotle, *Politics* 1269, 1271.
25 Athenaeus, *Deipnosophistai* 6.263.
26 Pausanias 3.3; Apollodorus, *Library* 2.4.
27 Euripides, fragment 1083 (Strabo 8.5).
28 Plato, *Laws* 684; Isocrates 6.22–3.

29 Tyrtaeus, fragment 5 (Strabo 6.3).
30 Pausanias 4.5–14.
31 Tyrtaeus, fragment 6 (Pausanias 4.14).
32 Pausanias 2.24.
33 Herodotus 6.127.
34 Strabo 8.4.
35 Pausanias 4.14–23.
36 Tyrtaeus, fragment 5 (Scholiast on Plato, *Laws* 629).
37 Tyrtaeus, fragment 11 (Stobaeus 4.9.16).
38 Tyrtaeus, fragment 10 (Lycurgus 1.107).
39 Tyrtaeus, fragment 11 (Stobaeus 4.9.16).
40 Plutarch, *Cleomenes* 2; *Moralia* 235; 959.
41 Tyrtaeus, fragment 23a (M. L. West, *Iambi et elegi Graeci* (Oxford: Oxford University Press, 1972), vol. 2).
42 Pausanias 4.16.
43 Pausanias 4.14.
44 Thucydides 1.134; Strabo 8.5.
45 Pausanias 4.18.
46 Polyaenus 2.31.
47 Pliny, *Natural History* 11.185.
48 Isocrates 6.27.
49 Herodotus 7.104.

2. Utopia on the Eurotas

1 Xenophon, *Hellenica* 2.3; Critias, fragment 14 (Libanius, *Orations* 25).
2 Plato, *Laws* 691–2.
3 Polybius 6.10.
4 Aristotle, *Politics* 1266.
5 Niccolò Machiavelli, *The*

Discourses, trans. Leslie J. Walker (Harmondsworth: Penguin, 1970), p. 122.

6 Haydn Mason, 'The Literary Reception of Sparta in France', in *A Companion to Sparta*, ed. Anton Powell (Malden, MA: Wiley-Blackwell, 2018), pp. 665–84 (p. 672), citing Jean-Jacques Rousseau, *Discours sur les sciences et les arts* (1750), iii. 12–13.

7 Ibid., p. 680, citing Robespierre, 'Report to the Convention', 7 May 1794.

8 Samuel Adams to John Scollay (30 December 1780), in *The Writings of Samuel Adams: Volume IV, 1778–1802*, ed. Harry Alonzo Cushing (New York: G. P. Putnam, 1908) p. 238.

9 Carl J. Richard, *Greeks and Romans Bearing Gifts: How the Ancients Inspired the Founding Fathers* (Lanham, MD: Rowman and Littlefield, 2008), p. 32.

10 Thucydides 1.6; Aristotle, *Politics* 1294; Athenaeus, *Deipnosophistai* 15.686.

11 Xenophon, *Lac. Pol.* 1; Plutarch, *Moralia* 237; Athenaeus, *Deipnosophistai* 12.550c.

12 Xenophon, *Hellenica* 7.1.

13 Aristotle, *Politics* 1294.

14 Plutarch, *Lycurgus* 16.

15 Xenophon, *Lac. Pol.* 2.

16 Xenophon, *Lac. Pol.* 3.

17 Xenophon, *Lac. Pol.* 2.

18 Plutarch, *Moralia* 234.

19 Xenophon, *Lac. Pol.* 2; Isocrates, *Panathenaicus* 211, 214; Plato, *Laws* 633.

20 Xenophon, *Anabasis* 4.6.

21 Xenophon, *Lac. Pol.* 5.

22 Isocrates, *Panathenaicus* 211; Plutarch, *Lycurgus* 17.

23 Plato, *Laws* 633.

24 Pausanias 3.14.

25 Xenophon, *Anabasis* 4.8.

26 Xenophon, *Lac. Pol.* 2.

27 Plutarch, *Moralia* 189.

28 Xenophon, *Lac. Pol.* 7.

29 Aristotle, *Rhetoric* 1367.

30 Plutarch, *Lycurgus* 12.

31 Plutarch, *Lycurgus* 12; Dicaearchus, fragment 23 (Athenaeus, *Deipnosophistai* 4.141).

32 Sir Henry Blount, *A Voyage into the Levant*, second edition (London, 1637), p. 105.

33 Plutarch, *Lycurgus* 12; *Moralia* 128.

34 Athenaeus, *Deipnosophistai* 4.138.

35 Molpis, fragment 2 (Athenaeus, *Deipnosophistai* 4.141); Xenophon, *Lac. Pol.* 5.

36 Plutarch, *Moralia* 210.

37 Xenophon, *Lac. Pol.* 5; Critias, fragment 10 (Athenaeus, *Deipnosophistai* 11.463); fragment 11 (Athenaeus, *Deipnosophistai* 11.483).

38 Plutarch, *Moralia* 233.

39 Plutarch, *Lycurgus* 28.

40 Aristotle, *Politics* 1266.

41 Herodotus 6.57; Xenophon, *Lac. Pol.* 15.

42 Plutarch, *Lycurgus* 12.

43 Isocrates, *Archidamus* 81; Plato, *Laws* 666.

44 Critias, fragment 13 (Eustathios on Homer, *Odyssey* 8.376); Plato, *Laws* 830; Lucian, *Anacharsis* 38.

45 Xenophon, *Lac. Pol.* 7.

46 Thucydides 1.6.

47 Dionysius of Halicarnassus, *Roman Antiquities* 7.72.

48 Tyrtaeus, fragment 10 (*Lycurgus* 1.107).

49 Athenaeus, *Deipnosophistai* 12.550.

50 Plutarch, *Agis* 8; *Cleomenes* 11.

51 Homer, *Odyssey* 13.412.

52 Herodotus 6.61; Pausanias 3.7.

53 Athenaeus, *Deipnosophistai* 13.566.

54 Xenophon, *Lac. Pol.* 1; Plato, *Protagoras* 342.

55 Plutarch, *Lycurgus* 14–15.

56 Pollux 4.102.

57 Ibycus, fragment 399 (Plutarch, *Comparison of Lycurgus and Numa* 3).

58 Plutarch, *Lycurgus* 15.

59 Pausanias 3.13–14.

60 Philostratus, *On Athletic Training* 9–10.

61 Plutarch, *Lycurgus* 21.

62 Athenaeus, *Deipnosophistai* 14.633.

63 Plutarch, *Lycurgus* 21.

64 Athenaeus, *Deipnosophistai* 14.630.

65 Plato, *Laws* 815.

66 Pollux 5.79; Athenaeus, *Deipnosophistai* 14.631.

67 Lucian, *De saltatione* 10–13.

68 Plato, *Protagoras* 342.

69 Isocrates, *Busiris* 17–18.

70 Agatharchides of Cnidus, fragment 10 (Athenaeus, *Deipnosophistai* 12.550).

71 Isocrates, *Panathenaicus* 181.

72 Pliny, *Natural History* 9.60; Pausanias 3.21.

73 Hesiod, *Theogony* 192.

74 Critias, fragment 11 (Athenaeus, *Deipnosophistai* 11.483).

75 Isocrates, *Panathenaicus* 178.

76 Aristotle, *Politics* 1271.

77 Plutarch, *Moralia* 223.

78 Thomas J. Figueira, 'Helotage and the Spartan Economy', in *A Companion to Sparta*, ed. Anton Powell (Malden, MA: Wiley-Blackwell, 2018), pp. 565–95 (p. 565).

79 Herodotus 6.63; Xenophon, *Hellenica* 5.4; Xenophon, *Lac. Pol.* 7.

80 Herodotus 6.75.

81 Herodotus 6.68.

82 Plutarch, *Agesilaus* 3; Xenophon, *Lac. Pol.* 1.

83 Herodotus 7.229; Thucydides 4.8, 4.16.

84 Critias, fragment 14 (Libanius, *Orations* 25).

85 Xenophon, *Lac. Pol.* 6; Aristotle, *Politics* 1263.

86 [Xenophon], *Ath. Pol.* 1.10–12.

87 Strabo 8.5; Pollux 3.83.

88 Critias, fragment 14 (Libanius, *Orations* 25).

89 Myron of Priene, fragment 2 (Athenaeus, *Deipnosophistai* 14.657).
90 Plutarch, *Lycurgus* 28.
91 Ibid.
92 Plato, *Laws* 633.
93 Thucydides 4.80.
94 Aristotle, *Politics* 1269.
95 Hesychius of Alexandria, *Lexicon*.
96 Thucydides 5.34.
97 Thucydides 4.80.
98 Xenophon, *Hellenica* 6.5.
99 Plutarch, *Lycurgus* 28.
100 Thucydides 1.18; Plato *Laws* 691–2; Xenophon *Lac. Pol.* 10; Polybius 6.10.
101 Herodotus 6.56–7; Xenophon, *Lac. Pol.* 15.
102 Herodotus 5.90.
103 Xenophon, *Lac. Pol.* 10.
104 Plato, *Laws* 691–2.
105 Aristotle, *Politics* 1270–1.
106 Plutarch, *Cleomenes* 9.
107 Aristophanes, *Lysistrata* 1072–3, *The Wasps* 475–7.
108 Xenophon, *Lac. Pol.* 15.
109 Aristotle, *Politics* 1270.
110 Aristotle, *Politics* 1313; Plutarch, *Lycurgus* 7.
111 Thucydides 1.87.
112 Plutarch, *Lycurgus* 6.
113 Herodotus 1.65; Thucydides 1.18.
114 Plutarch, *Lycurgus* 2–4.
115 Plutarch, *Lycurgus* 6.
116 Plutarch, *Lycurgus* 8.
117 Xenophon, *Lac. Pol.* 7; Plutarch, *Lycurgus* 9.
118 Pseudo-Plato, *Eryxias* 400.
119 Plutarch, *Lycurgus* 9.
120 Plutarch, *Lycurgus* 10.
121 Herodotus 1.66; Pausanias 3.15.
122 Herodotus 1.65.
123 Plutarch, *Lycurgus* 1.

3. Sparta's Rise to Dominance: 600–520 BCE

1   Herodotus 1.65–8.
2   Herodotus 1.66.
3   Ibid.
4   Herodotus 9.28.
5   Herodotus 1.66.
6   Pausanias 8.47.
7   Herodotus 9.26.
8   Pausanias 8.53; Polyaenus, *Stratagems* 1.8.
9   Herodotus 1.67.
10 Herodotus 1.67–8.
11 Pausanias 7.1.
12 Plutarch, *Cimon* 8.
13 Herodotus 1.68.
14 Thucydides 1.19.
15 Aeschines 2.116; Pausanias 10.8; Strabo 9.3.
16 Arthur S. Hunt, *Catalogue of the Greek Papyri in the John Rylands Library, Manchester, Volume 1: Literary Texts* (Manchester: Manchester University Press, 1911), No. 18.
17 Diodorus 9.10.
18 Pausanias 3.16.
19 Plato, *Protagoras* 342.
20 Herodotus 1.28.
21 Herodotus 1.94.
22 Herodotus 1.53.
23 Herodotus 1.69; Pausanias 3.10.
24 Herodotus 3.47.
25 Herodotus 1.80.

26 Xenophon, *Cyropaedia* 6.2.

27 Thucydides 5.41.

28 Sosibius, fragment 5 (Athenaeus, *Deipnosophistai* 15.678).

29 Herodotus 1.82.

30 Plutarch, *Moralia* 306.

31 Lucian, *Icaromenippus* 18.

32 *Inscriptiones Graecae* V.1.45.

33 Herodotus 1.141–2.

34 Herodotus 1.152–3.

35 Plutarch, *Moralia* 511.

36 Xenophon, *Cyropaedia* 1.2.

37 Herodotus 3.45-48, 54–7.

38 Plutarch, *Moralia* 215–16.

39 Herodotus 3.125.

40 Herodotus 3.148.

4. Royal Rivalries:
Cleomenes vs. Demaratus:
520–490 BCE

1 Herodotus 5.39–40.

2 Herodotus 5.42.

3 Plutarch, *Agesilaus* 1.

4 Herodotus 5.45.

5 Pausanias 3.19.

6 Herodotus 6.62.

7 Pindar, *Pythian Odes* 11.61–4; *Nemean Odes* 10. 55–6.

8 Herodotus 5.63.

9 [Aristotle], *Ath. Pol.* 19.

10 Thucydides 6.59.

11 Herodotus 5.63.

12 Herodotus 5.65.

13 Herodotus 5.69–72.

14 Herodotus 5.71.

15 Aristophanes, *Lysistrata* 275–80.

16 Herodotus 5.74.

17 Plutarch, *Moralia* 223.

18 Dionysius of Halicarnassus, *Roman Antiquities* 19.1.

19 Herodotus 5.77.

20 Herodotus 5.91.

21 Herodotus 5.49.

22 Herodotus 5.33–5.

23 Herodotus 5.50.

24 Herodotus 5.51.

25 Plutarch, *Moralia* 240.

26 Plutarch, *Agis* 7.

27 Aristotle, *Politics* 1269.

28 Plutarch, *Moralia* 241.

29 Ibid.

30 Xenophon, *Hellenica* 4.5.

31 Herodotus 5.97.

32 Herodotus 5.105.

33 Herodotus 6.76.

34 Herodotus 6.77.

35 Herodotus 6.78.

36 Herodotus 7.148.

37 Herodotus 6.78–9.

38 Herodotus 6.80.

39 Herodotus 6.75.

40 Stephanus of Byzantium ('Athana').

41 Herodotus 6.83.

42 Herodotus 7.202; 9.28.

43 Herodotus 6.49.

44 Herodotus 7.133.

45 Plutarch, *Pericles* 8.

46 Herodotus 6.50.

47 Herodotus 6.51.

48 Herodotus 6.65.

49 Plutarch *Lycurgus* 15

50 Herodotus 6.66.

51 Herodotus 6.67.

52 Herodotus 6.68–9.

53 Plutarch, *Themistocles* 29.

54 Herodotus 6.74–5.

55 Herodotus 6.84.

56 Herodotus 6.84.

57 Herodotus 6.58.

58 Herodotus 6.85.

59 Herodotus 6.86.

60 Herodotus 6.100.

61 Herodotus 6.106.

62 Plutarch, *Moralia* 861–2.

63 Plato, *Laws* 698.

64 Herodotus 6.112.

65 [J. S. Mill], Review of George
    Grote, *A History of Greece*,
    Edinburgh Review 84 (1846),
    343–77 (p. 343).

66 Isaac Asimov, *The Greeks:*
    A Great Adventure (Boston:
    Houghton Mifflin, 1965), p. 104.

67 Robert Graves, *Collected Poems:*
    1965 (London: Cassell, 1965),
    p. 187.

68 Herodotus 6.120.

69 Herodotus 7.61.

70 Xenophon, *Hellenica* 3.4.

71 Herodotus 6.120.

72 Herodotus 7.104.

5: Xerxes' Invasion: The
     Spartans Liberate Greece?
     481–479 BCE

1   Herodotus 7.239.

2   Aeschylus, *Persians*, 238–9.

3   Herodotus 7.226.

4   Herodotus 7.33–7.

5   Herodotus 7.54.

6   Herodotus 7.101–5.

7   Herodotus 7.104.

8   Herodotus 7.133.

9   Herodotus 7.135.

10 Esther 3:2–3.

11 Herodotus 7.134–6.

12 Herodotus 7.220.

13 Herodotus 7.149.

14 Herodotus 157–63.

15 Herodotus 7.129.

16 Herodotus 7.173.

17 Diodorus 11.2.

18 Herodotus 7.205.

19 Plutarch, *Moralia* 225.

20 Diodorus 11.4.

21 Herodotus 7.206.

22 Athenaeus, *Deipnosophistai*
    4.141.

23 Herodotus 7.208–9.

24 Xenophon, *Lac. Pol.* 12.

25 Xenophon, *Hellenica* 4.8.

26 Plutarch, *Agesilaus* 34.

27 Herodotus 7.210.

28 Herodotus 7.211.

29 Diodorus 11.4.

30 Herodotus 7.212.

31 Diodorus 11.8.

32 Herodotus 7.211.

33 Herodotus 7.213.

34 Herodotus 7.218.

35 Herodotus 7.220.

36 Herodotus 7.222.

37 Plutarch, *Moralia* 864.

38 Herodotus 7.223.

39 Diodorus 11.11.

40 Herodotus 7.225.

41 Diodorus 11.10.

42 Diodorus 11.9.

43 Herodotus 7.238.

44 Herodotus 8.24–5.

45 Pausanias 1.13.

46 Herodotus 7.228.

47 Simonides, fragment 531
    (Diodorus 11.11).

48 Herodotus 7.231.

49 Isocrates, *Panegyricus* 92.

50 Diodorus 11.11.

51 Herodotus 7.144.

52 Herodotus 8.2.

53 Herodotus 8.11–20.

54 Herodotus 8.61.

55 Plutarch, *Themistocles* 11.

56 Herodotus 8.75–6.

57 Herodotus 8.92.

58 Herodotus 8.93.

59 Herodotus 8.88.

60 Herodotus 8.123.

61 Herodotus 8.124.

62 Herodotus 8.144.

63 Herodotus 9.10.

64 Herodotus 9.9.

65 Herodotus 9.28.

66 Lycurgus, *Against Leocrates* 81;
   Diodorus 11.29.

67 Herodotus 7.235.

68 Herodotus 8.113; Diodorus
   11.30.

69 Herodotus 7.89.

70 Herodotus 8.114.

71 Herodotus 9.46–48.

72 Herodotus 9.51–56.

73 Herodotus 9.72.

74 Herodotus 9.62; Diodorus 11.31.

75 Plutarch, *Moralia* 873–4.

76 Herodotus 9.70.

77 Herodotus 9.64.

78 Arrian, *Anabasis* 1.9.

79 Herodotus 9.85.

80 Plutarch, *Aristides* 19.

81 Diodorus 11.33.

82 Herodotus 9.71.

83 Herodotus 9.78–9.

84 Herodotus 9.82.

85 Herodotus 9.102.

86 Diodorus 11.36.

87 Thucydides 1.132.

88 Vitruvius 1.1.

89 Pausanias 3.11.

**6: Sparta During the
'Fifty Years': Isolationist
and Isolated**
479–431 BCE

1 Thucydides 1.20.

2 Thucydides 1.21.

3 Thucydides 1.95.

4 Plutarch, *Aristides* 23.

5 Herodotus 9.106.

6 Diodorus 11.39.

7 Thucydides 1.128; Diodorus
   11.44.

8 Simonides, fragment 11 (*P.Oxy*
   2327 and 3695).

9 Thucydides 1.95; Plutarch,
   Aristides 23.

10 Pausanias 3.7.

11 Herodotus 6.72.

12 Herodotus 5.32.

13 Plutarch, *Aristides* 23; *Cimon* 6.

14 Thucydides 1.59.

15 Diodorus 11.50.

16 Thucydides 1.95.

17 Thucydides 1.128.

18 Plutarch, *Cimon* 6.

19 Lord Byron, *Manfred*,
   II.ii.182–6.

20 Thucydides 1.32.

21 Thucydides 1.132.

22 Thucydides 1.133.

23 Diodorus 11.45; Polyaenus 8.51.

24 Pausanias 3.17.

25 Aelian, *Varia Historia* 9.41.

26 *Athenaion Politeia* 23; Plutarch,
   Aristides 25.

27 Thucydides 2.13.

28 Meiggs and Lewis, *Greek Historical Inscriptions* 47.

29 *Inscriptiones Graecae* I3 39; 40.

30 Thucydides 1.98.

31 Thucydides 1.100; Diodorus 11.62; Plutarch, *Cimon* 12.

32 Herodotus 9.35.

33 Isocrates, *Archidamus* 99.

34 Diodorus 11.65.

35 Thucydides 1.101.

36 Thucydides 1.128; 3.54.

37 Plutarch, *Cimon* 16.

38 Diodorus 11.63.

39 Polyaenus 1.41.

40 Xenophon, *Hellenica* 5.3; Thucydides 2.27.

41 Thucydides 3.54.

42 Thucydides 2.27.

43 Plutarch, *Cimon* 16.

44 Aristophanes, *Lysistrata* 1137–42.

45 Thucydides 1.102.

46 Thucydides 1.113–14.

47 Diodorus 11.79.

48 Thucydides 1.108; Plutarch, *Cimon* 17.

49 Osborne and Rhodes, *Greek Historical Inscriptions* 112.

50 Thucydides 1.103.

51 Ibid.

52 Plutarch, *Lycurgus* 28.

53 Thucydides 4.80.

54 Thucydides 1.109.

55 Plutarch, *Pericles* 12.

56 Thucydides 5.14.

57 Thucydides 1.112.

58 Thucydides 1.113.

59 Plutarch, *Pericles* 22.

60 Thucydides 1.40; 1.115.

61 Plutarch, *Pericles* 23.

62 Plutarch, *Pericles* 22.

63 Thucydides 1.55.

64 Thucydides 1.56.

65 Thucydides 1.139; Plutarch, *Pericles* 30.

66 Thucydides 1.70.

67 Thucydides 1.86–7.

7: The Archidamian War: Humiliating Failure?
431–421 BCE

1 Thucydides 1.23.

2 See Graham T. Allison, 'The Thucydides Trap: Are the U.S. and China Headed for War?', *The Atlantic* (24 September 2015).

3 Thucydides 1.118.

4 Thucydides 1.139.

5 Thucydides 1.141.

6 Thucydides 2.13.

7 Thucydides 2.14.

8 Thucydides 4.5.

9 Thucydides 4.26–7.

10 Plutarch, *Nicias* 8.

11 Thucydides 4.28.

12 Thucydides 4.29.

13 Thucydides 4.33.

14 Pausanias 4.26.

15 Thucydides 4.37.

16 Thucydides 4.40.

17 Pausanias 1.15.

18 Thucydides 7.18.

19 Thucydides 2.25; Diodorus 12.43.

20 Thucydides 2.85.

21 Thucydides 4.12.

22 Anton Powell, 'Sparta's Foreign – and Internal – History, 478–403', in *A Companion to*

Sparta, ed. Powell (Malden
MA: Wiley-Blackwell, 2018),
pp. 291–320 (p. 312).

23 Thucydides 4.81.
24 Thucydides 4.70–3.
25 Thucydides 4.86.
26 Thucydides 4.117.
27 Thucydides 5.9.
28 Plutarch, *Moralia* 219.
29 Thucydides 5.10.
30 Plato, *Symposium* 221.
31 Plutarch, *Moralia* 240.
32 Thucydides 4.93.
33 Thucydides 5.15.
34 Thucydides 5.19.

**8:   The Athenian War:
       Sparta Betrays Greece?
       421–404 BCE**

1   Thucydides 5.27.
2   Thucydides 5.43.
3   Thucydides 5.47.
4   Thucydides 5.48–50.
5   Thucydides 5.56.
6   Aristophanes, *Peace* 1066–7.
7   Thucydides 5.60.
8   Plutarch, *Alcibiades* 15.
9   Thucydides 5.63.
10 Thucydides 5.65.
11 Thucydides 5.68.
12 Thucydides 5.73.
13 Diodorus 12.79.
14 Thucydides 5.75.
15 Thucydides 5.76–80.
16 Thucydides 5.89.
17 Thucydides 6.15.
18 Thucydides 6.1.
19 Thucydides 6.16.
20 Thucydides 6.88; Plutarch,
    Alcibiades 23.

21 Thucydides 6.96–7.
22 Plutarch, *Alcibiades* 23.
23 Thucydides 6.91.
24 Plutarch, *Nicias* 19.
25 Thucydides 7.86; Plutarch,
    Nicias 28.
26 Thucydides 8.2.
27 Thucydides 8.3.
28 Thucydides 8.18.
29 Thucydides 8.37.
30 Thucydides 8.58.
31 Plutarch, *Alcibiades* 23.
32 Xenophon, *Hellenica* 1.1.
33 Xenophon, *Hellenica* 1.5;
    Plutarch, *Lysander* 4.
34 Diodorus 13.71.
35 Plutarch, *Alcibiades* 39.
36 Diodorus 13.76.
37 Plutarch, *Moralia* 229.
38 Xenophon, *Hellenica* 1.6.
39 Plutarch, *Lysander* 6.
40 Xenophon, *Hellenica* 1.6.
41 Diodorus 13.99.
42 Xenophon, *Hellenica* 1.6.
43 Xenophon, *Hellenica* 1.7.
44 Xenophon, *Hellenica* 2.1.
45 Plutarch, *Lysander* 9.
46 Xenophon, *Hellenica* 2.1.
47 Plutarch, *Lysander* 18; Pausanias
    3.17–18.
48 Pausanias 10.9.
49 Xenophon, *Hellenica* 2.2.
50 Polycrates, fragment 2a
    (Scholiast on Aristotle, *Rhetoric*
    1401 a33).
51 Xenophon, *Hellenica* 2.3.
52 Xenophon, *Hellenica* 2.2.
53 *Inscriptiones Graecae* II2 1388.
54 Plutarch, *Lysander* 14.
55 Xenophon, *Hellenica* 2.2.

56 Diodorus 14.10.
57 Strabo 8.5.

9: **'Glad to Eat Them, Even Raw':**
    Inequality and the Downfall
    of Sparta
1   Xenophon, *Hellenica* 3.3.
2   Polyaenus, *Stratagems* 2.14.
3   Xenophon, *Hellenica* 3.3.
4   Aristotle, *Politics* 1306.
5   Ibid.
6   Thucydides 1.6.
7   Aristotle, *Nicomachean Ethics*
    1127.
8   Xenophon, *Lac. Pol.* 5.
9   Molpis, fragment 2c
    (Athenaeus, *Deipnosophistai*
    4.140).
10 Xenophon, *Lac. Pol.* 6.
11 Aristotle, *Politics* 1263.
12 Herodotus 6.103; Pausanias
    6.10.
13 Herodotus 6.70.
14 Pausanias 6.1.
15 Pausanias 3.15.
16 Polycrates, fragment 1
    (Athenaeus, *Deipnosophistai*
    4.139).
17 Xenophon, *Agesilaus* 8.
18 Xenophon, *Agesilaus* 9;
    Plutarch, *Agesilaus* 20.
19 Plutarch, *Moralia* 242.
20 Aristotle, *Politics* 1270.
21 Athenaeus 15.555b.
22 Aelian, *Varia Historia* 12.53;
    Athenaeus, *Deipnosophistai*
    6.271.
23 Plutarch, *Lysander* 2.
24 Plutarch, *Lysander* 16.

25 Aristotle, fragment 544
    (Diodorus 7.12).
26 Herodotus 6.72.
27 Herodotus 3.148; 5.51.
28 Herodotus 8.5.
29 Plutarch, *Pericles* 22.
30 Aristotle, *Politics* 1270.
31 Aristotle, *Politics* 1271.
32 Plato, *Alcibiades* I 122–3.
33 Dionysius of Halicarnassus,
    Roman Antiquities 20, excerpt
    13.
34 Xenophon, *Agesilaus* 8;
    Plutarch, *Moralia* 210.
35 Xenophon, *Agesilaus* 1.
36 Aristotle, *Politics* 1270.
37 Plutarch, *Agesilaus* 26.
38 Plutarch, *Cimon* 16.
39 Plutarch, *Lycurgus* 8.
40 Plato, *Alcibiades* I 122–3.
41 Aristotle, *Politics* 1270.
42 Aristotle, *Politics* 1272.
43 Aristotle, *Politics* 1270.
44 Ibid.; Aelian, *Varia Historia* 6.6.
45 Xenophon, *Lac. Pol.* 1.
46 Polybius 12.6.
47 Plutarch, *Lycurgus* 15.
48 Athenaeus, *Deipnosophistai*
    13.555.
49 Plutarch, *Moralia* 227.
50 Aristotle, *Politics* 1270.

10: **Spartan Hegemony:**
    Empire at Last?
    404–386 BCE
1   Theopompos, fragment 23
    (Theodoros Metochites, *Essays*
    and Didactic Notes 116).
2   Xenophon, *Anabasis* 6.6.
3   Plutarch, *Lysander* 18.

4 Plutarch, *Lysander* 15.

5 Xenophon, *Hellenica* 2.4.

6 Ibid.

7 Ibid.

8 Pausanias 3.5.

9 Xenophon, *Anabasis* 1.4.

10 Plutarch, *Artaxerxes* 6.

11 Xenophon, *Anabasis* 2.6.

12 Plutarch, *Artaxerxes* 18.

13 Plutarch, *Agesilaus* 2.

14 Xenophon, *Lac. Pol.* 2.

15 Plutarch, *Moralia* 237.

16 Aristophanes, fragment 907
(Photius, *Lexicon* K 1263);
Hesychius, K 4735; Plato, *Laws*
836.

17 Cicero, *Republic* 4.4.

18 Plutarch, *Lycurgus* 16.

19 Gerhard L. Weinberg, ed.,
*Hitler's Second Book: The
Unpublished Sequel to 'Mein
Kampf'* [*Hitlers Zweites Buch:
Ein Dokument aus dem Jahr
1928* (Stuttgart 1961)], trans.
Krista Smith (New York:
Enigma, 2006), p. 56.

20 Xenophon, *Hellenica* 3.3.

21 Plutarch, *Agesilaus* 1.

22 Plutarch, *Agesilaus* 2.

23 Plutarch, *Moralia* 241.

24 Xenophon, *Hellenica* 3.3.

25 Plutarch, *Agesilaus* 6.

26 Xenophon, *Hellenica* 3.4.

27 Plutarch, *Agesilaus* 6;
Xenophon, *Hellenica* 3.4.

28 Xenophon, *Hellenica* 3.4.

29 Xenophon, *Agesilaus* 5.

30 Xenophon, *Hellenica* 3.4.

31 Plutarch, *Agesilaus* 10.

32 Xenophon, *Hellenica* 4.1;

Agesilaus 1.36; Plutarch,
Agesilaus 15.

33 Polybius 1.2.

34 Xenophon, *Hellenica* 3.5;
Plutarch, *Lysander* 29.

35 Strabo 8.5.

36 *Hellenica Oxyrhinchia* 7.2–3.

37 Xenophon, *Hellenica* 4.2.

38 Xenophon, *Lac. Pol.* 11.

39 Xenophon, *Agesilaus* 7.4–5.

40 Xenophon, *Hellenica* 4.3;
Agesilaus 2.2.

41 Plutarch, *Lycurgus* 13.

42 Xenophon, *Hellenica* 4.5.

43 Xenophon, *Hellenica* 5.1.

44 Ibid.

45 Xenophon, *Hellenica* 5.2.

11: Sparta's Decline and Fall 386–371 BCE

1 Xenophon, *Hellenica* 5.2.

2 Thucydides 1.43.

3 Xenophon, *Hellenica* 5.2.

4 Diodorus 15.5.

5 Xenophon, *Hellenica* 5.2.

6 Ibid.

7 Ibid.

8 Diodorus 15.19.

9 Xenophon, *Hellenica* 5.2.

10 Diodorus 15.19.

11 Diodorus 15.20.

12 Xenophon, *Hellenica* 5.3.

13 Plutarch, *Moralia* 775.

14 Tod, *Greek Historical
Inscriptions* 120.

15 Xenophon, *Hellenica* 5.3.

16 Xenophon, *Hellenica* 5.4.

17 Ibid.

18 Ibid.

19 Plutarch, *Agesilaus* 24.

20 Rhodes and Osborne, *Greek Historical Inscriptions* 22.
21 Xenophon, *Hellenica* 5.4.
22 Ibid.
23 Plutarch, *Agesilaus* 26.
24 Xenophon, *Hellenica* 5.4.
25 Plutarch, *Moralia* 230–1.
26 Diodorus 15.35.
27 Xenophon, *Hellenica* 6.1.
28 Plutarch, *Pelopidas* 16–17; *Agesilaus* 27; Diodorus 15.37.
29 Diodorus 15.46.
30 Xenophon, *Hellenica* 6.3.
31 Ibid.
32 Plutarch, *Agesilaus* 28; Pausanias 9.14.
33 Polyaenus 2.3.
34 Pausanias 4.32.
35 Xenophon, *Hellenica* 6.4.
36 Plutarch, *Moralia* 210.
37 Diodorus 15.55.
38 Diodorus 15.55–6; Plutarch, *Pelopidas* 23; Xenophon, *Hellenica* 6.4.
39 Pausanias 9.13.
40 Cicero, *De inventione* 2.69.
41 Diodorus 13.24.
42 Diodorus 15.63.
43 Rhodes and Osborne, *Greek Historical Inscriptions* 30.
44 Plutarch, *Agesilaus* 30.
45 Xenophon, *Hellenica* 6.4; Plutarch, *Agesilaus* 30.
46 Plutarch, *Agesilaus* 31.
47 Ibid.
48 Plutarch, *Agesilaus* 32.
49 Diodorus 15.65.
50 Xenophon, *Hellenica* 6.5.
51 Aristotle, *Politics* 1269.
52 Plutarch, *Agesilaus* 32.
53 Ibid.
54 Xenophon, *Hellenica* 6.5.
55 Plutarch, *Pelopidas* 24.
56 Diodorus 15.66–7.

Epilogue: No More Heroes?
1 Xenophon, *Lac. Pol.* 1.
2 William Golding, *The Hot Gates and Other Occasional Places* (London: Faber, 1965; 1974), p. 20.

Select Bibliography

Cartledge, Paul, *Agesilaos and the Crisis of Sparta* (London: Duckworth, 1987).

—, *Sparta and Lakonia: A Regional History, 1300–362 BC* (2nd edition; Abingdon: Routledge, 2002).

—, *Spartan Reflections* (London: Duckworth, 2001).

—, Nikos Birgalias, and Kostas Buraselis, ed., Η συμβολή της αρχαίας Σπάρτης στην πολιτική σκέψη και πρακτική [*The Contribution of Ancient Sparta to Political Thought and Practice*] (Athens, 2007).

—, and Anton Powell, ed., *The Greek Superpower: Sparta in the Self-Definitions of Athenians* (Swansea: Classical Press of Wales, 2018).

—, and Antony Spawforth, *Hellenistic and Roman Sparta: A Tale of Two Cities* (London: Duckworth, 1989).

Cavanagh, William G., Christopher Mee, and P. James, ed., *The Laconia Rural Sites Project, Annual of the British School at Athens*, Supplement 36 (London: British School at Athens, 2005).

—, and S. E. C. Walker, ed., *Sparta in Laconia: The Archaeology of a City and its Countryside. Proceedings of the 19th British Museum Classical Colloquium* (London: British School at Athens, 1998).

Christien, Jacqueline, and Françoise Ruzé, *Sparte: Géographie, mythes et histoire* (Paris: Armand Colin, 2007).

Cooley, M. G. L., ed., *LACTOR 21: Sparta* (London: London Association of Classical Teachers, 2017).

Davies, Philip, *Standing Among the Spartans: Institutions and Status within the Spartiate Community* (London: Bloomsbury Publishing, 2025).

—, and Judith Mossman, ed., *Sparta in Plutarch's Lives* (Swansea: Classical Press of Wales, 2023).

de Assumpção, Luis Filipe Bantim, ed., *Esparta: Política e Sociedade* (Curitiba: Editora Prismas, 2017).

Doran, Timothy, *Spartan Oliganthropia* (Leiden: Brill, 2018).

Ducat, Jean, *Spartan Education: Youth and Society in the Classical Period* (Swansea: Classical Press of Wales, 2006).

Figueira, Thomas J., ed., *Spartan Society* (Swansea: Classical Press of Wales, 2004).

Fitzhardinge, L .F., *The Spartans* (London: Thames & Hudson, 1980).

Hodkinson, Stephen, *Property and Wealth in Classical Sparta* (Swansea: Classical Press of Wales, 2000).

—, ed., *Sparta: Comparative Approaches* (Swansea: Classical Press of Wales, 2009).

—, and Ian Macgregor Morris, ed., *Sparta in Modern Thought: Politics, History and Culture* (Swansea: Classical Press of Wales, 2012).

—, and Anton Powell, ed., *Sparta: New Perspectives* (Swansea: Classical Press of Wales, 1999).

—, and Anton Powell, ed., *Sparta & War* (Swansea: Classical Press of Wales, 2006).

Kennell, Nigel M., *The Spartans* (Malden, MA: Wiley-Blackwell, 2010).

Lévy, Edmond, *Sparte: Histoire politique et sociale jusqu'à la conquête romaine* (Paris: Seuil, 2003).

Lupi, Marcello, *L'Ordine delle generazioni: Classi di età e costumi matrimoniali nell'antica Sparta* (Bari: Edipuglia, 2000).

—, *Sparta: Storia e rappresentazioni di una città greca* (Rome: Carocci editore, 2017).

Luraghi, Nino, *The Ancient Messenians: Constructions of Ethnicity and Memory* (Cambridge: Cambridge University Press, 2008).

—, and Susan E. Alcock, ed., *Helots and their Masters in Laconia and Messenia: Histories, Ideologies, Structures* (Washington, DC: Centre for Hellenic Studies, 2003).

Luther, Andreas, Mischa Meier, and Lukas Thommen, ed., *Das Frühe Sparta* (Stuttgart: Franz Steiner Verlag, 2006).

Nafissi, Massimo, *La nascita del kosmos: studi sulla storia e la società di Sparta* (Naples: Edizioni Scientifiche Italiane, 1991).

Ogden, Daniel, *Aristomenes of Messene: Legends of Sparta's Nemesis* (Swansea: Classical Press of Wales, 2004).

Pothou, Vassiliki, and Anton Powell, ed., *Das antike Sparta* (Stuttgart: Steiner Franz Verlag, 2017).

Powell, Anton, ed., *Classical Sparta: Techniques Behind Her Success* (London: Routledge, 1989).

—, ed., *A Companion to Sparta* (Malden, MA: Wiley-Blackwell, 2017).

—, and Paula Debnar, ed., *Thucydides and Sparta* (Swansea: Classical Press of Wales, 2021).

—, and Stephen Hodkinson, ed., *Shadow of Sparta* (London: Routledge, 1994).

—, and Stephen Hodkinson, ed., *Sparta: Beyond the Mirage* (Swansea: Classical Press of Wales, 2002).

—, and Stephen Hodkinson, ed., *Sparta: The Body Politic* (Swansea: Classical Press of Wales, 2010).

—, and Nicolas Richer, ed., *Xenophon and Sparta* (Swansea: Classical Press of Wales, 2020).

Rahe, Paul, *The Spartan Regime: Its Character, Origins, and Grand Strategy* (New Haven: Yale University Press, 2016).

Richer, Nicolas, *Les éphores: Études sur l'histoire et sur l'image de Sparte (VIIIe–IIIe siècles avant Jésus-Christ)* (Paris: Publications de la Sorbonne, 1998).

—, *La religion des Spartiates: Croyances et cultes dans l'Antiquité* (Paris: Belles lettres, 2012).

—, *Sparte: Cité des arts, des armes et des lois* (Paris: Perrin, 2018).

Rusch, Scott M., *Sparta at War: Strategy, Tactics, and Campaigns, 550–362 BC* (Barnsley: Frontline Books, 2011).

Sekunda, Nick, *The Spartan Army* (Oxford: Osprey Publishing, 1988).

Thommen, Lukas, *Sparta: Verfassungs- und Sozialgeschichte einer griechischen Polis* (Stuttgart/Weimar: Metzler, 2003).

Welwei, Karl-Wilhelm, *Sparta: Aufstieg und Niedergang einer antiken Großmacht* (Stuttgart: Klett-Cotta, 2004).

Whitby, Michael, ed., *Sparta* (Edinburgh: Edinburgh University Press, 2002).

Acknowledgements

There is an old joke among ancient historians that everyone, at one time or another, thinks that it would be a good idea to write a book about Sparta. It is such a good idea that I wrote a short one back in 2020. So this book simply would not exist if my wonderful agent, Adam Gauntlett, had not reached out to me back in 2021 to see if I was interested in writing a longer book on Sparta. I was, and I hope that the end result justifies Adam's enthusiasm for the initial idea that grew out of our discussions.

This book would also not exist without my fabulous commissioning editor at Profile, Nick Humphrey. I am immensely grateful to Nick for offering me the opportunity to write this book, for his patience with me in delivering the manuscript, and for his many editorial interventions that have led to what is a vastly improved tale of Sparta's rise and fall.

The manuscript was also improved immeasurably by the equally fabulous Jessica Yao at Norton, who offered wise counsel about how to arrange a narrative, an astute editorial eye, and helpful pointers to make the narrative more suitable for an American audience.

Many thanks are also due to Nick de Somogyi for his keen eye as a copy editor, especially his many suggestions to improve long, sometimes clunky sentences. Nick's enthusiasm for his work made the final copy-editing process genuinely enjoyable.

I am also grateful to Georgina Difford for her care and attention, which has made the entire publishing process so smooth.

I would also like to thank my students at the University of Birmingham, who were sometimes the unwitting victims of new lectures based on draft versions of the narrative chapters of this book, and the staff at the various libraries and cafes where much of this book was written.

Finally, I would like to thank my family and friends for tolerating my long absences from social activities while I was writing and finishing this book. I would especially like to thank my wife Vicky, who as usual never tires of being my sounding board, thesaurus and sense checker, often at the most random and inconvenient of times. Without her support – in all aspects of life – not a single word written in this book would have made it to print.

Picture Credits

Figures: Prologue (p. 1): BM 1977,0101.8. Chapter 1 (p. 17): Sparti Museum / Getty 1223162265. Chapter 2 (p. 41): Alamy W7E8HA. Chapter 3 (p. 71): Antikensammlung, Staatliche Museen zu Berlin 3404 / Alamy WH9TJ9. Chapter 4 (p. 93): Sparti Museum 3365 / Getty 5877658877. Chapter 5 (p. 127): Alamy HXXKJ4 (Inv. ASb3312-21, Louvre). Chapter 6 (p. 165): BM 1880,0917.1. Chapter 7 (p. 197): Wikimedia. Chapter 8 (p. 217): Wikimedia. Chapter 9 (p. 249): Alamy 2HCD857. Chapter 10 (p. 269): BM 89333. Chapter 11 (p. 297): Alamy 2A5R18Y. Epilogue (p. 321): BM 1923,0212.245.

Plates: 1. Andrew Bayliss. 2. Alamy DY8J68. 3. Getty 501585831. 4. Wadsworth Atheneum Museum 1917.815. 5. Alamy B45213. 6. Bridgeman 9067778. 7. BM 1954, 1018.1. 8. BM 1842,0407.7. 9. Wikimedia. 10. Getty 918943500. 11. Wikimedia. 12. Wikimedia. 13. Alamy T4E790. 14. BM 1877,0201.1.

Index

Page references in *italics* indicate images.